Caribbean Migrants

Caribbean Migrants

Environment and Human Survival on St. Kitts and Nevis

Bonham C. Richardson

The University of Tennessee Press

Knoxville

Frontispiece: A small landowner on Nevis. *Photograph by the author.*

*Clothbound editions of University of Tennessee Press
books are printed on paper designed for an effective
life of at least 300 years, and binding materials
are chosen for strength and durability.*

Library of Congress Cataloging in Publication Data
Richardson, Bonham C., 1939-
  Caribbean migrants.
  Bibliography: p.
  Includes index.
  1. St. Christopher and Nevis—Emigration and immigra-
tion—History. 2. St. Christopher and Nevis—Social
conditions. I. Title.
JV7339.S75R52   304.8'097297'3   82-7078
ISBN 0-87049-360-4   AACR2
ISBN 0-87049-361-2 (pbk.)

For Linda Buchholz Richardson

Contents

Illustrations

Photographs

Figures and Maps

Tables

Preface

THE VACATION POSTCARD image of the small islands of the Commonwealth Caribbean ignores their tragic histories. The half millennium of external control over Caribbean lands and peoples has witnessed the annihilation of the aboriginal population, the importation of slaves, environmental devastation, and relentless plantation repression. The region's laboring classes have always resisted, and their resistance has taken many forms, including migration. Reacting to outside control of local resources and declining insular carrying capacities, West Indians have for generations migrated from and returned to their islands to sustain their local societies. In many smaller Caribbean islands, migration traditions are so pervasive and of such long standing that they are a way of life.

This book is a historical geography of human migration on the islands of St. Kitts and Nevis in the northeastern Caribbean. It stresses, at the microscale, the ways in which Afro-Caribbean slaves and their descendants have dealt creatively with environmental and human-induced problems for centuries. The historical perspective employed in this book differs from other Caribbean migration studies, whose intent often seems to be to show the ways in which contemporary West Indians are attracted to London, New York, and elsewhere. I have attempted to document here that the roots of human migration in the small islands of the Caribbean are far deeper. Further, I discuss throughout how subsequent generations of migrants from St. Kitts and Nevis have created a historical continuum leading to a migration ethos that underpins the societies of the two islands today.

This study also differs from other works on Caribbean migration by emphasizing the ecology of the people and their islands. On St. Kitts, Nevis, and other small West Indian islands, local environments traditionally have been controlled by a planter elite. Plantation deforestation and subsequent soil erosion have reduced severely the lands' capabilities of sustaining local populations. A sad and important incongruity therefore has persisted between peoples and lands in the Caribbean, an incongruity that stimulates migration and, in some cases, exacerbates ecological devastation.

I have organized this book to proceed from general to particular and back again to general. Chapter 1 presents an overview of historical and contemporary human migration in the Commonwealth Caribbean. Chapter 2 describes the contemporary migration cultures of St. Kitts and Nevis. Chapters 3–6 then tell how these migration cultures evolved in four different time periods beginning with earliest English colonization and plantation slavery. Chapter 7 is an interpretive essay that attempts to place back-and-forth human movements from St. Kitts, Nevis, and other small West Indian islands into a broader human ecological perspective.

The fieldwork, archival research, and writing of this book have been done over a period of several years. In 1974 and 1975 I formulated a research proposal for work in St. Kitts and Nevis based on my earlier work in Guyana, Trinidad, and Carriacou. From January through July 1976, my wife, our one-year-old-daughter, and I resided in St. Kitts and Nevis, a research sojourn made possible through generous financial assistance from the National Geographic Society and the Rutgers University Faculty Academic Study Program. Extremely helpful individuals on St. Kitts were Washington Archibald, E.S. Bridgewater, William Dore, Livingstone James, Donald McLachlan, Tom Molyneaux, and Oliver Spencer. On Nevis, Johnny Clarke, Simeon Daniel, Calvin Howell, Evan Nisbett, and Samuel Parris were very generous with their time and assistance.

The historical information at the government archives in Basseterre—notably in early newspapers and handwritten colonial records—led me to continue historical research after I returned to the United States. I have subsequently done archival work at the William R. Perkins Library at Duke University and the Carol Newman Library at Virginia Polytechnic Institute and State University. I owe much to Don Daidone at the latter library for his help.

As I have written this book I have sought advice, help, and criticism from others. Early chapter drafts and the manuscript at various stages have been read and commented upon from a variety of viewpoints by Sarah Blanshei, Mavis Bryant, Roger Buckley, Robert Dirks, Larry Grossman, Frank Mills, Bernard Nietschmann, and Linda Richardson. William Green and Dirks unselfishly lent research notes. R. Christopher Goodwin provided photographs at a crucial time. Karen Waldrop drew final maps. Glenna King and Jane Vyula typed drafts, revisions, and corrections well beyond the call of duty. Joanne Ainsworth provided splendid copyediting.

Special mention must be made of the work of anthropologist Richard Frucht, whom I never met. Frucht died of a heart attack in March 1979. He did the pioneering social anthropological work on Nevis, developed ideas about the interrelationships of twentieth-century migration and social change on Nevis, and was actively researching on St. Kitts almost until his death. I have relied on Frucht's fine work, as I have relied on the work of others, in parts of this book. To my knowledge, however, I have not misconstrued Frucht's original ideas, or anyone else's, for my own.

As with any long-term project such as this, the information, help, advice, and encouragement from many persons have improved the study greatly. On the other hand, I accept full responsibility for any errors and misinterpretations.

Bonham C. Richardson
Cave Hill, Barbados
February 18, 1982

Caribbean Migrants

CHAPTER ONE

Migration, History, and Environment in the Commonwealth Caribbean

Beginning with columbus's voyage into the Caribbean, and even earlier with Amerindian movements north from Central and South America, the Caribbean has been as well known for its travel routes as for its destinations. The fragmented nature of the region's insular geography only partially explains this fact. More important is the Caribbean's centuries-old status as an economic colony of Europe and North America. Conquistadores, buccaneers, planters, slave traders, merchants, diplomats, colonial administrators, businessmen, tourists, and commissioners all have traveled through the Caribbean, but comparatively few have settled there permanently. Most of the area's inhabitants are the Afro-Caribbean descendants of the Atlantic slave trade, the most fearsome forced migration in world history. In more recent times hundreds of thousands of Asian immigrants, from China, India, and Indonesia, have been brought to the Caribbean, principally as indentured workers.

Much of the human movement into and through the Caribbean can be directly attributed to the plantation, the metropolitan-focused institution that has dominated the region for centuries.[1] Variations of the plantation once held sway from coastal Brazil to the southern United States, and many similarities in racial composition, economic inequities, land policies, and crop combinations throughout Atlantic America can be considered, at least indirectly, plantation legacies. Nowhere, however, were the plantation and plantation slavery as pervasive and intense as in the Caribbean. And nowhere are the remnants of an earlier plantation system so obvious today.

Many observers have suggested that current Caribbean patterns of migration have their origins in the region's externally controlled plantation history. Not only did the plantation originally bring into the Caribbean region European planters and an African labor force but it also exported crops for processing and marketing. And Caribbean plantation profits routinely have been exported to enrich metropolitan, not Caribbean, regions. Today most lines of communication and transportation from the Caribbean still lead to Europe and North America.

Although American, Dutch, French, Spanish, Swedish, and Danish Caribbean islands all have sustained plantations, British islands imported more slaves and have exported raw sugar for a longer continuous period than any except the earliest Spanish colonies of the Greater Antilles. In a variety of subtropical environments, from the early seventeenth century to the present, British West Indian planters have combined land, labor, machinery, and capital under changing commercial and technological conditions. Each of the former British colonies of the Caribbean, however, has its own unique history and ecology that often includes earliest colonization by other European powers. Jamaica and Trinidad were first colonized by the Spanish, the Windwards by the French, and Tobago and Guyana by the Dutch. British colonial policy and its aftermath in the West Indies are therefore complicated by the persistence of Dutch land law, Spanish place names, and a French-based patois in ex-British colonies, depending upon the particular island or coastal zone. Difference among the states of the former British Caribbean is, then, more the rule than the exception, and in this way the Commonwealth Caribbean is highly typical of the region as a whole.

The "Commonwealth Caribbean" is meant here to include those former British dependencies of the West Indies with similar plantation histories. Most are now politically independent, and all have by now been granted some type of political autonomy. They include Jamaica, the British Virgin Islands, the Leewards (Anguilla, Antigua-Barbuda, St. Kitts–Nevis, and Montserrat), the Windwards (Dominica, St. Lucia, St. Vincent, and Grenada), Barbados, and Trinidad and Tobago (Figure 1). A history of British colonialism and plantation slavery, a socioeconomic system based partly on color, ecological deterioration, and the official language are common to all. However, differences among these Caribbean states—differences usually between the larger and smaller islands—have continuously frustrated attempts at political or economic federation.

The contemporary states of the Commonwealth Caribbean are also well known as points of origin for recurring human migration, and any attempt at understanding migration from and within the region must begin by contemplating the importance of the plantation in the region's history and

Figure 1. The Commonwealth Caribbean

geography. It was, of course, the institution to which laborers originally were forced to migrate, but it has also generated internal movement of its own. From earliest colonial days the plantation and its repressive labor systems have naturally repelled its workers. The runaway slave was a ubiquity of the Caribbean plantation. In the late nineteenth century in Trinidad and Guyana, indentured Indian workers often fled from their estates, preferring a clandestine existence to servitude under harsh plantation masters. Since emancipation in the Caribbean, former slaves and their descendants have been similarly repelled by and yet partially dependent upon the plantation and have sought refuge and their own social and economic identities outside its physical boundaries. The hundreds of small island villages throughout the Caribbean today represent, among other things, an earlier movement away from direct plantation control. This resistance to a plantation regime, manifested in this case by an independent village adaptation, has been suggested by the anthropologist Sidney Mintz as an overarching theme that might be used to study the "reconstituted peasantries" of the Caribbean.[2]

The establishment of postemancipation villages in the Caribbean did not free their inhabitants from the wider plantation economy. Although the hillside peasants of Jamaica and the freedmen[3] of Guyana's coastal mudflats inhabited their own village communities, they were partly dependent on the cash derived from seasonal estate work as well as from the sale of their farm surpluses at plantation markets, which necessitated traveling back and forth between village and plantation. Newly freed slaves on some of the smaller and more densely populated islands of the British Caribbean, however, faced different circumstances. In several of the smaller islands, little if any land was available for subsistence plots or for truly independent village communities. Freed slaves on these small islands of the eastern Caribbean—including St. Kitts, Nevis, Montserrat, Barbados, Grenada, St. Vincent, and the others to a lesser extent—commonly chose to migrate away for better wages and to return with money earned elsewhere in order to support families left behind. In other words, on several of the smaller islands a "migration adaptation" served a function roughly analogous to a "village adaptation." Migrating away for wages, although the earliest destinations were often other plantation islands, was an assertion of independence. It was not a complete escape from the larger plantation sphere, but neither did it represent a docile willingness to accept local conditions dictated by former plantation masters. The movement of people back and forth among the small Caribbean islands and beyond continues to the present day.

The islanders accomplished their back-and-forth voyages after emancipation on small and exceptionally dangerous sailing craft. Since then, both men and women of the smaller Caribbean islands have reacted to the stresses, the uncertainties, and the monotony of their particular island environments by traveling away for work, often under trying conditions. Although many of these labor migrants have departed altogether, probably many more have returned or maintained close contact with the home community. Most important, their travels have been crucial in sustaining the local societies. We are, therefore, not dealing simply with movements or migrations of people from one place to another but with a mobile livelihood system that has evolved within the broader framework of, and partially in opposition to, the continuing domination of the Caribbean by outside forces. Livelihood migration from several small West Indian islands has long since become legitimated by time. It is now a traditional process, a process that paradoxically calls for people to leave, though often to return again, in order to maintain and improve what they had left behind.[4]

A search for the origins of a Caribbean migration tradition must begin with plantation slavery. Planter and slave on the islands, though mutually interdependent, faced a continuous struggle with one another—one for cheap labor, the other for freedom. The struggle continues today in the Caribbean between foreign power holders, who continue to dominate the region in a variety of ways, and the individual islanders, who attempt to wrest their livelihoods from a world they do not control. This search, beginning with slavery, also underlines the Caribbean-based nature of the struggle. Although the first planters were European and the slaves were African, their interaction took place on the islands and rimlands of the Caribbean. And although West Indians have drawn upon and borrowed from a number of traditions, predominantly from Africa but also from Europe, Asia, and elsewhere, their cultures are uniquely Caribbean— locally adaptive systems of livelihood, kinship, and ceremony that have evolved in West Indian settings.

The insularity of the Caribbean islands has enabled each place to develop its own cultural traditions, yet it has also helped encourage the human migration common everywhere in the region. A combination of history and local environments, however, have produced more migration in some places than in others. For instance, on the British Leewards after emancipation, local land law left virtually all of the islands' lands in the hands of planters; this situation led to the early migration adaptation by freedmen.

The relationships between people and land in the Caribbean lack the historical continuity found in most other ex-colonial regions. The indigenous population of the West Indies was eliminated shortly after Europeans took control of the area, then African slaves were imported. Although black slaves, to be sure, interacted directly with the islands' physical environments, the forms of this interaction were invariably mediated and determined by a white planter class. The memory of this imposition, according to agricultural development dogma in the Caribbean, makes young people today "refuse" to work the land. Yet there is enough countervailing evidence to qualify, if not reject, this notion. In case after case, when small land plots have become available on the islands, West Indians have spent their saved earnings to obtain them. Ownership of one's own land in the Caribbean signifies pride, prestige, and a sense of rootedness: "The aim of runaway slaves was more than flight; it was recognized sovereignty over the land itself."[5] A refusal to work as a laborer on another's estate is one thing; personal control over one's own land is entirely another.

Today the newly independent states of the Commonwealth Caribbean are taking control of most of the islands themselves after centuries of expatriate control. Most observers find local ownership and control a positive approach if there is to be economic self-sufficiency in the region. At the same time, we must again look to the Caribbean's plantation history for perspective on current and future land use in the region and the implications for its people. Caribbean island ecosystems, like the region's common people, have been subject to outside control since the late fifteenth century. As plantation profits have flowed to metropolitan centers, the islands of the Caribbean, especially the smaller islands, have undergone systematic ecological change. Forests have been converted to canelands, and, in some cases, to cotton fields and subsequently to grazing lands. Deforestation, soil erosion, and greater susceptibility to hurricanes and droughts reinforce the islands' dependency on external food sources. The area's physical environments—destabilized, modified, and depleted by centuries of colonial control—do not support and cannot guarantee the success of livelihood strategies based entirely on local resources and opportunities. This leaves little to interpose between the demands of the outside world and the needs of Caribbean islanders. The persistence of human migration as livelihood is therefore one of the few alternatives available to West Indians of the smaller islands in coping with a precarious and ongoing economic dependency that they have inherited from the Caribbean's plantation past.

The Early Caribbean Setting

The Caribbean has been appropriately described as a rimland, an area whose constituent parts may be referred to by cardinal compass points but never a center.[6] The mountains of Cuba, Hispaniola, and Puerto Rico are geological extensions of the highlands of southern Mexico. Most of the Lesser Antilles chain, however, lies along an intersection of two of the earth's crustal plates, thereby explaining its igneous cores, high earthquake frequencies, and occasional volcanic eruptions. These generalities account for only the broad physiographic patterns of the Caribbean. Exceptions are the dry outlying islands of the northeastern Caribbean, Barbados, which is associated with older marine sediments, and Trinidad, which is geologically related to Venezuela.

Rainfall generally increases from north to south through the Caribbean with maximum seasonal precipitation usually occurring in the late summer and fall of the Northern Hemisphere. Annual hurricanes (from the

Carib *furacan)* travel through the region in a generally south-to-north trajectory from August to October. Island topography is as important as latitude in determining annual rainfall; the higher peaks trigger rain from the prevailing easterly winds, while the lower islands suffer from more frequent drought. Recurring drought throughout the region as a whole is especially noticeable on the smaller islands, its effects exacerbated by the ecological changes in the Caribbean during the region's half millennium of European domination.

The biogeography of the Pre-Columbian Antilles was quite different from today's. In general the islands were more heavily forested, the larger islands possessing the greater variety of tree species. Forest complexes varied from island to island, highlands to lowlands, and from wetter to drier areas. True rainforests were rare, since most forests were seasonal.' On the leeward sides of the larger islands, and more generally on the smaller, low-lying islands, forest cover gave way to thorn scrub and grasses. The native fauna of the region was similarly more numerous and involved greater variety than in post-conquest times. Rodents and bats were the only land-dwelling mammals except in Trinidad. Wild birds were plentiful, and fish, shellfish, turtles, and waterfowl apparently abounded in the shallow waters around each island.[8]

Fishing and aquatic collecting probably attracted the first people into the Caribbean region. The early Ciboney collecting people perhaps sailed or drifted to the Greater Antilles, following large sea mammals from Yucatán and Central America possibly as early as 5000 B.C.[9] At about the time of Christ other Amerindians from Venezuela and the Guianas were island-hopping into the Caribbean, reinforced by the security of being able to see each successive island on their way north.

The Caribbean economy encountered by the first Spanish explorers was a mixture of cultivation and fishing. Four subtribes of Arawaks farmed subsistence plots in the Greater Antilles and the Bahamas. The smaller islands of the Lesser Antilles were inhabited by the Caribs, who had more recently migrated from the south. The Caribs exploited coastal reefs and deepwater banks from their dugout canoes with a complex array of hooks, lines, and traps. In later decades Carib fishermen passed techniques on to slaves of French planters, a cultural transfer that has perpetuated, at least in part, a Pre-Columbian fishing tradition in the Caribbean of today.[10]

Although the Spaniards were soon preoccupied with the aboriginal civilizations of highland Mexico and Peru, their contact with the Caribbean changed the region irrevocably. On Hispaniola the Arawaks mined gold and cultivated food for the Spanish and died from enslavement, disease, and overwork. Their high mortality rates led the Spanish to raid neighboring Caribbean islands for more workers. In 1509, slave-raiding parties traveled to the Bahamas and Jamaica. Two years later the inhabitants of Trinidad were declared cannibalistic "Caribs" in order to justify the activities of Spanish slavers there.

Spanish crops, animals, and lumbering activities altered the native vegetation of the Antilles.[11] Wood was necessary for fuel, building material, and gold smelting. The increase in agriculture, moreover, called for forest removal. A shipbuilding industry was sustained by native hardwoods of the region. Deforestation and the introduction of animals, especially on Hispaniola, doubtless played supporting roles in the near-extinction of the aboriginal population, in effect causing them to be outcompeted for their native lands.

Columbus brought sugar cane to Hispaniola on his second voyage. This expansion into the Caribbean was a "logical continuation" of the sugar-cane industry, which had been coupled with slavery in the eastern Mediterranean by the twelfth century and had moved as far as Portuguese Madeira on the eve of Columbus's first Atlantic voyage.[12] Several black African slaves were introduced to Hispaniola as early as 1505 to replace the "weak" and declining native population. Almost upon arrival a few of the Africans escaped into the mountains.[13] The new slaves were hardy and strong workers in the gold mines, and they were soon being brought to the island in larger numbers from the Cape Verde Islands and directly from Africa. After the gold was gone, the Africans were set to work on the sugar estates on the southern side of the island. Spanish colonial interest, however, was soon focused strongly toward colonizing Central America and South America. Sugar cane and imported Africans had nevertheless been joined almost immediately after the European intrusion into the New World, an enduring Caribbean association that predates Plymouth Rock by a full century.

Plantations and Slavery: The Profits of Environmental Change

Sugar cane was introduced to English Barbados in the 1640s, and sugar cultivation using slave labor spread to other islands of the English Caribbean in an institution different from the earlier Spanish colonies in both location and economic intensity. Tied closely to London and other Atlantic regions of the empire through monopoly capitalism, the plantation of the British Caribbean became a source of spectacular individual and national wealth. The West Indian plantation was a new creation in a subtropical setting, not simply extracting local products but introducing factors of production from all over the world: an Asian crop (sugar cane); African labor, cultivating techniques, and foodstuffs; North American food supplies and building materials; and European capital, equipment, and technology.[14]

The sugar-cane plantation of the British Caribbean has experienced inevitable technological change during three and one-half centuries. In the mid-seventeenth century on an estate of two hundred acres, canes were planted and harvested by slaves, then were carried to the plantation settlement where they were crushed by mills powered by animals, water, or wind. Variations of this relatively simple mode of sugar production persisted until the early nineteenth century. By that time, techniques more commonly associated with the European and American industrial revolutions had been introduced to reinvigorate the Caribbean plantation. Steampowered mills, improved boiling pans, chemical fertilizers, macadam roads, and cog rails appeared in Trinidad and British Guiana by the first half of the nineteenth century. Formerly Spanish and Dutch possessions, these new territories were unfettered by the erosion, obsolete equipment, and outdated infrastructures of the original small plantations on other British islands. Large-scale sugar-producing technologies eventually spread to much of the rest of the Commonwealth Caribbean.

The development of cane plantations in the British Caribbean called for large-scale clearing of the native vegetation. The overall ecological effect of this massive change was to convert the multispecies island ecosystems into those favoring a limited number of cultivated plants. The earlier activities of aboriginal woodsmen and even Spanish colonists had slight effect in comparison with the sharp ecological discontinuity that accompanied the British plantation clearing. Entire forested areas were removed with axes, and then the underbrush was cleared and burned, leaving exposed ground.[15] African slaves accomplished the forest clearance itself. The task of felling thousands of acres of tropical forest using handaxes was so arduous as to be a possible contributing factor to the unusually high death rates among slaves during the early stages of plantation development.[16]

Beyond initial clearing, the plantation placed other demands upon native vegetation. Building materials were necessary for dwellings, processing buldings, animal pens, and seasonal repairs. Most important, loads of firewood were burned to fuel the sugar-juice boilers during the processing season. In several of the smaller plantation islands the timber was rapidly exhausted, and forested zones were denuded to the most precipitous slopes. The need for firewood then led to the clearing of parts of nearby nonplantation islands. After much of the Antilles' original forest had been felled and burned, crushed canes and cane leaves were commonly used as boiler fuel, although there were occasional supplements of British coal imported as ship ballast.

Besides serving the utilitarian functions of making way for and fueling the production of raw sugar, Caribbean forest clearance was also thought to promote better health among European settlers. Unhealthy "fevers" and "airs" were thought to abound in woods because of poor wind circulation. French sailors burned the whole island of St. Croix in the mid-seventeenth century in order to render it more fit for human habitation![17] Indiscriminate and apparently widespread burning was possibly a reaction to the high mortality and morbidity experienced by Europeans entering a new disease environment. Whatever the reason, burning led to major environmental change, especially in some of the smaller and drier islands.

Soil depletion and erosion inevitably resulted from forest clearance in the early British Caribbean. The earlier cultivation of tobacco, cotton, and food crops on Barbados had already decreased the fertility of some of its soil. by 1689, several Barbadian estates had been abandoned, partly because of a decline in soil productivity.[18] The removal of island vegetation had eliminated the protective forest microclimates that had both ameliorated the climatic extremes of the region and allowed insular soils to develop, and the climatic perturbations of the area now became environmental hazards. The late summer and autumn rains that had once nurtured native forests were now pounding, erosive agents, washing tons of topsoil into the sea. Droughts were also more serious, quickly evaporating trickles of water from mountain streams in the northern islands; a law in Montserrat in 1702 called for the preservation of vegetation near streams to protect local sources of water.[19]

The steepest islands endured the most sensational cases of soil erosion. Forest clearance on higher slopes led to damaging sheet erosion during rainshowers. By the early nineteenth century, cane cultivation on Nevis had been pushed into intermediate and high elevations. Rainfall then stripped the unprotected hillside slopes, actually enriching the lands of the estates at lower elevations.[20] Some local colonial governments on the steeper islands enacted laws restricting the use of elevated forest areas, restrictions that would eventually limit the potential for the development of free villages after slave emancipation.

The hogs that the Spaniards had left on Barbados were "quickly hunted out for sport and food" in the seventeenth century.[21] The wild pigs were, however, quickly replaced by a complex of alien animals—horses, mules, and oxen—that powered cane-grinding mills. The effects of grazing and trampling by these larger animals added additional stress to the insular environments. Smaller yard animals came from Africa and Europe. West African vervet monkeys, introduced to St. Kitts and Nevis by the French, are given credit for extinguishing several native bird species. The mongoose, introduced to Trinidad in 1870 and Jamaica in 1872 and now found on most of the islands, played a similar role.

The transformation of the islands from forests to cultivated lands created an environment ripe for the introduction of alien grasses. Furthermore, the continuous animal-browsing along cultivated margins and into forested areas tended to favor sun-loving plants, both native and introduced. Grasses and thorn scrub established themselves quickly after deforestation, and natural forest succession was inhibited by continued human and animal disturbance. Deforestation notwithstanding, after colonization the islands appeared drier.

In a broad sense then, the ecological change in the British Caribbean was a destabilizing process. Once begun, soil erosion was difficult to stop. The natural wealth of the region—precious metals, aboriginal populations, and the minerals and nutrients of forests and soils—had been destroyed or seriously modified or had flowed away in the form of tropical staple crops. Economically, the British Caribbean had become a subtropical adjunct of a European-centered economy, and market demand exerted by Europeans made few concessions to Caribbean island environments. Although actual cultivation took place on the islands themselves, little thought was given to soil conservation or similar local corrective action. Planters could, and occasionally did, transport their slaves to new estate holdings on other islands after experiencing low yields from worn-out soils. Metropolitan demand continued for the tropical crops—and profits ran high—for at least two centuries, without regard for the environmental stability of the region.

The forced labor system of the plantation was similarly interrelated with plantation profitability. By the early nineteenth century, slavery "had become the very basis of organized society throughout the British West Indies. . . ."[22] Planters on some islands routinely replenished their labor stocks with new slaves from Africa when high death rates or sexual imbalance led to a decrease in their slaveholdings, favoring such purchases over a more benign but more expensive strategy of slaveholding that would have possibly allowed for a natural increase of slaves. In an exhaustive and trenchant analysis of nineteenth-century slave demography in Jamaica, B. W. Higman suggests that a calculating attitude of the white West Indian planter toward the black slave was simply one side of an ambivalent viewpoint that regarded a slave as a fellow human being and at the same time "a mere unit of power to be weighed against a steer, mule, plough, or wheelbarrow."[23]

An estimated 1.7 million Africans, and possibly more, were transported on slave ships to the British Caribbean during the era of the Atlantic slave trade.[24] Tens of thousands of African slaves suddenly arrived on the islands in the seventeenth century. Their presence and the associated revolution in sugar-cane cultivation swept aside the small-scale tobacco and subsistence farms that had been established by English yeomen. The demographic character of the colonies was irrevocably altered. by 1684 on Barbados, each square mile held an average of 280 slaves. A century later the figure for St. Kitts was 360 per square mile. These averages are remarkable when one considers that most of the land in both places was devoted to export crops. Barbados, St. Kitts, and other smaller islands had become specialized agricultural production units involving the geographic juxtaposition of slaves and canes, with much of the food imported. High human population densities and local food deficits were thus established as features of colonial plantation strategies on the British Caribbean islands—conditions that persist on those same islands today.

Slave dwellings were commonly located near the plantation processing buildings but on ground unfit for more profitable use. In Guyana, for instance, the slave "logies" were invariably situated near the mud sea-walls, continuously threatened by inundation. The plantation equipment and owner's house stood nearby, on slightly elevated and safer sand reefs. On Barbados, the slaves were usually responsible for erecting their own wattle-and-daub huts, with little help from the planters.[25]

The quantity and quality of slave food, both imported and locally produced, varied from one plantation to another. On Jamaica, hillside cultivation grounds for slaves were required by law in 1678. These subsistence areas, where slaves cultivated yams, cassava, potatoes, and bananas, were supplemented by kitchen gardens nearer the slave villages in which a variety of vegetable and tree crops were grown. By the early nineteenth century on Jamaica, slaves owned poultry, pigs, and even cattle. On St. Vincent, slaves subsisted on a wide array of vegetables, eggs, imported foods, and fresh fish from inland streams.[26] Subsistence farming was least important, especially in the early days of slavery, where islands were small, where most land was amenable to cane cultivation, or both. On Barbados, much of the corn fed to slaves came from abroad during the first century of sugar-cane plantations. Thereafter many estates cultivated their own corn. Salt fish from the fishing banks of North America arrived in Barbados periodically, often in a spoiled condition.[27]

Relatively little is known of the domestic family units maintained by Afro-Caribbean slaves. Almost certainly they differed according to local conditions and historical periods. At the same time they must have been linked by an invariant and underlying commitment to kin and friends, based on their common fate of slavery. Fictive kinship ties probably resulted from relationships among those who had been on board slave ships together from West Africa. In some cases the ties may have been more than "fictive," since individual cargoes certainly included captives from common regions, villages, and even families. Several scholars have suggested that the Afro-Caribbean plantation family was, and is, unstable and mother-oriented, owing to the insurmountable oppression associated with slavery.[28] Evidence from two plantations on Jamaica, on the other hand, indicates that the majority of slaves there in the early nineteenth century "lived in simple family households, most of them nuclear units."[29]

The maintenance of family and friendships seems to have been an expression of individuality and humanity in what were often inhuman conditions—and therefore an expression of continuous resistance and adaptive survival. The ultimate form of resistance was escape. Maroons, runaway slaves, were adjuncts of every West Indian slave society, and where a sufficiently large and impenetrable land area lay adjacent to the plantation zone, such as on Jamaica and the Guianas, maroon societies of formidable size and tenacity emerged.[30] Maroons staged raids from their palisaded villages, cultivated their own crops, and occasionally achieved formal autonomy from the colonial governments. It is probably safe to assert that the freedom and independence associated with *marronage* was an irresistible and unending source of inspiration for the plantation slaves. The possibility of rebellion and escape was therefore probably as much a part of daily plantation life in the Caribbean as were agricultural chores; planters had continuously to be on the watch. During inter-European wars for the sugar colonies, for instance, planters were reluctant to arm their slaves to defend against enemy invasions, a fact suggesting that planters and slaves were not always in complete accord about just what and whom to defend.[31]

Prestige among slaves and their differing treatment from planters were generally based on a combination of color and occupational status.[32] On Trinidad and British Guiana, skillful boilermen and mechanics were crucial to the operation of complex machinery on each estate and thus to the very life of the plantation. On the smaller islands, fishermen may have formed a kind of slave elite. The very nature of fishing, apart from the technical and navigational skills involved, would have been attractive to the slaves, since it meant periodic physical removal from the islands and even chances for escape.[33]

Escape by emigration was rare though not unknown. In 1699, twenty Jamaican slaves escaped to Cuba in a canoe. In the last years of slavery, when freedom was imminent, extraisland escape became more feasible. In 1826 an Assembly bill on Nevis regulated local boats, canoes, and waterfront personnel to prevent the escape of debtors or slaves. A folk legend on Carriacou centers around a slave hero who swam there from Grenada after escaping reprisal for an abortive rebellion.[34] In the early nineteenth century a brisk interisland slave trade took thousands from the older, worn-out islands of the British Caribbean to the new sugar-cane plantations on Trinidad and British Guiana.[35] Selected slaves had traveled as far as England with their masters and returned to the West Indies.[36] These travel experiences were doubtless recounted among island slaves, providing a possible basis for the emigration from the smaller British islands upon slave emancipation.

Emancipation and Migration, 1834–1900

Slavery was legally abolished in the British Empire in 1833, and the law was implemented in the following year. Under the British Emancipation Act, planters claimed financial compensation for the 540,559 slaves on the British Caribbean islands and British Guiana. Complete freedom, except on Antigua, where slaves were freed unconditionally, would not come until 1838; a transitional period of "apprenticeship" called for workers above the age of six to perform estate labor as before in exchange for food, clothing, housing, and medical care. Apprenticeship was enforced clumsily by a few special magistrates who investigated claims and counterclaims by both planters and laborers concerning work rules and benefits. The former slaves balked and resisted through this period, understandably "perplexed" at this peculiar kind of freedom.[37]

On August 1, 1838, full emancipation took effect in the British Caribbean. Ex-slaves were now free, but planters invariably continued to dominate the best land. On the larger islands where there was idle land, thousands of former slaves moved away from the estates, forming their own free settlements. A "highland adaptation" on Jamaica and the Windwards saw newly freed blacks build dwellings and establish subsistence farms on the hillsides above the lowland plantations.[38] In British Guiana's "lowland adaptation," former slaves purchased defunct estates and erected their own houses along the public road adjacent to the remaining sugarcane plantations.[39] Though highland and lowland settlement types imposed contrasting ecological demands upon the new residents, both represented a physical withdrawal from the plantation. Many villagers continued to work part-time on nearby estates, but they were now free from the physical constraints of residing there and from the associated planter-imposed sanctions over daily life.

Large-scale peasant resettlement placed new environmental stresses on the plantation-altered islands. Highland zones, heretofore unoccupied (save for occasional maroons), now supported root crops, vegetables, and corn, and were therefore susceptible to runoff erosion during rainshowers. The farming plots were also subject to drought. In 1844, prolonged aridity on Jamaica forced a larger than usual number of hillside farmers to seek work on the plantations below. During the next decade drought created unusual hardship on Antigua. Peasant settlements on Trinidad, established three decades later by indentured Indians, were in swampy areas adjacent to better-drained cane plantations. Subsistence pressures there led to the rapid depletion of fish and crabs in lowland swamps and rivers.[40] Both highland and lowland peasant adaptations led to the exploitation of marginal ecological zones that had previously acted as buffers against climatic extremes. The modification of these areas by the new settlements magnified the problems of erosion, drought, and flooding.

On the smaller islands of the British Caribbean, local peasant adaptations similar to those on Jamaica and Guyana were not possible. Most, if not all, land remained in the hands of the planters, although specific tenure arrangements varied from island to island. On St. Kitts, Nevis, and

17

Montserrat essentially all land remained in the hands of the planter class, who rented house plots to former slaves. On Barbados comparatively few black freedmen acquired independent holdings, giving them no local alternatives to continued estate work. A combination of small island size and an almost complete lack of free land led inevitably to migration. The need to resist, to escape, and generally to assert individual freedom—needs thwarted throughout slavery—could be expressed only by going away.

Despite abortive attempts by small-island planters to immobilize local blacks, migration by freedmen to higher-paying jobs in Trinidad, British Guiana, and, to a slight extent, Jamaica, occurred almost immediately upon full emancipation. The migrants from the small islands thus denied their former masters the full captive labor force they had had during slavery. The ex-slaves did not escape from the larger Pan-Caribbean plantation system, but they made the best of things—asserting their freedom and also taking advantage of relatively high wages (one dollar per day on Trinidad versus fifty cents in the Leewards) offered elsewhere. Their migration was not necessarily permanent. Much of it was seasonal, involving periodic travel back home. Although many freedmen did take up residence in their new workplaces, most of the others returned to family and friends. As early as 1837, freedmen from Antigua had emigrated to Demerara and had sent messages to friends and relatives staying behind.[41]

Planters of Trinidad and British Guiana eventually "solved" the claimed postemancipation labor shortage by importing hundreds of thousands of indentured workers from India over the next several decades. Immediately after emancipation, however, the southern Caribbean planters sought to entice workers from Barbados and the Leewards. In 1840, for example, Governor Light of British Guiana offered to convey, at government expense, the entire population of Anguilla to his colony![42] The combination of small islanders wishing to emigrate and southern planters seeking labor led to a movement of thousands to the southern areas.[43]

The voyages themselves were hazardous journeys on light wooden sailing vessels, and death by drowning and mishap was doubtless as routine as it is today in the Lesser Antilles. Limited navigational abilities of novice long-range sailors and the storms and squalls of interisland passages must have killed hundreds or more. Avoiding Guadeloupe and Martinique, where slavery was not terminated until 1848, possibly entailed sailing far out from land in rough and unprotected waters or a night passage, both strategies fraught with danger. In short, successful labor migration from small British islands, especially from the Leewards, which were far from work destinations, was dangerous and required considerable courage in dealing with both natural and human hazards. When a successful migrant returned, after a journey characterized by the same dangers as the one going out, it is inconceivable that he or she was received with anything but admiration and respect. It is therefore entirely reasonable to suggest that migrants who returned were held in greater esteem than those who had remained. Those who had gone away and successfully returned with gifts for loved ones and tales of perils overcome had beaten the system, while those who had stayed behind had not. Thus, in the small island societies of the British Caribbean, a laboring elite, associated precisely with successful labor migration and return, quite possibly had been formed within a decade after slave emancipation. This elite would have derived its prestige independently of, and as a result of opposition to, the European-oriented society that formally controlled the area.

Interisland labor migration in the West Indies continued throughout the remainder of the nineteenth century and increased as steamship travel became more common. In 1879, regular steamer travel was established between Jamaica and New York, but the steamship had already connected the major Caribbean islands before then. Those prosperous enough began to travel outside the West Indies, some settling in the eastern United States, notably in New York and Boston. Poorer black islanders booked passage as "deckers," traveling from one island to another. In 1877 the steamer *May Flower* began regular service between crowded Barbados and British Guiana, reinforcing migration links already established.[44] By 1884, almost 35,000 Jamaicans had traveled to Panama as part of the French effort to buld the Panama Canal. And workers from Jamaica had already begun to travel by steamship to the American-owned banana plantations in the Limón district of eastern Costa Rica.[45]

At least two major differences existed between migrations from small islands at the time of emancipation and interisland movements later in the nineteenth century. First, the early small-island movements were free, adventuresome sailing voyages controlled by black West Indians; steamer travel, on the other hand, involved white corporation agents shuffling itinerant laborers back and forth to meet business-decreed labor needs. Second, the small-island migrations represented initial, postemancipation cultural imprints; in contrast, on Jamaica and in the Windwards, the early village "highland adaptations" symbolized the first freedom from planter control. These two differences help explain why small islanders, whose ancestors accomplished the earliest migration adaptation, seem to continue to place greater emphasis on migration than do those from larger places, although the latter subsequently have accounted for a greater volume of exported labor.

Migration in the Twentieth Century

In 1897, the Royal Commission investigating social and economic conditions in the British Caribbean suggested that cotton be considered as a potential cash crop for the smaller islands, which were unable to sustain large-scale sugar industries, owing to both size and aridity. Sea-island cotton from the Carolinas was therefore cultivated on St. Lucia and the Leewards in 1901 and 1902.[46] The experiment seemed successful, and because of relatively high cotton prices, portions of Nevis, Antigua, and Montserrat were converted from cane to cotton. This conversion was a reflection of changing sugar-cane technology that now needed larger areas for sustained profits. Lands on small islands, heretofore devoted to cane, now came under cotton and also peasant-produced rootcrops and vegetables. As a result, local farmers on small islands have since had greater autonomy over their islands' lands, although cultivation of cotton and other crops requiring clean, open-row tillage has accelerated soil erosion and nitrogen depletion. Sugar cane is a grass; it generally shades, anchors, and maintains the soil better than crops requiring clean-cropping. The conversion of small Caribbean islands from cane to other crops, combined with growing livestock populations, has led to ever more serious environmental degradation, further encouraging human emigration.

Labor migration from the islands in this century has been both permanent and temporary, encompassing millions of individual journeys. It has, moreover, ameliorated the unending population pressures on the islands while also serving metropolitan labor needs. Migrating West Indian workers have since 1900 served North Atlantic capitalism in the Caribbean region and beyond. International corporations have built highways, railroads, oil refineries, tourist hotels, sugar mills, and other facilities around the Caribbean, creating brief but intensive construction periods in different places. These boom and bust wage labor cycles have called for thousands of semiskilled West Indians to travel from one place to another for employment.

The Panama Canal is perhaps the most dramatic testimony to any of the work ever performed by migrating West Indian laborers. The few remaining old men of the islands who worked there refer to themselves with fraternal pride as veterans of the "Panama Gang." From 1905 to 1913, "a constant number . . . of 35,000" mainly from Jamaica and Barbados, worked on the canal.[47] And between 1906 and 1916, more than 13,000 British West Indians died in the Canal Zone from disease and accidents, mishaps duly reported in contemporary West Indian newspapers:

> The following are the names of the West Indians killed or injured in the explosion at Bas Obispo, Panama, early last month: John Brown, black, Barbadian, fireman, mutilated; Charles Sylvester, black, Antiguan, injured; Henry Allen, black, Montserrat, injured; Abraham Phillips, black, St. Kitts, injured; Wilfred Harrison, black, Jamaican, killed; James Thomas, black, Antiguan, injured; George Cole, black, Antiguan, injured. The bodies of four blacks were recovered, but they could not be identified owing to their shattered condition.[48]

A more important source of wage labor for residents of the Leeward Islands was the construction of the Bermuda naval dockyards beginning in 1900. Men and women, mainly of St. Kitts, Nevis, and Antigua, the closest Caribbean islands, arranged steamer deck passage to Bermuda. Proximity to work destinations generally has been important in helping to explain the migrants' islands of origin in intra-Caribbean movements in this century. The construction of the oil derricks of Lake Maracaibo, for instance, attracted laborers from Barbados, Trinidad, the Windwards, and the Grenadines. These were men familiar with work in and around the water, and their home islands were relatively close to Venezuela.

While British West Indian sugar companies attempted to modernize their industries on small, exhausted, and technically antiquated islands, they faced severe competition for their best laborers. American capital investment in Cuba and the Dominican Republic during the first three decades of this century developed enormous sugar cane estates. The harvest period during the first half of each year called for the exodus of tens of thousands of Haitians, Jamaicans, and small islanders of the British Caribbean to the large Hispanic islands and back again. Black cane-cutters from the British islands supported both themselves and their families at home from their annual work sojourns to Cuba and the Dominican Republic, although they met abuse and prejudice as a black, predominately male, linguistically alien, large, itinerant population. In both places they were regarded as agents of foreign capitalists, and acts of violence between guest and host populations were not uncommon. At the beginning of the world economic depression both Spanish-speaking islands decreed immigration quotas denying entry to and deporting "colored" workers from the British West Indies.

Racial restriction to labor emigration was not new to the British Caribbean. But in the 1930s the depression curtailed the outlay of investment capital in the Caribbean area and the job prospects for what was by now a veteran migrant force. The pent-up frustration of men who had emigrated annually but who now had no place to go ignited the explosive political character of the British Caribbean in the 1930s. The first of a series of West Indian labor disputes, the St. Kitts riots in 1935, was partially attributed to Basseterre's function as a transshipment point for cane cutters to the larger Spanish-speaking islands and therefore a town where there was normally a large crowd of unemployed men.

World War II provided slight relief in the form of a few short-lived labor migration destinations within the Caribbean area. United States armed forces bases at Atkinson Field in British Guiana, Coolidge Field in Antigua, and the Chaguaramas complex in Trinidad attracted local men and women as well as those from nearby islands. Also in the 1940s black West Indians—mainly from Grenada, St. Vincent, and the Grenadines—were traveling to oil refinery jobs in the Netherlands Antilles. In the following decade refinery automation on Aruba and Curaçao led to the by now familiar layoffs and subsequent deportation for black British West Indians.

The decade of the 1950s marks the period of massive human emigration from the British Caribbean to the United Kingdom. The estimates of total Caribbean migration to the United Kingdom from 1951 to 1961 range between 230,000 and 280,000. The smaller islands contributed the highest percentages of their total populations; Montserrat lost over 30 percent of its people to England in this decade.[49]

Afro-Caribbean emigrants to the "mother country" were initially enthusiastic about moving. Since then, high rates of unemployment, low social status, and a complete lack of assimilation into the population at large, generally have replaced enthusiasm with alienation. The West Indian community in Britain enjoys a certain social insularity; closer kin and friendship patterns are maintained among those from particular islands than with the Caribbean community at large.[50] But remarkably high percentages of Afro-Caribbean British suggest that they would prefer returning to the West Indies.[51]

Caribbean blacks emigrating to North America seem in general more satisfied with their choice than those who have emigrated to Britain. West

Indians have traveled to and settled in the eastern United States since the late nineteenth century. After the Commonwealth Immigrants Act of 1962 (which essentially stopped West Indian migration to Britain) and the United States' revisions of its immigration policies in 1965, the flow of Caribbean migrants has been focused more than ever toward North America. Between 1950 and 1972 roughly 100,000 British West Indians went to Canada. During that period 200,000 entered the United States legally and possibly an additional 150,000 illegally.[52]

The most recent work destination within the Caribbean has been the United States Virgin Islands. A tourist boom in the 1960s called for construction work on St. Thomas, and the Hess oil refinery on St. Croix has similarly attracted labor migrants. Other migrants work as taxi drivers, tour guides, waiters, maids, refinery laborers, and domestics. In 1975, semiofficial population estimates on the Virgin Islands put the number of West Indian "aliens" at 10,000, the majority from the Leeward Islands of Antigua, St. Kitts, Nevis, and Anguilla.

A chronology of principal destinations for migrating West Indians since slave emancipation understates the interisland mobility that is vital to West Indian livelihood. For instance, seasonal cane-cutters traditionally travel from Nevis to St. Kitts and from the Windwards to Trinidad, and Barbadians are found throughout the Caribbean as artisans, professionals, and laborers. Hundreds of workers from Dominica find seasonal employment in Guadeloupe and Martinique. Thousands of West Indians have harvested crops in the United States and Canada for years.

The Resultant Migration Cultures

The more recent Commonwealth Caribbean emigrants to metropolitan destinations have been equated, in the minds of their predominantly white hosts, with the larger islands. To some Londoners all black West Indians are "Jamaicans," and rural Americans apply the same lack of distinction to seasonal West Indian farm laborers. Indeed, the larger and more populous islands have exported the greatest absolute numbers to North America and England. From 1950 to 1972, for instance, 110,000 Jamaicans emigrated legally to the United States, and only 22,000 emigrated from the Leewards and Windwards combined.[53] Within the Caribbean region itself, on the other hand, it is the smaller places where a migration ethos, as well as more tangible attributes of migration, underpin entire island communities. Expatriate social scientists invariably have been struck by the importance of migration on small islands of the Commonwealth Caribbean. Within the last two decades, anthropologists on Nevis, Carriacou, St. Lucia, Dominica, Montserrat, St. Vincent, and Grenada have spent lengthy research periods dealing with aspects of human migration.[54]

The term *migration culture* as used here refers to locally adaptive traits pertaining to the particular island society in question. Though all of the islands have generally similar human and environmental qualities, each place is distinct. Generations have been born, lived, and died, in both slavery and its aftermath, on their particular islands. And modes of livelihood, interpersonal relationships, and ceremony have evolved in unique physical settings. A West Indian distinguishes himself from others on the basis of his home island, which is often the broadest allegiance that he knows.[55]

Migration from the smaller islands obviously connotes going away, but there is usually return, and, more important, migration is economically and socially fundamental to insular ways of life. Small size and ecological deterioration doubtless explain much of this movement. Owing to a lack of diversity both economically and ecologically, residents of smaller islands constantly must seek work elsewhere given even minimal drought, depression, or other perturbations. Successful migrations and returns reinforce the tradition of earliest triumphant returnees from Trinidad and British Guiana. Today on smaller islands, such as Montserrat, elaborate parties or fetes continue to mark a migrant's departure and homecoming.[56]

A black migrating elite formed immediately after slavery would have derived its status independent from a European planter-dominated prestige system. Although migrating black men have earned money and achieved success abroad, their social standing has been confined mainly to their home islands. On the other hand, individuals of the mixed-blood middle class that was first formed during slavery derive their standing within a wider, European-oriented prestige system based on skin color, occupation, and accumulated wealth. This distinction between groups based on color and class may help explain general differences between permanent and temporary migration from the islands that persist today. "Getting ahead" for an individual of mixed blood calls for conventional education, the acquisition of job skills, and the accumulation of enough money eventually to leave the island permanently. Indeed, a disproportionate amount of the permanent emigration to extra-Caribbean regions seems to have been accomplished by middle-class West Indians of mixed blood.[57] Lighter-skinned West Indians also have found it easier to assimilate into British, Canadian, or American societies than have their darker counterparts. "Lower-class" black islanders have, on the other hand, usually migrated away temporarily for wage labor, and they have then returned. This, of course, perpetuates the "freedmen elite" tradition of postslavery. In the case of Nevis, Richard Frucht presented an intriguing discussion of contemporary black smallholders, locally known as special people.[58] This group, a local "lower-class elite," migrates predominantly to other Caribbean islands, eventually to return, while much of the "colored" middle class has left the island permanently.

Individuals, usually men, have perpetuated the tradition of a migration elite in the smaller Caribbean islands. Their travels, to be successful, have required achievement based on individual intelligence, acuity, and skill, combined with physical strength and job abilities, in the face of ever-changing economic circumstances. The outside world, upon which migrating islanders have depended for sustenance and success, has presented a fluid array of obstacles, hazards, and rewards. Successful migration has required a keen understanding of the way the outside world operates and fails to operate. Economic specialization has had few long-term rewards. Strength and endurance may be necessary on only one job, while the ability to haggle successfully with immigration officials or foreign supervisors may be crucial to avoid being deported or laid off. In the face of continuing uncertainty, migrating islanders have usually foregone permanent commitments in any one direction except for eventually returning home. Since successfully coping with the many hazards facing extraisland migrants requires them to display a variety of talents and to overcome formidable obstacles, returning men are understandably proud of their achievements. "So when men gather together in rum shops or beneath the palm trees on the beach much of their conversation is taken up with stories of their exploits—mostly those that occurred abroad."[59]

Economic underspecialization, a calculated lack of permanent job commitment in the face of continuing uncertainty, is found throughout the British Caribbean.[60] To the interviewer's question about what one does for a living, the respondent might answer by indicating a particular job type, but many small islanders then add "also working all about." The lack of individual aspiration for a particular profession or job type is, of course, less a lack of ambition than it is a keen awareness of future uncertainty. Ideas about underspecialization are often passed from one generation to the next; in interviewing schoolchildren on Montserrat,

Stuart Philpott learned that one boy wished to become eventually a mechanic, a chauffeur, a policeman, *and* a carpenter.[61]

The astonishing sums of money remitted to home islands by West Indians working elsewhere are evidence of economic achievement abroad, and they provide vital support for those left behind. Barbadian emigrants were sending postal money orders home as early as 1865. In 1968 alone, Jamaicans working in the United Kingdom sent £6.5 million home in postal and bank money orders.[62] Relative figures show that remitted money actually is more vital to the smaller islands. In 1973 in Carriacou (resident population 6,000), I found that the equivalent of slightly more than U.S. $500,000 had been sent to the residents of the island the year before in both postal money orders and through the island's single bank.[63] Almost certainly as much or more was sent or brought back as cash. Gifts are also sent home, especially at Christmas—clothing, furniture, and used household appliances. Islanders abroad thereby maintain prestige *in absentia* by sending family members money and gifts. Every small island has similar anecdotal "treasure tales" told often about faithful returning migrants who sewed thousands of dollars or pounds of foreign currency into their clothing to avoid currency regulations or who smuggled expensive goods into the island to benefit their families. Remitting money from abroad is not simply a means of earning local prestige. It is also an adaptation to uncertainty abroad. Changing rules in host countries can lead to deportation. A young man or woman who has regularly remitted money in his or her absence receives a warmer homecoming than one who has not.

Money earned abroad becomes a source of economic prestige for returning labor migrants, since it elevates them to relatively prosperous positions as taxi drivers, shopkeepers, or landowners. Many men work abroad until they have earned enough to purchase a fishing boat (which they then invariably name *Success, Endeavor,* or *Courage)* as well as lines, nets, traps, and an outboard motor. Houses and rum shops are occasionally named in honor of the particular work place where the funds were earned to build them. Names from St. Thomas and St. Croix ("Crucian Moon") dot the countryside on St. Kitts and Nevis. Concrete block "Curaçao" houses are found in Montserrat. Dwellings on Carriacou with relatively elaborate water catchment systems and expensive concrete cisterns are "Aruba" houses.

The absence of so many family members and friends for such long periods is reflected in family relationships and demographic patterns. The smallest islands often appear to be societies of grandparents and grandchildren. Parents are away working, sometimes for years, and grandparents are left to look after the young. Island officials deplore this situation, suggesting that children misbehave because the old folks cannot look after them properly. Family structure also is affected by migration. Mother-centered households predominate on the small islands of the Caribbean, especially during the times when many of the men are absent seasonally or for longer periods. No simple classification or typology "explains" family structure on the basis of differential migration; rather a variety of family forms exists in the Caribbean under varying economic conditions.[64] This variety itself represents resilience and adaptability in the face of change and uncertainty.

Local systems of work and production are altered when many of the younger, more vigorous islanders have gone away. Many younger men of St. Kitts recently have worked in the Virgin Islands, so that the men and, increasingly, women in Kittitian cane-cutting gangs often average fifty years of age and older. On Montserrat reciprocal family exchange systems, such as mutual cotton harvesting, are difficult, if not impossible, to maintain as more and more people have emigrated.[65] Then there is the possibility that family and friends will never return and be lost to the outside world forever. Though permanent departure has relieved local population pressures and associated ecological stress, the continuous loss of loved ones inevitably leads to a certain despair.[66]

None of the smaller islands of the Commonwealth Caribbean faces complete depopulation through emigration, especially since many of the traditional legal emigration outlets now are closed. Nevertheless, high rates of permanent emigration probably will continue to characterize these islands, at least in the near future. The fact of permanent emigration does not necessarily invalidate the migrating black elite hypothesis. Because people are attracted away and leave permanently does not mean that this tradition is not felt by those who stay. On Nevis, for instance, the voluntary departure of much of the middle class has left most of the island resources in the hands of the special people. Indeed, as formal colonial controls recede and as political autonomy for even the smallest islands becomes imminent, it seems possible that the ultimate in island-based prestige, full political control, will fall to the descendants of the migrating black elite, or at least to those who follow this cultural tradition.

Several political leaders of the Leeward and Windward islands have themselves been labor migrants. The most notable example is former Prime Minister Eric Gairy of Grenada, who emigrated to Trinidad during World War II to work on an American base; he later became a union organizer in the Aruban oil refining industry. Gairy describes himself as being from among Grenada's "decent poor."[67]

Population Pressures, Insularity, and Environmental Deterioration

With the systematic termination of most formal, large-scale emigration outlets, the recurring dilemma of too many people for too little land has become acute in the Caribbean. The problems of Caribbean overpopulation and related social and political stress have drawn attention even from the metropolitan news media. Stories on population pressures and resource-related problems of the Caribbean, however, almost invariably neglect to mention that such "crises" are not new to the region. The immediate need for a migration "safety valve" was reported at least three decades ago.[68] Before World War II, Caribbean island populations were alarmed that imminent warfare might restrict shipping and therefore diminish supplies of imported food. In September 1938, the *Voice of St. Lucia* published an editorial entitled, "If War Comes—We May Starve." And virtually all Caribbean agricultural reports and soil surveys in this century have been prefaced with the immediacy associated with the area's high human population densities and limited local resources.

An emphasis on the recurring nature of the population-resource problems of the Commonwealth Caribbean is not an attempt to minimize the gravity of current problems there. Unemployment rates of, commonly, 20 to 30 percent mask both the tenuous nature of most jobs in the region as well as the widespread underemployment. Here again the lack of jobs is a traditional characteristic of the region—not circumstances precipitated by unforeseen or sudden economic events. The general age structure of the population suggests that unemployment and underemployment rates already are rising faster and higher than the most recent figures provided by the local governments. The 1970 Population Census of the Commonwealth Caribbean, for instance, shows that roughly 55 percent of all Jamaicans are twenty years old or younger, a percentage slightly *lower* than those for most of the smaller islands. Population control programs were sponsored by the Barbados government in 1955; Jamaica and Trinidad and Tobago followed in the next decade with similar programs.[69]

Most of the smaller islands now also have at least government acceptance of population control programs, often implemented or sponsored by the representatives of international agencies.

In light of the recurring population pressures on the islands, the associated and ever-present need to import food becomes crucial. A historical emphasis on cash crops or an unwillingness of the populace to work agriculturally because of the memory of slavery usually are suggested "reasons" for a relative lack of locally grown food on Caribbean islands. Both seem partially correct, although they underemphasize the persistence of the "introduced overpopulation" that characterized plantation slavery and the subsequent lack of encouragement of, and even discrimination against, subsistence agriculture by earlier colonial governments. Recently independent island states, with limited international economic leverage, are therefore left to reorient food deficit economies created by centuries of colonial rule. Food deficits vary from one island to another, and there is usually a general and worrisome lack of information about how much food is imported compared with that locally produced.

Frozen meat from Australia and New Zealand and canned goods from the United States and elsewhere are purchased by the reasonably affluent, but the "flour boat" from Canada regularly visits the Lesser Antilles, providing a staple for the great majority of the peoples of the islands. In 1970, external sources of food for Jamaica, mainly from the United States, made up 47 percent of calories and 67 percent of all protein consumed on the island.[70] Percentages of imported food on the smaller islands are even higher.

Since independence, Caribbean governments relentlessly have emphasized self-reliance in food production, promoting countless self-help garden programs, grow-more-food campaigns, and the like. These have met with limited local success, and although the poor results defy simplistic analysis, several factors bear on the problem: little prime agricultural land has actually been given over to subsistence crops; local marketing facilities are poor; and many potential cultivators perceive government programs as more rhetorical than substantive. One exception is on Jamaica, where the government restricted the importation of a number of food items in 1973 and 1974, and currency inflation drove the prices of many imports well beyond the reach of most consumers. Encouragingly, local food production was thus increased in rural St. James parish, which then saw less, nor more, malnutrition among children.[71] Jamaica's relatively large size, however, discounts the possible extrapolation that similar self-reliance in local food production would automatically follow throughout the rest of the Commonwealth Caribbean if the volume of imported food were suddenly reduced.

The future for any Caribbean agriculture, whether for home consumption or for export, is clouded by the region's continuously declining carrying capacity. The historically induced soil erosion and depletion, the general deforestation, and the necessary exploitation of marginal environments by growing populations create a vicious circle between people and land. The continued cultivation of sloping hillsides by farmers in upland villages has led to constant erosion; twenty years ago in one rural district of the Blue Mountains of eastern Jamaica, the topsoil already had been completely washed away.[72] On the smallest islands, ecological degradation is acute. Growing livestock herds now browse through thorn scrub on Nevis and Carriacou where forests once stood. On Montserrat the relatively recent cotton cultivation has reduced much of the land's productive capacity for any agriculture.[73] A regional drought in 1977, leading to starvation in Haiti and producing crop and livestock loss south to Trinidad, was severe only partly because of the lack of rain. Grasses and shrubs afford little protection against the sun and thus cannot help the soil to retain moisture in the face of periodic drought. Neither do they inhibit soil loss.

Human migration is an understandable response to such conditions, but migration and ecological change have now become interrelated in the Caribbean, not simply the former following on the heels of the latter. In times of peak migration, such as during the 1950s exodus to England, a declining labor force made livestock-keeping economically attractive, especially on lands already depleted from previous cultivation. Animals are, moreover, ready sources of cash and represent "resources on the hoof," as on Barbuda.[74] And they can be sold to finance further travel. The soaring livestock populations on the smaller, drier islands, however, contribute to further environmental deterioration. Emigration itself has thus indirectly fed the ongoing devastation of the island environments, and some of the changes seem irreversible. Parts of the smaller islands already resemble moonscapes. They seem simply unable to sustain their local resident populations, not to mention future generations or those working abroad who may someday be forced to return for good.

No buffers insulate the island peoples of the Caribbean from the outside world and never have. Centuries of colonial control have left the islands with inherited overpopulation and impoverished environments. Economic dislocation has attracted capital away from most of the smaller islands so that they seem faded relics of a richer colonial past. Continued migration, either permanent or part-time, seems the only realistic alternative for the island cultures, save for the occasional island refinery which reinforces outside control.

Although these islands may seem sleepy and antiquated in physical appearance, they are nonetheless historically linked for survival to a world economy. Locational incongruity between people and the resources they consume is normal in most human societies, magnified in insular states, and fundamental in the Commonwealth Caribbean. International markets for tropical staples affect local wages and living standards there. Quotations from distant banking centers eventually inflate local prices, which in turn means that one must work more to earn more wages to obtain the same imported item.[75] Decisions made abroad create jobs to which local people gravitate for a few years, and similarly distant decisions send them home or on to a new destination. The West Indian lives in a world that is precarious, ever-changing, and beyond his control. And demands from this outside world are relentlessly immediate. It is a curious case of isolated proximity. Everything is near and dear, yet it is also far away.

CHAPTER TWO

The Contemporary Migration Cultures of St. Kitts and Nevis

St. KITTS AND NEVIS (Figure 2) together comprise the British Caribbean's sole remaining Associated State, a political arrangement that calls for internal political autonomy with foreign relations controlled by London. Although only two miles apart, the two islands offer dramatic geographic contrasts, microcosms of the landscape extremes found today in the Commonwealth Caribbean. At first glance, St. Kitts (formally "St. Christopher") appears more "modern" than Nevis—the larger island's ongoing sugar-cane industry creating a protoindustrial atmosphere that is entirely lacking on the smaller island. In terms of Caribbean landscape evolution, however, Nevis is farther along than St. Kitts. Nevis has passed through a sugar-cane plantation period, its lands given over to small producer crops and livestock decades ago. On Nevis, where a local saying has it that "if you buy land, you someone,"[1] there is an almost sentimental attachment to the land. There is little reason for such an outlook on St. Kitts. Land-use contrasts between the two islands are therefore reflected by cultural differences between Kittitians and Nevisians. The islanders themselves recognize these differences, interpreting them as culminating in a St. Kitts–Nevis political rivalry, which is discussed at the conclusion of Chapter 6.

In spite of their differences, the people of St. Kitts and Nevis have much in common. Perhaps most important is a heavy reliance upon human migration. As a visitor to St. Kitts and Nevis becomes more familiar with the two neighboring islands, he or she begins to realize that migration provides the very basis for their contemporary cultures.

The Outsider's View: Arriving on St. Kitts and Nevis

St. Kitts and Nevis offer few gaudy tourist trappings for vacationing North Americans. Neither has the tinsel facade of the duty-free emporium

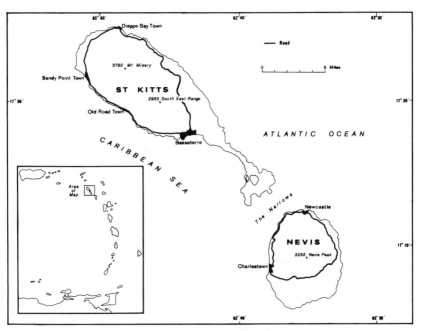

Figure 2. St. Kitts and Nevis

of the American Virgin Islands or the casino atmosphere of St. Martin. St. Kitts has a new jetport and golf resort, and Nevis stresses its tranquility in travel advertisements. But neither island has undergone a major transformation to attract North Americans to visit in droves. A few small boutiques and craft shops have appeared on both islands in the last few years as concessions to the two islands' incipient tourist industries.

Some visitors even stay for a while, despite a dearth of beach parties and limbo contests. A two-hour taxi ride around St. Kitts affords views of the canelands covering the alluvial aprons beneath volcanic Mt. Misery, the evenly spaced villages of wooden houses along the perimeter road, and Brimstone Hill, a spectacular eighteenth-century colonial fortress in the northwestern corner of the island. In direct contrast to the trim neatness of St. Kitts's canelands, Nevis's landscape of coconut palms, open range, and provision farms, scattered around Nevis Peak (the volcanic centerpiece of the island) gives the smaller island an even slower and sleepier appearance. Nevis boasts Alexander Hamilton's birthplace in Charlestown and the ruins of an old bathhouse, formerly a vacation spa for the planter class of the early Caribbean. A small but influential and highly visible colony of

33

Americans and Canadians have buit homes and taken up residence on Nevis in the last fifteen years. They employ a few local maids, gardeners, and construction workers.

Although there are flights between St. Kitts and Nevis, normal passenger travel between the two islands is by boat. A new shallow–draft, diesel–powered vessel, the *Caribe Queen,* covers the twelve miles between Basseterre and Charlestown in about 45 minutes. A limited amount of cargo can be carried on board as well. Other cargo vessels, both motor as well as sailpowered, carry food, lumber, hardware, automobiles, and appliances from St. Kitts to Nevis. Stevedores offload cargo at the pier with winch and slings, an operation invariably accompanied by a great deal of pushing, shouting, and cursing.

Census takers in 1970 counted 33,737 residents on St. Kitts and 11,147 on Nevis. The population is overwhelmingly of African descent. A tiny white elite—bank managers, retail outlet managers, and government advisers from abroad—live in the Basseterre district. A handful of cloth merchants of Mediterranean origin resides in Basseterre. Middle-level economic positions in the capital town are occupied by lighter-skinned persons of mixed blood as are shopkeeper positions in Basseterre and some villages of the St. Kitts countryside. St. Kitts is otherwise populated exclusively by dark-skinned blacks. With a few exceptions, Nevis has been given over entirely to a black population, and "class" there is based on occupational status rather than skin color. The shopkeepers and merchants on Nevis are landowners as well, the special people of the island, all of whom recollect their grandfathers migrating to work abroad, usually to the Venezuela goldfields before the turn of the century.

With a population of 12,000, Basseterre is the unquestioned metropolis of St. Kitts and Nevis. Basseterre, St. Kitts, is a sun-bleached, tired-looking town of stone, stucco, and wood. Vehicular traffic is slight except for the Saturday morning market along the waterfront. Basseterre is the seat of local government, the site of the cable and wireless office, several modern grocery stores, and dry goods and specialty stores. The main hospital is immediately to the west, and east of town is the island's central sugar mill and refinery next to the electricity generating plant. Basseterre's residents are well to do in a relative sense, although there are pockets of "lower-class" housing in the town.

The trip from Basseterre, St. Kitts, to Charlestown, Nevis, seems to involve a passage back in time. The many land rovers and jeeps give Charlestown an almost frontier look at first glance. Charlestown (population about 2,000) offers little in the way of shopping, recreational, and educational amenities. Walking ashore from the town's (and island's) pier, one passes the cotton gin and goes on to Charlestown's single main street. The courthouse building, post office, and small grocery stores surround a tiny square. In the house yards and streets that intersect Charlestown's main thoroughfare, an extraordinarily large number of dogs, cats, chickens, sheep, and goats wander about under varying degrees of control.

Rural dwellings and settlements of St. Kitts and Nevis are typical of the Commonwealth Caribbean. The houses are neither "primitive" thatch or mud nor do they approach North American opulence. Yet is it less helpful to locate St. Kitts and Nevis houses along a theoretical primitive-to-modern continuum than it is to suggest that houses on the two islands reflect local livelihood strategies: dwellings are adapted to the local environment yet they are built with imported materials. Rural dwellings are constructed of wooden planks and consist of two or three rooms with a wooden cooking structure outside. Bamboo fences often surround house yards, especially in St. Kitts. Even the poorest houses contain some kind of manufactured furniture. Sofas and plastic curtains indicate a certain prosperity or at least the regular receipt of remittances from abroad. Almost every house has a glass-fronted case containing souvenirs, curios, and family photographs. A number of rural houses now have small refrigerators, since electricity has recently been extended to all of the settled areas of both islands.

Few village households have running water. Each community is served by communal waterpipes and faucets served by gravity-powered water systems emanating from catchment areas or springs in nearby mountain areas. On Nevis the spring-fed water reservoirs are only seasonally reliable owing to periodic drought, and the more elaborate dwellings in rural Nevis have their own water cisterns. There are usually community showers in the village areas of both islands, and most houses have private latrine pits. Tenure arrangements for house plots differ from one village to the other. In general, Nevisians own their own houseplots, and Kittitians, whose village communities are often technically on estate land, are renters, paying a nominal fee to nearby plantations.

Both islands are precariously dependent upon imported food, fuel, clothing, and building materials. And although no one seems to know the quantitative extent of the two islands' dependence on outside food, everyone agrees that food imports are vital to daily subsistence. Upper- and middle-class groups of both islands are particularly dependent on food imports. On Nevis there is a generally greater subsistence element in the local diet than on St. Kitts, although everyone on both islands depends heavily upon imported flour from Canada and imported rice from Guyana and the United States. In a descending order of monetary value, the most important imported commodities are flour, milk, poultry, and fish.[2] Imported clothing is popular for special occasions, although children's shirts, trousers, and dresses are usually sewn by village tailors and seam-stresses. Shoes and hats are imported and store-bought. Small transistor radios are within the means of most local families. Automobiles are owned by foreigners, the most affluent local residents, or persons involved in transportation. While village shops normally carry small items for daily use—soap, kerosene, cooking oil, powdered milk, crackers, cigarettes, and rum—any more important purchases call for a trip by taxi bus into Basseterre or Charlestown. The economies of both islands are based strictly on cash; although some food is cultivated locally and some very rudimentary processing and manufacturing goes on within each house-hold, few economic transactions on either island occur without money changing hands.

The monetary character of the local economy reinforces its precarious, outward-focused, and externally controlled nature. The Eastern Carib-bean dollar lost 35 percent of its value relative to the United States dollar from mid-1975 to mid-1976, and St. Kitts and Nevis depend upon Puerto Rico, the U.S. Virgin Islands, the United States, and Canada for more than 20 percent of imported goods.[3] By June 1976, rural shopkeepers were no longer able to stock certain canned goods and powdered milk that had traditionally been imported from the United States and Canada. Local savings also have been seriously eroded by a combination of inflation and a decline in emigration possibilities. In 1965, when emigration possibilities were brighter, local bank accounts showed a collective balance of E.C. $1,337,000. In 1973, the collective balance of local depositors had dwin-dled to E.C. $505,000.[4]

A visitor to St. Kitts and Nevis sees little evidence of ill health among the populace, although relatively high incidences of malnutrition afflict the very young and very old. Among 2,094 children who were taken to government sponsored "child welfare" clinics on the two islands in 1972, 536 showed signs of some kind of malnutrition. A number of adults suffer from a combination of poor nutrition and gastrointestinal disease. The infant mortality rate in 1972 was 86 per 1,000 live births.[5] There is one hospital on each island and three smaller infirmaries on St. Kitts and one on

Nevis. Child innoculation campaigns are carried out by the government with the aid of international organizations. Once an individual passes the critical first year of life, assuming adequate diet, longevity is quite common on the two islands, many older men and women living into their 80s and 90s.

The extremely high percentage of children in the local population is perhaps most apparent at the end of a school day in a rural area of either island, when throngs of uniformed schoolchildren are walking home. There are thirty-five primary and secondary schools on St. Kitts and Nevis with a combined enrollment of 13,551. Despite limited educational resources and crowded classrooms, students of both islands are particularly interested in education, and there is a modicum of literacy among all the families of the two islands. Successful completion of secondary school qualifies one for the few local civil servant or clerical positions available or, very rarely, university training abroad. The teachers and principals on the two islands hold some of the few positions of locally based prestige and are looked upon for leadership and wisdom by both students and adults, especially in the rural communities.

Contrasts in Land Use and Livelihood

A mild earthquake startled St. Kitts in early 1975, causing slight damage to the Anglican churches in Basseterre and Middle Island and to a few other buildings in the capital town. Although actual damage was minimal, the quake was strong enough to remind residents of St. Kitts and Nevis of past tremors and of the earthquake on Nevis during slavery that sent an entire plantation and its village sliding into the ocean, an event unconfirmed by historical records but real enough in Nevisian folklore to help shape attitudes about living in the countryside there. Prior to the passage of Hurricane David in the autumn of 1979, the only serious hurricanes in living memory were those of August 1899 and August 1924, although everyone is quite aware of the hurricane vulnerability of the two islands every year from July to October. Rainfall is unpredictable. Annual averages are from 40 inches in the settled lowlands of Nevis to 100 inches at the highest points on Nevis Peak and from about 50 inches in the St. Kitts coastal villages to 150 inches at its highest elevations.[6] High rainfall variability is so typical of both islands that "average" precipitation totals become meaningless, especially during the frequent periods of drought. The windward sides of both islands suffer from wind desiccation and salt spray, and Nevis's conical peak deflects rain-bearing winds unpredictably so that one part of the island may have a downpour while another area remains dry. Environmental uncertainty is therefore part and parcel of the physical underpinning for the two islands.

Although both are volcanic in origin, St. Kitts (67 square miles) and Nevis (36 square miles) are quite different in general topography and soil types. The smaller island is steeper and stonier with a considerable clay component in the soil. These conditions have always inhibited agricultural activities, especially those calling for mechanization, and fields in Nevis are often separated from one another by stonewalls built with the rocks taken from the fields during cultivation. The Nevis clays are less permeable to water infiltration than are the loamy soils of St. Kitts, helping to explain why Nevis has experienced more soil erosion than the larger island, whose fine-grained volcanic soils have been remarked upon for their fertility since earliest plantation days. St. Kitts has sustained sugar-cane crops continuously for more than three centuries, and soil depletion is becoming a serious problem; thousands of tons of chemical fertilizers are now imported annually from the United States and Trinidad to enrich the fields. "Natural" vegetation on the two islands is confined to the areas just below the highest peaks, Nevis Peak (3,232 feet) and Mt. Misery (3,792 feet) on St. Kitts. The early colonial forest clearance and more recent cutting for firewood and charcoal has modified the forest cover at all but the highest elevations.

Unlike Nevis, where sugar cane is no longer grown commercially, St. Kitts's arable land has been in cane since earliest colonial days. During the twentieth century, the estates all have shipped their cane to the one central mill near Basseterre so that the island essentially has been one large agro-industrial production unit with the resident black labor force, their efforts coordinated and mediated by a handful of planters, producing canes for the single sugar factory. St. Kitts is one of the sole remaining sugar-cane monocultures in the Commonwealth Caribbean, almost all other islands now actively seeking major land-use diversification. Even the locations of most St. Kitts village communities are explained more because of their lack of potential for cane rather than their suitability as settlement sites. On the eastern side of the island, villages are located in the dank drainage channels, or "ghauts," that intersect the gently sloping canelands. Where the land is suitable for cane but where houses are needed for fieldworkers, the dwellings are packed tightly along the roadside.

On St. Kitts the sugar-cane cuttings are planted by hand after tractors prepare the soil. Five principal cane varieties are planted on the island in order to guard against possible pest or disease attack focused on a single genotype. Hand weeding of the cane fields is a job often performed by women and children. Harvesting, lasting from February to June, is accomplished by hand, by male cane-cutting gangs and single cutters and now occasionally by female cutting gangs.[7] Usually three or four ratoon crops will be cut from a single planting. After the crop is harvested it is loaded aboard the cane cars of the narrow-gauge railway that circles the island. The cut cane is thereby delivered to the central sugar factory east of Basseterre, where it is processed into semirefined sugar and then transported via ocean-going vessels to England for final refining.

The typically seasonal sugar-cane industry of St. Kitts is the island's main business. Cane workers, truck and tractor drivers, and factory hands are active during the first half of the year, and underemployment characterizes the island during the other half, although the estates have generally maintained agricultural practices to give sporadic rural employment during the "out-of-crop" season.[8] Individual productivity varies widely: a typical cane-cutter harvests two and one-half to three tons of cane daily and is paid E.C. $3.50 (about U.S. $1.30) for each ton. The relatively low average output for Kittitian harvesters is because the cane is not burned before harvest. Burning reduces sharp foliage and makes cutting easier, but the cane leaves are preserved in St. Kitts in order to retain soil moisture and retard soil erosion.

Major structural change has occurred recently in the management of the Kittitian sugar industry. The state took control of all of the canelands in December 1975. In late 1976 the government assumed control of the central sugar factory. All phases of St. Kitts sugar production have thus come under full local control. One of the avowed aims of the government's "rescue" operations for the sugar-cane industry is to begin to diversify St. Kitts's agriculture. In 1976 an estimated 10,000 acres of sugar cane were reaped. But nearly 600 acres more were grown in peanuts, carrots, potatoes, root crops, peas, and corn.[9]

Provision farming on St. Kitts, heretofore extremely limited in acreage and tightly controlled by the lowland estates, traditionally has been restricted to the hills above the cane. Highland plots have been tilled by the estate workers, who have rented the land from the individual estates, since the latter have controlled all of the island's land up to the mountain crests. In 1975 there were 2,466 highland farms in St. Kitts, 1,968 of which were less than one acre in size.[10] The cultivation of a highland plot traditionally has been contingent upon work on the adjoining sugar-cane estate. Even then, the estate owner has usually taken one-third of the plot's produce as rent, selling the confiscated food locally. Highland garden plots are sometimes rented for E.C. $10–15 per year, although cash renting is rare. The hillside farming itself is almost invariably accomplished with a heavy hoe, although plots above some of the windward settlements can be reached by rented tractors. Women tend plots in the cool of the morning, and older men often spend weekend days at these gardens. Each plot is characterized by variety. Potatoes, beans, eggplant, pumpkins, peppers, pineapples, and bananas are all cultivated for home consumption with a little extra for cash sale. Drought, soil erosion from highland rainshowers, and crop theft by both neighbors and monkeys pose recurring hazards to provision farming on St. Kitts.

Highland garden farming on St. Kitts is strictly a livelihood necessity rather than a commitment to the land. Villagers say that highland agriculture on the island is a throwback to plantation days when mountain plots were allocated for slave farming, and some old men still refer to the estate-owned plots as "the nigger grounds." The Kittitian villager is relieved of the necessity to work the provision lands when cash is available from abroad to purchase food. During the 1960s when many young people were working in the Virgin Islands and sending money home, some highland provision areas were almost abandoned.

Less noticeable livelihood activities within Kittitian villages supplement the more visible cash-earning jobs and supplementary provision farming. Chickens are kept in many house yards and fed table scraps. Grazing animals are often tethered alongside cane fields where they can eat weeds and grass. Pigs are commonly kept, and several of the more prosperous pig farmers on St. Kitts import feed from the Virgin Islands. Village breadfruit, coconut, citrus, and mango trees, although normally considered the property of a single individual or family, are often picked clean by village children and may constitute an important nutritional supplement for them.[11]

Fishing has never occupied large numbers of men from either St. Kitts or Nevis, although it is an occupation to which many aspire, possibly because of its relative prestige as much as the financial rewards. On St. Kitts, fishermen are found in Dieppe Bay, Sandy Point, Old Road Town, and Basseterre, and they are also in the Charlestown area of Nevis. Small fishing boats and an occasional sailing schooner are constructed locally on the beaches. The smaller boats, powered by outboard motors, take fishermen as far north as the Saba banks and occasionally south to Montserrat. Fishing is potentially profitable and always risky. A man can earn up to E.C. $300 per week or catch nothing. The catch is sold to local villagers at the beach or market, and recent inflation (E.C. $2,000 for an outboard motor) has raised prices for most locally caught fish to E.C. $1.50 per pound.

Although the St. Kitts economy is centered around sugar cane, Basseterre provides enough work for stevedores and for those working in manufacturing and service jobs to generate a light but steady stream of vehicular traffic to and from the capital town during the morning and late afternoon. This is not the case on Nevis because livelihood on the smaller island is focused on village agriculture and livestock husbandry. Nevis was originally a sugar-cane island, but its last muscovado sugar mill closed in 1958. Canes from Nevis were thereafter sent to the St. Kitts sugar factory by sail-powered barge, and the canes often soured or deteriorated from pest attack before they arrived. The last such shipment to St. Kitts was in 1969. Nevis was producing only patches of sugar cane by the late 1970s, for home use and animal feed.

Nevis is an island of small landholders. During this century many of the former estate lands have been broken up into large to medium-sized land parcels, which have become available to individual farmers. The most recent agricultural census of the Commonwealth Caribbean showed 1,690 individuals on Nevis who either owned (904) a plot of land of less than five acres or who controlled such a plot under conditions of "mixed tenure" (786).[12] Land is also rented out by individuals and by officials who administer fifteen different government estates. In 1976 there were 364 different tenants on the government lands, using it mainly for grazing animals.[13] On Nevis, ownership of a piece of land, however small, is a measure of prestige. On St. Kitts, little land is available for purchase by would-be smallholders.

The symmetry and homogeneity of the St. Kitts canelands are in direct contrast to the ragged, unmanaged, and overgrown appearance of Nevis. On closer inspection the land appears overgrown because individual small holdings are characterized by variety. It is not uncommon on Nevis to see yams, pigeon peas, corn, and a few stalks of cane growing in the same small plot, interspersed with banana plants and citrus trees. This is, of course, a typical subsistence adaptation that provides crop variety for family use and some extras for sale, as well as insurance against pest attack, plant disease, and market insecurity.

41

Sea-island cotton is Nevis's principal cash crop, accounting for more acreage than any other crop on the island. It is cultivated exclusively on small land plots, either by the owners or through sharecropping or hired hand arrangements if owners are absent or too old to work the land. In August 1975, 450 acres on Nevis were planted in cotton. By the following May, 117,662 pounds of sea-island cotton lint had been sold to the Nevis Agricultural Department, the island's sole buyer. In 1976 there were 501 producers of cotton on Nevis, 298 of them women, whose output ranged from 1,415 pounds down to 5 pounds.[14] Cotton is generally cultivated in the gentler sloping lands of Nevis, below the 600-foot contour but above the drier coastal zones. It is usually planted in August, but when cane was still a cash crop on Nevis, cotton was planted in May and harvested in the fall so that harvest periods did not overlap.[15] Cotton is hand-harvested, and then the stalks are burned to rid the following crop of the pink bollworm, a pest that has ravaged sea-island cotton on the island for half a century.

No one on Nevis denies that cotton cultivation is ultimately harmful to the island's soil. Older farmers recall that soil erosion became much more serious as cotton began to take over from cane in the first decade of this century. Younger cultivators remark about the problems of sheet erosion of the unprotected, exposed soil between the rows of cotton. The annual burning reduces ground moisture and is detrimental over a long period of time. Burning also disturbs hundreds of flying insects, which then move on to other fields.

As on St. Kitts, the main food crops on Nevis are starchy tubers—yams, sweet potatoes, and cassava. It would appear economically ideal for a two-island state to have one island specializing in a cash crop and the other in food. Provision farmers on Nevis, however, suggest that their relationship with St. Kitts inhibits rather than encourages their food production. Almost all foodstuffs, to be sold in bulk, must be sold to the government's Central Marketing Corporation in Basseterre. Nevisian farmers say that their yams, for instance, could be sold for much higher prices in St. Martin and the U.S. Virgin Islands. They also suggest that government buyers of foodstuffs are incompetent and lazy, often delaying buying trips to Nevis that leave delivered goods rotting at the Charlestown pier.

Nevis's most striking feature is its ubiquitous livestock population. Cattle, and especially the smaller grazing animals—sheep and goats—appear everywhere, but they are most heavily concentrated in the drier parts of the island. There were an estimated 3,700 cattle, 10,000 sheep, and 6,000 goats on the island in 1971, roughly twice the numbers for 1946.[16] The livestock, owned by every rural farmer, are tethered in pasture areas during the day and then brought back to the owner's house at night to feed upon grasses or weeds that have earlier been cut for them along the roadsides. Animals are readily sold to butchers on both islands, and they are also shipped to Guadeloupe and Martinique. Beef export to the French islands is monitored and controlled by the government. Cattle are commonly stolen and butchered in the Nevis countryside.

The high livestock density in the southern and eastern parts of Nevis has led to a complete loss of topsoil through the elimination of all but the most hardy foliage in these drier zones of the island. The landholding system of hundreds of tiny plots has been the setting for inevitable disputes over marauding animals that occasionally roam at will through neighboring garden plots. Nevisians who own rural acreage and who return after a lengthy sojourn abroad sometimes find their land denuded by their neighbors' voracious animals. Small herds of goats clamber over the island's garbage dumps, and sheep commonly outnumber children in the schoolyard of the Charlestown secondary school. Cattle feed is now imported to Nevis for herds used by the small tourist hotels. But this is only a tiny fraction of the island's animal population. The livestock carrying capacity of parts of Nevis has already been exceeded, and routinely now, several animals die whenever drought reoccurs.

The contrasts in land use between St. Kitts and Nevis are inevitably reflected in human livelihood activities, personal financial strategies, and the images or stereotypes that the islanders maintain of themselves and of each other. Everyone on St. Kitts and Nevis acknowledges that the Nevisian is more "rooted in the land" and has greater command over his own economic destiny than the Kittitian, who is typically a wage earner, although everyone is quick to point out that individual farming is very risky. Most Kittitians and Nevisians sharply disagree, however, about the relative virtue and vice associated with island stereotypes. Generally, most Kittitians consider themselves outgoing, generous, articulate, and fashionable as opposed to most Nevisians, who, they feel, are clannish, grasping, secretive, and old-fashioned; most Nevisians, on the other hand, find that they are prudent, family-oriented, trustworthy, and hardworking, in contrast to most Kittitians, whose principal interests they see as centered around drinking, dancing, boasting, and fighting.

Insular stereotypes notwithstanding, distinctions between the two islands and their residents are blurred because of the many family ties between St. Kitts and Nevis and also because many Nevisians have "crossed over" to reside permanently on St. Kitts. A considerable though unknown number of the adult population along St. Kitts's windward coast, for instance, were originally from Nevis and are now regarded as "cane cutters" and "no longer real Nevisians" by those who have stayed on the smaller island.

Financial Strategies and Migration

Residents of both St. Kitts and Nevis depend heavily on the cash earned or sent from abroad. Many families maintain passbook savings accounts of several hundred dollars, often kept in the mother's name. The account balance becomes larger when remittances are received and is often drawn down to almost nothing when little money is coming in. This usually does not lead to the development of even modest financial estates through incremental saving, but it does help avoid chronic indebtedness, a rare phenomenon on the two islands. A traditional savings medium on St. Kitts and Nevis has also been membership in quasi-religious burial groups or "friendly societies." They are open to adults of both sexes, who pay a few cents per week in return for either modest benefits in time of sickness or financial help with family burial costs. In the last twenty-five years the membership of and participation in local friendly societies has declined substantially owing to large-scale migration to England and the Virgin Islands, campaigns by both private insurance companies and a government-sponsored provident fund, and political differences among members of the societies.

Both similarities and differences exist in the investment of savings and earnings on St. Kitts and Nevis. House construction is by far the most common financial obligation a household head faces after the purchase of basic foodstuffs. Construction costs are high, since essentially all building materials are imported—cement from Puerto Rico and lumber from Belize, Guyana, and the Virgin Islands. In both places in 1976 a simple wooden plank house cost about E.C. $1,500 for materials and labor, while a spacious, more modern home with water connections and utilities, a great deal of imported cement, and corrugated iron roofing cost tens of thousands of dollars. In early 1976, the overwhelming majority of the latter houses that had been recently built or were under construction in the housing developments outside Basseterre were financed by Kittitians who were abroad or recently returned.[17] Similarly, modern houses in the Charlestown area are, more often than not, financed by "outside" money.

The money to buy taxis, rum shops, trucks, and fishing equipment can also be traced, almost invariably, to an original extraisland money source, and some small shops and stores have by now been passed on to the next generation. The case of a sixty-year-old shopkeeper from Old Road Town in St. Kitts is typical. He was a gardener and part-time estate worker in St. Kitts until he traveled to Trinidad in 1942 and worked as a cook for the U.S. Army. From there he went to the Shell refinery on Curaçao and stayed until 1958. During his absence he sent "everything" to his mother and then used these savings to establish his small grocery store. He has helped two daughters and a son to "get started" in England and hopes his youngest son will stay to inherit his shop.

The most obvious investment difference between the islands is that Nevisians purchase land plots, whereas land is generally not available on St. Kitts. Moreover, an intermediate class of landholders has emerged on Nevis, but there is little scope for the development of a similar class on the larger island: there are 118 private landholdings of five or more acres on Nevis compared with 36 on St. Kitts, and Nevis has 74 "specified farms" of an average 196 acres, whereas St. Kitts has few of comparable size.[18] Among black Nevisians, there has thus emerged a stratum of small land-owners who have attained prestige, not in legal status or life style, but in the amount of property held. Their special status, coming from the investment in land of migration money from abroad, is possibly a continuation of a "migration elite" formed in the Leewards immediately after slave emancipation. In more recent years this group has parlayed migration savings into positions of respect and financial profit on Nevis. According to Richard Frucht,

> Many of the returnees have bought large amounts of land, sell smaller plots to local buyers who are less affluent returnees, or laboring class people now receiving remittances from England. One estate, for example, was sold in 1953 to a Nevisian just returned from the Dutch islands, where he had spent the previous ten years. Between 1954 and 1962, he sold not less than 34 plots of various sizes to as many buyers. He used part of this capital to establish local businesses.[19]

Farm machinery, the effectiveness of which is severely limited by Nevis's rocky environment, is not a major capital investment there. Simple hand tools—forks, hoes, and spades—constitute the only cultivating equipment, although more prosperous cultivators own or rent trucks and vans to haul produce. Livestock on Nevis is a major form of invest-ment, regardless of the amount of land held or the availability of grazing acreage. Investing migration money in animals on the smaller island is a means of beating currency inflation as well as an adaptation to Nevis's deteriorated environment.

The development of a landed "migration elite" has been impossible on St. Kitts, since land has never been available. There are nonetheless notice-able differences between those who have successfully migrated away from St. Kitts and returned in comparison with those who have not. The man who has returned with enough money saved to become a shopkeeper, taxi driver, truck owner, or fisherman on St. Kitts has freed himself from field labor, while the man who has not "works on the estate and belongs to the estate." The admired return migrant of St. Kitts also has more cash to spend than others, and he is not reticent to share with family and friends. He occasionally purchases a bottle of rum and shares it with friends and acquaintances, who are, in turn, expected to listen in awe to stories of personal experiences set in London, New York, or Aruba. Admiration on St. Kitts is therefore partly associated with the man who is willing to "spree out" and share the money that he has earned abroad.

Migrants returning to St. Kitts have maintained a special status on the island through their political activities. They have been the driving force behind the St. Kitts Labour party. Party policies and programs have represented an organized response to plantation domination, which has traditionally inhibited the development of a class of small landholders. St. Kitts plantations have, however, provided a common foe against which workers' groups and, more recently, labor unions have organized. In each Kittitian village one finds the Labour party's key supporters—the old-line "labor men" of St. Kitts—who began their working careers in the cane fields of the Dominican Republic. They have always supported the Labour party with money contributions and, more important, their vocal support in the villages and towns of the island.

Besides the more tangible manifestations of prestige associated with migration on St. Kitts and Nevis, it is commonly acknowledged on both islands that more esteem or respect is accorded the return migrant than the person who has remained behind. The young men of St. Kitts who stay to cut cane are considered by many to be less intelligent than those who go abroad, and the advice of men and women who have worked away is commonly sought by village children. In a psychological comparison of cane cutters and fishermen of Dieppe Bay, St. Kitts, Joel Aronoff suggests that parents' migration from the island and leaving children behind under the care of relatives are detrimental to a child's psychological development, since it disrupts family structure.[20] This point is not totally convincing, since Aronoff makes no distinction between permanent and temporary emigration. His study emphasizes differences between the dependence and lack of confidence of local cane cutters and the independent, self-assured fishermen of Dieppe Bay. Aronoff analyzes these differences on the basis of local livelihood pursuits, although in his discussion he points out that village fishermen have had backgrounds of more varied work experience and began fishing as relatively older men, suggesting strongly that he is really contrasting those who have "made it" abroad and those who have stayed at home.

Migration, Remittances, and Family

Table 1 reflects the relative population imbalance in sex and age usual in the Commonwealth Caribbean and typically related to emigration. But static population figures do not begin to show the mobile nature of the populace of St. Kitts and Nevis. In 1975, for instance, residents of the two islands generated 17,309 separate trips abroad (7,253 to the U.S. Virgin Islands), almost exclusively by air, and 17,328 returns (7,461 from the U.S. Virgin Islands).[21] These data do not include the heavy back-and-forth travel between the two islands themselves.

A recent United Nations report, using data collected before the tightening of immigration laws in the U.S. Virgin Islands, indicates that the migration rate from St. Kitts and Nevis (17,572 from the two islands from 1960 to 1970) is almost twice as high as the rate for the Commonwealth Caribbean in general. The report also states that no longer do only the young men of the two islands migrate away in order to achieve local success. Young women now have an almost equal propensity to emigrate.[22]

Young people who go away are expected to provide financial support for family and friends left behind, and almost everyone left on the two islands depends, at least in part, upon the success of those, old and young, who have emigrated. Local land use and livelihood in the two islands therefore provide a very incomplete picture of the means by which individuals are sustained economically. In 1960 a local newspaper, the *Labour Spokesman,* reported, "It is not uncommon to hear people say: I don't have to depend on anybody here; I have me father—or mother, sister or

Table 1. Population of St. Kitts and Nevis, 1970

	St. Kitts				Nevis			
Age	M	%	F	%	M	%	F	%
0–9	5,510	50.1	5,478	49.9	1,757	50.4	1,731	49.6
10–19	4,453	49.6	4,530	50.4	1,536	48.1	1,656	51.9
20–29	1,298	45.6	1,549	54.4	360	44.6	448	55.4
30–39	890	42.7	1,193	57.3	230	41.4	326	58.6
40–49	1,149	43.9	1,468	56.1	284	39.8	429	60.2
50–59	1,265	46.6	1,450	53.4	402	42.7	540	57.3
60–69	950	42.9	1,265	57.1	361	42.5	488	57.5
70–79	329	35.6	594	64.4	136	34.3	260	65.7
80 and over	73	19.9	293	80.1	61	30.0	142	70.0
Total	15,917	47.2	17,820	52.8	5,127	46.0	6,020	54.0

Source: 1970 Population Census of the Commonwealth Caribbean, III, 146–53.

brother, son or daughter as the case may be, in America, Curaçao, Aruba or the United Kingdom who is supporting me: It ain't St. Kitts or Nevis money that me eating."[23]

The amount of money sent from abroad is the best measure of the importance of migrants' support, although no data are available to show all of the money sent to the two islands. Postal remittances (see Table 10), almost all from the United Kingdom, during 1975 totaled more than E.C. $1,000,000 to persons on St. Kitts and E.C. $550,000 to those in Nevis.[24] Personal bank checks are sent mainly from the United States and the Virgin Islands. Migrants also send cash through the mail and take money home personally or send it with a friend. It is common for a Kittitian or Nevisian working in the Virgin Islands to wait at the airport on St. Thomas or St. Croix until he finds an acquaintance flying home with whom he can entrust cash for his family.

Some local residents of St. Kitts and Nevis speculate that outside remittances account for more disposable income on the two islands than any other source, including the St. Kitts sugar industry. Money sent home is sometimes considered more valuable than that earned locally. It enables residents to purchase imported frozen meat, gifts for children, a bright square of linoleum, or even a bicycle—items over and above subsistence needs. Merchandise, too, is sent home to the two islands. During each Christmas season, the Basseterre roadstead taken on a carnival atmosphere as "the boats" bring shipments of furniture, used kitchen appliances, and clothing sent from family members working abroad. The relatives them-selves often return to spend Christmas, bringing money and swelling the local population, which appears to triple.

Inevitably, a long tradition of labor emigration has led islanders to expect, not simply to hope, that persons leaving will periodically send back money and gifts. In earlier days it was generally a case of male migrants supporting those left behind, who were mainly female. Today it is not uncommon for a father to use his savings to help a daughter go abroad and then for the daughter to send money home. Parents expect their sons and daughters, and children their mothers and fathers, to send money home, and siblings also expect gifts from abroad. Family members make no pretense about relative favor and disfavor of kin abroad in terms of remittances received. One old woman in Basseterre remarked, "I have five children away, but I really have only four—one never sends any-thing." Similar comments are heard time and again on the two islands. Commitments to kinsmen left behind are usually weakened when obliga-tions are assumed abroad: a typical interview response in this regard is, "My daughter is in the Bronx, but she got married, so we hear from her only once or twice a year."

Male migrants from St. Kitts and Nevis have traditionally sent remitt-ances home to mothers, wives, or girlfriends for their personal expenses, for safekeeping, and for supporting children. This reinforces the mother-centered family, widespread among the "lower-class" black families of the Commonwealth Caribbean. High "illegitimacy" rates on both islands and traditional male absenteeism help lead to matrifocal family types on St. Kitts and Nevis. Formal marriage is most common among, but not confined to, the small middle class on both islands. Marriage never has been regarded as a necessary precondition for poor couples of St. Kitts and Nevis to live together and raise a family. Of 916 live births on St. Kitts in 1974, 774 were from unwed parents; on Nevis 172 of 227 babies were born out of wedlock.[25] On St. Kitts, the birth of a child to an unwed mother results in only slight and temporary disapproval or embarrassment. Often the infant's maternal grandmother immediately assumes responsibility for care of the child, especially if the young mother emigrates.[26]

It is not uncommon among the poorer folk on both islands for a woman to have children by several males, and each successive male may be a temporary resident in the woman's house, which she owns or rents. This therefore provides a temporarily "stable," though not legalized, mother-father arrangement. The women know who the children's fathers are, use

49

the father's surname for his children, and make a rough allocation of funds received from the father for each child, even though the father may be absent. The mother's child-rearing responsibilities are financed from what she earns and from the money her husband or mates furnish. On St. Kitts and Nevis, and throughout the Caribbean, the mother will return to her parents' or mother's household if her mate or mates do not regularly provide money.[27] Later she will most likely come to depend upon money that her children send from overseas. The mating and family system on St. Kitts and Nevis is complex and difficult to categorize. The system whereby the mother comes to depend upon several different sources of cash should be considered more flexible and functional than promiscuous.

Child care is the sole responsibility of the mother if the father is absent, and if both parents emigrate, the job of rearing children falls to the grandparents (usually the grandmother) or to other relatives or friends, with remittances coming from the child's parents. It is often difficult for grandparents to "keep up" with their grandchildren, and much of the school misbehavior on both islands is attributed to the aggressiveness of children who are being raised by mothers alone or by grandparents. Moreover, the lack of "intact families" has been deemed the cause of deep-seated anxiety among young Kittitians whose parents work abroad.[28] In terms of sentiment or obligation, an aunt or grandmother who rears a child on St. Kitts or Nevis may eventually be favored over the child's biological parents and will often be the eventual recipient of remittances from overseas.

Traditionally, many young fathers of "illegitimate" children on the two islands have ignored their offspring until they were one or two years old, then the young father and mother have often established a household together. This, however, may be changing. Young fathers now regularly accompany mothers to government health clinics and care for their babies in public. In fact, the importance of the father in "lower-class" Caribbean families may have been seriously underestimated if information from St. Kitts and Nevis is representative of the area as a whole. The father, though absent out of necessity, has often set an example for his sons by working away. Many of the older men on the two islands recall first meeting their fathers in Cuba or the Dominican Republic when they themselves migrated. More recently, many fathers from the two islands have arranged jobs for their sons in Aruba, Curaçao, or the Virgin Islands.

Household and family in St. Kitts and Nevis cannot be assessed except in the context in which these institutions have evolved. Since slave emancipation, the personal prestige, success, and survival of the common people of the two islands have depended upon emigration to short-lived jobs and the ability to cope with periods when jobs were in short supply. The accumulation of cash, to satisfy survival or subsistence needs, has been a primary goal for an individual, male or female, on both islands. A typical adult male has therefore held some kind of local job while being flexible enough to respond to calls for laborers from abroad, knowing that he will probably return eventually. A typical female, in order to maximize her cash-receiving position in the light of economic uncertainty, has depended on herself, on a male mate—sometimes more than one—and eventually on children working abroad. Individual needs have been fulfilled more often than not by establishing male-female "family" alliances. These flexible alliances, supported by children and other relatives, have seen family members geographically dispersed beyond St. Kitts and Nevis. This dispersal further enhances a cash receipt position for individuals and might be considered an adaptation to the economic circumstances surrounding the common people of the two islands. "Family" on St. Kitts and Nevis is an elusive and ever-changing structure and a social adaptation to change and uncertainty.

A geographic dispersal of family members over a wide area calls for periodic reuniting of the family unit. In many cultures, the celebrations of birth and marriage call family members together. In St. Kitts and Nevis, however, birth is not widely celebrated and marriage is uncommon among members of the "lower-class" black population. This leaves death as the milestone in life celebrated by all Kittitians, Nevisians, and their kin abroad, regardless of their social status or family form. The local funerals on the two islands are not only religious ceremonies where grief is ritualized but also important socioeconomic events that reunite members of spatially dispersed families and thereby bring considerable sums of money back to the two islands.

Migration and Death Ceremonies

Three times each day on radio ZIZ, the only local commercial radio station on St. Kitts and Nevis, death announcements, accompanied by mournful organ music, inform listeners of local deaths and enumerate grieving relatives (and their locations) left behind.[29] When the death announcements are aired, everyone—whether in houses, rum shops, or markets—stops to listen. The broadcast obituaries are so much a part of daily life that many Kittitians and Nevisians believe they are legally bound to report the death of a family member to officials of ZIZ. Table 2 shows the geographic distribution of relatives abroad of 120 people who died on St. Kitts and Nevis during a four-month period in 1976. All the relatives were enumerated in the particular death announcement, often including aunts, uncles, and cousins as well as members of the nuclear family.

The death announcements usually specify details about funeral arrangements to listeners on St. Kitts, Nevis, and nearby islands. Although the listening range of ZIZ is limited, the station is usually audible at higher elevations in St. Thomas. Listeners there notify friends, and the news travels quickly through the Kittitian-Nevisian population in the Virgin Islands. It is not unusual for relatives from St. Thomas or St. Croix to arrive on St. Kitts by airplane on the same day that a family member's death has been announced. Relatives in the Virgin Islands and those residing in the United States, Canada, or the United Kingdom are most often notified by telephone or telegram within hours after a death. Air travel from these places allows a return for a funeral within two or three days.

Attendance at a family member's funeral, especially a funeral of a

Table 2. *Locations of Relatives Abroad of Persons Dying in St. Kitts and Nevis, March 20 to July 19, 1976*

				Locations of Relatives Abroad				
	Deaths[a]	United Kingdom	United States	Canada	St. Thomas	St. Croix	Tortola	Netherlands Antilles
St. Kitts								
Males	38	37	23	8	36	8	1	9
Females	60	45	18	16	31	13	5	13
Nevis								
Males	9	10	13	5	16	7	2	1
Females	13	5	11	4	9	6	3	1
Total	120	97	65	33	92	34	11	24

Note: Other locations mentioned where relatives of deceased lived: Anguilla, Antigua, Bahamas, Barbados, Belize, Bermuda, Brazil, Cuba, Dominican Republic, Jamaica, Montserrat, Netherlands, Puerto Rico, Spain, Surinam, Trinidad.
[a]Eighteen of the deceased persons had no relatives abroad specified.
Source: "Death Announcements," Radio Station ZIZ, Springlands, Basseterre, St. Kitts. With permission of the *Journal of Cultural Geography.*

parent, on St. Kitts and Nevis is expected of those residing abroad, an expectation as strong or stronger than the expectation of remittances. Young people abroad will "sacrifice anything" to return for a funeral, since they will be "scorned" if they do not come. Local social pressures are thereby brought to bear on all distant kin to return when relatives die. The funeral is only one part of a wider social event. As in other cultures, family funerals also involve the telling of stories, the renewal of friendships, the incurring and payment of debts, and the discussion of business. Not incidentally, family members returning for funerals usually bring money and gifts. Their appearance at the funeral solidifies their places in the local society. This is especially important for young people working temporarily in the Virgin Islands. If they are eventually forced to return, their welcome will be warm if they have returned for funerals in the interim.

The funerals themselves are Christian rites, religious affiliations on the two islands being legacies of missionary activity that began before emancipation; Methodists predominate in Basseterre, and Anglicans are the most numerous Christian group in rural St. Kitts and Nevis. Fundamentalist sects have gained adherents from both islands over the past four decades. Almost every funeral is coordinated by one of three undertakers, two on St. Kitts and one on Nevis. The recent innovation of corpse refrigeration (since 1961 on St. Kitts and since 1973 on Nevis) leads to considerable expense. More often than not returning migrants pay for the funeral of a family member. The undertakers on the two islands, in fact, often reckon funeral expenses according to where the deceased's kin are located. A "Virgin Islands" funeral costs roughly E.C. $600, while a "U.K." funeral can cost the bereaved as much as E.C. $2,000. Not arbitrary, these costs reflect refrigeration expenses associated with the time and distance involved in traveling from, for instance, England or North America to the Caribbean.

Before the days of high speed international air travel and corpse refrigeration, relatives working away from St. Kitts and Nevis returned home for periods of mourning; the actual funeral was almost always on the same day as the death. Now, as means of travel and funeral technology have become more sophisticated and as workers' incomes have increased, the death ceremonies on the two islands have become more elaborate and more highly attended. The mortuary aspect of religious ceremony, often regarded as a "traditional" element of symbolic culture, appears closely related to the ongoing migration tradition on the two islands. It therefore seems safe to assert that the contemporary importance of local funerals in St. Kitts and Nevis has as much to do with a migration tradition as it does with fulfilling religious and psychological needs.

The Insider's View: A Talk with Isaac Caines

Death ceremonies, family relationships, and the other elements of the contemporary migration cultures of St. Kitts and Nevis are the cumulative products of the activities and experiences of individual Kittitians and Nevisians for more than three centuries. Men and women from the two islands always have had to cope with a host of uncertainties and hostilities at home and abroad. Interviews with older people on the two islands therefore reveal remarkable life histories. One such individual is Isaac Caines, now sixty-seven years old, who lives in a village settlement north of Basseterre. Seated on the side of an antique flatbed truck in his yard, Caines recalled a life of adversity, travel, and hard work.[30]

Isaac Caines was born in 1914 in St. Peter parish, northeast of Basseterre. Before he was born his father went to the Dominican Republic to cut cane and never returned. Caines lived with his mother and his older brothers and sister until he was old enough to leave for the Dominican Republic: "It was the only place to go if you had no money." This was in 1929 when he was fifteen. He traveled to Anguilla via sailing schooner, then on to Santo Domingo via steamer with a larger group of men. In the Dominican Republic he cut cane at the La Romana estate near San Pedro de Macorís in the southeastern part of Hispaniola. Unlike most, Caines "disappeared into the interior" of the Dominican Republic during the off-season and worked there rather than returning to St. Kitts each year after the cane harvest. He came back to St. Kitts in 1932. For the next ten years Caines was a crew member aboard a cargo vessel between St. Kitts and Trinidad. Although he visited all of the intervening islands briefly, he rarely stayed, except for one four-month period when he worked at the cotton gin on Carriacou. During World War II he made U.S. $45 per week for three years as a messenger boy for the U.S. Army's air base at Coolidge Field in Antigua. After returning to St. Kitts, he was imprisoned for six months for drawing a pistol on a local policeman in the midst of a dispute for the attention of a young woman. He then worked for a while on St. Kitts as a fisherman and stevedore, although his local prison record made finding work difficult. In 1955 he traveled to England where he first stayed at a boardinghouse in Ipswich. Then a friend found him work as a mason's assistant in London. Caines, "a man for the money," held a number of laboring jobs in various places in the United Kingdom, always changing jobs if another offered more pay. Every two to three months he sent money home (up to £60 each time) to his mother for safekeeping for his eventual return. While a dock worker in Cardiff, Caines became involved in a gambling dispute with a fellow West Indian and stabbed him (the wound took seventy-eight stitches to repair), an incident that led to his imprisonment for three years. After his release Caines married a woman from St. Kitts in England, but they soon separated. He eventually returned to St. Kitts as he was suffering from arthritis and "wasn't getting any younger." His mother had spent the remitted money in his absence, although he had brought enough home with him to purchase a small boat *(Return)*, outboard motor, and fishpot equipment. Caines now lives with another woman and her children. He has traded his boat and fishing equipment for a truck, which he cannot afford to have repaired, and he obtains occasional laboring jobs through the government. He has always been a steadfast supporter of the St. Kitts Labour party, as have most of the older men who have traveled away and returned. Men who migrate away are more "politically minded" than those who stay.

Isaac Caines (a fictitious name, although one that is recognizably Kittitian) is a real person, and to point out gratuitously that his case is "typical" detracts from the individual tenacity, resilience, and aggressiveness that he has shown throughout his life. Caines has been in trouble with the law more often than most, but this seems more a source of pride than remorse. The Kittitian policeman "had never been anywhere" and was ridiculing Caine's tailored khakis that he had purchased in Antigua. The knifing incident in Wales happened because the other fellow was cheating, and the seventy-eight stitch stab wound is clear evidence that Caines has always been able to resolve his own problems in the face of a host of uncertainties and hostilities.

Since slave emancipation in 1838, men and women, like Caines, of these two small Caribbean islands have traveled away and returned and have remained underspecialized in light of the many changes and hazards in their paths. Mobility, underspecialization, resilience have thus become traits of the migration cultures of St. Kitts and Nevis—cultures that represent these peoples' historical experiences beginning with the establishment of English plantations on the two islands in the early seventeenth century.

CHAPTER THREE

Slaves, Slavery, and Plantation Ecology

Abrupt ecological and demographic transformations marked the European colonization of St. Kitts and Nevis. In the early seventeenth century, white settlers annihilated the aboriginal peoples and introduced an African slave labor force. Slave gangs subsequently stripped away native vegetation to make way for sugar cane. By the early 1700s the two islands had become sugar-cane colonies with only the most inaccessible forest zones left untouched. St. Kitts and Nevis had thereby been swiftly converted from insular, multispecies ecosystems to semi-industrial production units with field arrangements, settlement patterns, and communication networks all focused toward the production of a single tropical staple crop. Similarly, the peoples of the two islands were by now irrevocably linked to a transatlantic economic system—the planters for profits, the slaves for survival. Finally, in 1833, two centuries after first colonization, the British Emancipation Act was passed and £20,000,000 from the British treasury were paid to individual Caribbean slaveholders as compensation for their losses in human property. The 1,202 owners of the 15,667 slaves in St. Kitts received £329,000 of this sum, while the 399 slaveholders on Nevis accepted £151,000 for their 7,225 slaves. These payments were a final reward to the system of plantation slavery that had served the plantocracy of the two islands for two centuries and had irreversibly altered the lands.

An ecological perspective is helpful in describing interrelationships between slaves and the physical environments of the two islands in the earlier years of slavery, because the planter class of St. Kitts and Nevis considered slaves, at least partly, as interrelated units with the land itself. In 1732 one Nevis planter, had observed that while his normal annual slave "loss" was one in fifteen, the ratio increased to one in seven "in dry seasons when provisions were scarce."[1] Two years later William Mathew, governor of the Leeward Islands, noted that all of St. Kitts's arable land had already been cleared, and he suggested that as soil fertility decreased a denser slave population would be necessary.[2] In other words, as the physical environment deteriorated, cane production levels could be hypothetically maintained simply by importing more slaves and forcing them to drive the land harder. Later in the eighteenth century, John Pinney, a Nevis plantation owner, suggested that even marginal, sloping, and somewhat infertile land "well dunged and properly worked" with intensive slave labor would usually provide sufficient muscovado sugar output for worthwhile and continuous profit.[3]

Ecological perspectives aside, the ultimate goal of each planter—and therefore of the entire system of slavery on St. Kitts, Nevis, and throughout the British Caribbean—was monetary reward. Just as estate owners regarded the insular soils as vehicles of profit, they considered their slaves in the same light: "The master . . . only really wanted the best years out of a slave's life."[4] And in the early years of slavery it was more profitable for most planters continuously to replenish slave populations with new imports from Africa rather than to maintain the good health of burdensome slaves who were either too old or too young to work. The Reverend James Ramsay, who lived on St. Kitts in the late eighteenth century, observed that plantation owners usually opposed slave breeding because pregnancy reduced the efficiency of female field slaves. Female slaves who became pregnant were, according to Ramsay often "upbraided, cursed, or ill treated."[5] Extreme callousness and cruelty were not, however, in the planters' best interests, since overt physical abuse of one's labor force was self-defeating. This was especially true after the slave trade was abolished in 1807. Even when the Reverend Mr. Ramsay was making his observations, local laws called for at least minimal protection and care of all slaves. Some planters of both islands, noting the long-term benefits of large, homegrown slave populations, actively rewarded their female slaves for giving birth and thereby bolstering the estate's future workforce. British Caribbean slavery and "natural" human population increase were, however, incompatible and possibly mutually exclusive. On St. Kitts, Nevis, and throughout most of the British Caribbean, regardless of some planters' efforts to stimulate slave reproduction, demographic decline had led to aging slave workforces by the time the slave trade was abolished.[6]

Captivity, and its correlates of overwork and physical and psychological abuse, doubtless partially explains the low slave reproductive rates. But captivity on St. Kitts, Nevis, and the other islands did not extinguish the slaves' spirit to survive as humans. During the two centuries of slavery, they survived and resisted not as penned animals, nor as prison inmates, but as a human society. As in other human societies, slaves were born, grew older, behaved and misbehaved, had friends and families, made love, observed ceremony, and, in a limited way, achieved success or failed. Of course, slave activities were severely curtailed and ultimately controlled by white planters, but the latter were almost certainly profoundly ignorant of the extent and nature of the interpersonal ties and many of the activities of their own slaves. For instance, in describing Worthy Park, a sugar-cane plantation of central Jamaica, Michael Craton has hypothesized that "many a slave plantation population, after four or five generations, must have been virtually one huge extended family."[7]

By the end of the slavery era on St. Kitts and Nevis, an insular society had developed that was composed of a white planter class that identified itself more closely with Britain than with its local habitats, a small but growing group of freedmen, and a black slave population. Unlike the planter class, the two latter groups had no other geographic frame of reference. Although daily slave existence was characterized by oppression and brutality, the plantation islands themselves were the locales of home and family. Escape from slavery into the hills or to other islands—events occurring with accelerating frequency by the early nineteenth century—was not, therefore, without its social cost. Among slave punishments, the one considered most punitive next to death was, ironically, deportation. Similarly, the interisland slave trade among the British Caribbean colonies in the last years of slavery "was described as the most cruel of any," because it separated families and loved ones.[8] Thus, in the 1830s, the newly freed black populations of St. Kitts and Nevis must have viewed their home islands with a certain ambivalence: on both islands the repulsion of plantation oppression—which would endure long beyond slavery—and the attraction of friends and kin were emotions felt simultaneously. This feeling of ambivalence, formed during slavery and focused on the particular geographic habitats of St. Kitts and Nevis, would demonstrate itself over and over again among future generations of Kittitians and Nevisians migrating from and returning to their home islands.

The Aboriginal Setting

Pre-Columbian St. Kitts and Nevis is difficult to reconstruct with certainty, partly because of the sudden and massive environmental modification that accompanied European intrusion in the early seventeenth century. At that time both islands were wooded to the water's edge in most places.[9] Xerophytic plants predominated in the low-lying southern peninsula of the larger island and in lower elevations of the windward coasts of both islands, where vegetation was subject to wind desiccation and salt spray. Contemporary observations from the rain forest, which remains at the highest elevations, may suggest the original vegetation patterns of both islands. St. Kitts and Nevis forests are composed of relatively few tree species—40 percent are gumlin trees *(Dacryodes excelsa)*—and a floristic simplicity typical of small insular ecosystems.[10] At lower elevations the "prickly tree," whose exact identity is not known, proved especially troublesome to clear.

Animal life was similarly more abundant and of greater variety on the two islands and in surrounding waters before the Europeans came. Except for bats, the agouti *(Dasyproctidae)*, a forest rodent now extinct on the two islands, was probably the only native mammal. The Pre-Columbian human inhabitants of St. Kitts and Nevis directed their subsistence hunting and collecting toward an assortment of fish, including tuna and barracuda, as well as a variety of shellfish. Sea turtles were common off St. Eustatius, and the earliest European settlers of St. Kitts and Nevis made regular sailing forays to trap them.

Both St. Kitts and Nevis were inhabited from about the first century A.D. by the Island Caribs, whose distinctive "Saladoid" ceramic ware is found throughout the Lesser Antilles and into Venezuela, the probable area of its origin. St. Kitts seems to have had a considerably more dense aboriginal population than Nevis. Carib villages were composed of oval or rectangular thatched huts, and settlement sites were often located near coastal areas to facilitate fishing and shell collecting. On both islands aboriginal woodsmen cleared limited areas of forest with stone axes for plantings of cassava and corn. The Island Caribs spoke two languages, one for each sex, a possible outgrowth of Carib men capturing Arawakan-speaking women of other islands.[11]

A much earlier and more complex prehistory for St. Kitts is currently being unraveled from evidence from an archaeological site east of Basseterre. There in 1976 the archaeologist R. Christopher Goodwin accidentally encountered a shell midden below a layer of volcanic ash that has been tentatively dated from before 2000 B.C. The early "Archaic" Indian inhabitants of St. Kitts who left these middens and whose area of origin is not yet known apparently subsisted in part on shellfish. Goodwin's evidence also suggests that these peoples may have been forced to evacuate the area in haste in response to an eruption and subsequent lava flow from Mount Misery in the center of the island.[12]

European Intrusion and Ecological Change

Columbus "discovered" and named St. Christopher on his second voyage in 1493. He also sighted Nevis and is said to have named it Nieves because the omnipresent clouds around its central mountain were reminiscent of snow. During the next century European sailing vessels occasionally passed the two islands and probably made stopovers for wood and water. In 1607, Captain Newport, bound for Virginia, landed on Nevis and camped for six days, allowing his men to replenish the ship's foodstores with locally gathered birds and fish. In January 1623 an Englishman, Thomas Warner, a veteran of earlier colonization efforts in South America who had heard of St. Kitts's fertility, established the first permanent English colony in the Caribbean.

Warner's Englishmen were joined two years later by French settlers, with whom they partitioned the island, the French occupying either end and the English the middle. A joint Anglo-French sneak attack and massacre of the Caribs of St. Kitts eliminated many of the aborigines. The local Europeans were far more successful in this military operation than they were in resisting an attack on the island by the Spanish in 1629, which led to the devastation of buildings and crops. Nevis was permanently colonized by Englishmen from St. Kitts in 1628, and both islands and the rest of the lesser Antilles were hotly contested by the English and French during the first century of their colonization.

The competition between English and French in the Leewards in the seventeenth century helps explain the somewhat late arrival of sugar cane. Cane cultivation, which had revolutionized the landscape and the demography of English Barbados beginning in the 1640s, was brought to Nevis in about 1655 and to St. Kitts shortly after. The earliest cash crop on St. Kitts had been tobacco and was followed by cotton, which was then transplanted from St. Kitts to the other Leewards. As late as 1682, Christopher Jeaffreson, a planter on St. Kitts, preferred the cultivation of indigo to sugar cane because the former could be cut five times per year and it suffered less from hurricane damage.[13] Throughout the seventeenth century, cash crops and subsistence crops were of almost equal concern, the latter including European peas and potatoes as well as the aboriginal staples of cassava and corn.

In August 1681, a hurricane washed away Jeaffreson's cash crops, cassava and newly planted potatoes. The Europeans on both islands were by this time accustomed to the heavy rains and damage to life and property associated with these autumn storms. A hurricane had destroyed the first European tobacco crop on St. Kitts in 1624, and subsequent hurricanes had damaged buildings and crops on both islands in 1657, 1658, 1660, 1665, and 1667. By the early eighteenth century some planter families routinely sought refuge from hurricanes in their specially constructed, stonewalled "hurricane houses." European planters had, moreover, learned to expect occasional jarring tremors from earthquakes in their new environment. In 1690 an earthquake rocked Nevis, destroying all of the stone buildings in Charlestown.

Earthquakes and hurricanes, although dangerous, were nevertheless random or seasonal. A more immediate, daily environmental concern in the first decades of European settlement was the clearing of the natural vegetation. Deforestation was more difficult on St. Kitts and Nevis than on flatter islands such as Barbados or Antigua because of the slopes and steep-sided drainage channels. The English and French had initially hacked a road around the perimeter of St. Kitts and began chopping "lanes" through the island's forest in 1625. By the middle of the seventeenth century, the clearing of the two islands was well under way: St. Kitts's cultivated land was beginning to resemble contours paralleling the littoral, and the land had been cultivated to the steeper slopes, a scene not unlike that today; Nevis boasted dwellings on all sides, although where the land became steeper the forest was unbroken to the summit of Nevis Peak.[14] Within decades the problem of too much vegetation on the two islands had suddenly become a problem of too little. The French destruction of St. Kitts's plantations in 1666–67 had included a calculated deforestation of slopes in order to deprive the English of future building material. On Nevis in 1687, Sir Hans Sloane of Jamaica, seeking botanical specimens, hiked through cleared fields almost all the way to the island's summit, where he found a patch of trees.[15]

Seventeenth-century vegetation removal on St. Kitts and Nevis by fire, axe, and shovel involved several sequential steps and a substantial expenditure of human labor. Trees had to be felled, undergrowth chopped away and burned, and stumps grubbed from the soil. The first settlement sites and forest trails had been cleared by white men, but the subsequent and massive deforestation of St. Kitts and Nevis was accomplished by African slaves. As trees, bushes, and vines were cleared from the low and intermediate elevations of both islands, their African slave populations grew accordingly; gangs of slaves were necessary not only to strip the natural vegetation from the land but also to cultivate tropical staple crops in its place. Nevis was the slave mart of the English Leeward Islands in the late seventeenth century. From 1674 to 1689 the Royal African Company delivered 6,902 slaves to Nevis and only 624 to St. Kitts. The two English colonies probably also received slaves smuggled via St. Eustatius.[16]

During subsequent decades of the "development" of St. Kitts and Nevis, planter demand for slaves remained nearly insatiable. The increasing demand on the two islands reflected a transformation from small-scale, partly subsistence economies in the seventeenth century to full-blown, metropolitan-focused sugar-cane colonies in the eighteenth. St. Kitts planters alone imported 10,358 slaves between 1721 and 1730, but in that decade the absolute slave population of St. Kitts increased by only 7,000 (Table 3),[17] which suggests that many slaves were needed simply to replace those who died each year. Indeed, the slave death rate was incredibly high on the two islands during the latter part of the seventeenth century—an aggregate rate estimated as one-quarter per annum in 1684 and even higher among males.[18] "Reasons" for the exceptionally high slave mortality rates at this time include malnutrition exacerbated by drought, disease prevalence, execution, and accident. Almost certainly an additional factor was the excessive energy required of male slaves in forest clearing. During this period slaves were given little respite after their arrival from Africa; since forest clearing required little training or "seasoning," they were set to work immediately. The combination of new foods (which were often in short supply), a new disease environment, the social constraints of slavery, and the enormous amounts of labor often resulted in early death. The conversion of the insular forest ecosystems to open cropland had thus been accomplished by expending a nearly inexhaustible supply of human energy—and human life—imported from Africa.

Slaves cleared the forests on St. Kitts and Nevis to make way for large-scale sugar-cane cultivation, not the tobacco, cotton, and indigo of earlier days. As sugar profits soared, much of the islands' lands became too valuable for anything else. A planter's capital consisted primarily of his land and slaves, not plantation equipment; in 1700, simple cattle-powered wooden rollers were used to squeeze juice from the canes. An inevitable result of the evolution of sugar-cane monocultures on the two islands was

Table 3. Population of St. Kitts and Nevis during the Slave Era

	St. Kitts		Nevis	
	White	Slave	White	Slave
1672	—[a]	352	1,411	1,789
1678	1,234	1,436	—[a]	—[a]
1707	1,416	2,861	1,104	3,676
1720	2,740	7,321	2,358	5,689
1729	3,677	14,663	1,296	5,646
1734	3,881	17,335	—[a]	6,330
1756	2,713	21,891	1,058	8,380
1774	1,900	23,462	1,000	10,000
1787	1,912	20,435	1,300	8,000
1807	—[a]	26,000	1,300	8,000
1834	1,612	15,667	700	7,225

Note: For other recent population estimates for the two islands in the slave era, see Pares, *A West-India Fortune*, 22–3; Cox, "In the Shadow of Freedom," 12, 59; and Sheridan, *Sugar and Slavery*, 150.
[a] No data available.
Source: Deerr, *The History of Sugar*, II, 279; Oliver, *Caribbeana*, II, 77; Watkins, *Handbook of the Leeward Islands*, 33.

the elimination of small-scale European farmers. In 1713, when the Treaty of Utrecht stipulated that all of St. Kitts was to become British, 12,000 acres of "French lands" suddenly became available to British buyers. Various schemes were subsequently suggested for allocating the lands, among them an abortive proposal for 10-acre plots for military veterans. By 1721 the majority of the "French lands" had been sold to buyers in plots of more than 150 acres each.[19]

A reduction in natural environmental diversity for the sake of economic monoculture was mirrored by the simplicity of the stark bipolar society of the two islands. Although internal differentiation within the white free class and the black slave class of St. Kitts and Nevis would become more apparent by the time of slave emancipation, the essential duality of the insular societies had become set by the early 1700s and would persist far into the future.

Plantation Environment and Routine

The ecological, economic, and social dimensions of the slavery era on St. Kitts and Nevis were most apparent on the plantations, which were the islands' basic human settlement units. The "urban" areas of Basseterre and Charlestown were small complexes of wharfs, warehouses, markets, and shops geared exclusively to expediting the export of plantation sugar and the import of plantation supplies. On her visit to Basseterre in 1789, Maria Riddell found that the town had only 800 houses lining narrow, dirt streets—an inauspicious capital town for a wealthy island with more than 22,000 inhabitants.[20]

The size of a Kittitian or Nevisian sugar-cane estate could not expand indefinitely, owing to the transportation and processing requirements of the cane itself. Sugar cane's sucrose content sours a day or so after harvest, and oxcart accessibility to the mill at harvest time thereby limited the extent of each plantation. By 1828 the typical plantation of St. Kitts was, roughly, 200 acres, 150 planted in cane and the remainder in grazing, mountain, provision, or "waste" land. The compact layout of each plantation unit was also related to its quasi-industrial organization. Usually at the center, or at the estate's most accessible point, was the grinding mill, powered by wind by the eighteenth century and increasingly by steam in the nineteenth. Close by the mill were the boiling and curing houses, storehouses, animal pens, the owner's and manager's dwellings, and the plantation hospital or "hothouse." The slave huts were often some distance from the nucleus of an estate and on land unsuited for anything else. The cane fields themselves were intersected by cart trails, which created a gridded appearance for each plantation unit and also represented regularly spaced firebreaks.

Figure 3 shows, in valuable detail, part of the windward coast of St. Kitts in the decade prior to slave emancipation. Of particular interest are the locations of the slave huts, many of which are next to the windswept, saline littoral or, more often, in the dank drainage ghauts. During early slavery days on St. Kitts the slaves lived in "flimsy little huts, generally valued at £2 apiece."[21] Slave housing had improved by the late eighteenth century to wattle-and-daub structures supported by posts in the ground, with some of the slave dwellings boarded and shingled. On both islands, planters allotted small, peripheral land plots so that slaves could cultivate rootcrops and vegetables and keep goats, hogs, and poultry—provisioning activities to reduce the expensive importation of foodstuffs. Provision grounds were always of marginal quality and often located in mountainous areas far from huts—in Nevis's drier areas or in the sandy drainage ravines of St. Kitts. In the latter, torrents of water rushed through the channels after rain showers, causing the same kinds of damage inflicted

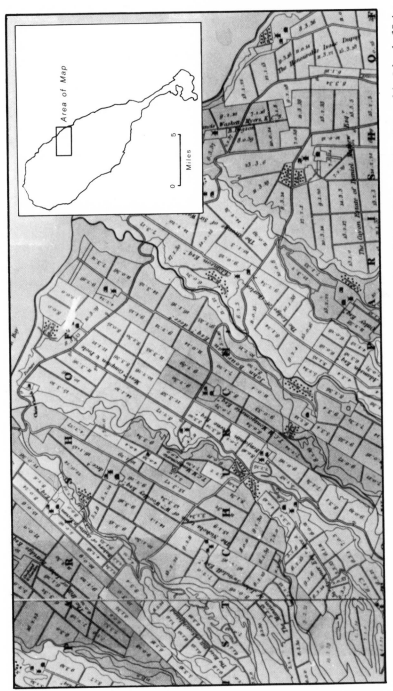

Figure 3. Part of the windward coast of St. Kitts in 1828. From William McMahon, *A New Topographical Map of the Island of Saint Christopher, 1828,* C.O. 700, St. Christopher and Nevis, no. 8. Reproduction of Crown-copyright records in the Public Record Office appear by permission of the Controller of H.M. Stationery Office.

today to the Kittitian peasants' houses, which remain relegated to these marginal zones.

Some planters of both islands rotated provision crops on canelands, although the best lands—those that were fertile, well-drained, and not too steep—were invariably planted in sugar cane. Hillside areas, especially on Nevis, were occasionally devoted to cane because of greater rainfall reliability at higher elevations, although this led to inevitable soil erosion to the detriment of the entire island.[22] As landholdings became larger, individual planters, such as John Pinney of Nevis, planted canes on lands extending from lowlands to highlands or held separate parcels at different altitudes, a landholding strategy adapted to the variability in precipitation from one area to another. Some planters of both islands expressed concern that excessive deforestation had reduced rainfall, but the opposite concern of too much rainfall prevailed during the hurricane season of late summer and autumn. Hurricane damage was one of the risks faced by all planters. The hurricane of August 31, 1772, for instance, caused £3,000 in damage to Pinney's plantations "though it let him off lighter than most."[23]

The autumn rains supplied the moisture for newly planted canes, and October to January was the optimum planting season. Although there were occasional experiments with ox-drawn plows on both islands, gangs of slaves usually prepared the fields with spades and hoes.

Routine typified plantation labor on both islands. The slaves were aroused at dawn and worked until slightly before sunset with intervals of rest or light tasks during the morning and afternoon. On St. Kitts in the 1790s an estate with 300 slaves saw 150 in the fields each day with the rest sick, too young, or employed as tradesmen or watchmen.[24] On one of Pinney's Nevis plantations, 45 (23 male and 22 female) of a total of 122 slaves were designated as members of the field gang and roughly 20 were in the weeding gang.[25]

On Nevis, John Pinney replaced cattle with a windmill to power his main estate's grinding factory in the 1790s. By this time most planters preferred windmills because they operated faster and were cheaper in the long run than cattle. The harvest season, assuming steady breezes from the northeast trade winds, would thus not have to be extended into the rainy period of late summer. Windmills needed neither rest nor food, so grinding and boiling could, and often did, last through the night during the harvest period.

The sights, sounds, and smells of the plantation nucleus at harvest time at night would have become seasonally familiar to any resident of the West Indies in the slavery period. The plantation yard, busy with dozens of slaves loading and unloading canes and cane trash, was illuminated by the flickering light from the boiling house while the canvas sails of the grinding mill creaked and groaned overhead, and the atmosphere hung heavy with the stifling sweetness of sucrose vapors. To the planter this familiar scene symbolized progress, profits, and possibly a return to England with the wealth he had "earned" in the Indies. To the slave the scene meant harder work than ever, although his food rations were generally more plentiful than at any other period of the year.

The Life and the Death of a Slave

After the era of Antillean forest clearing and as Caribbean slave societies "matured," newly arriving Africans were not immediately set to work with the rest of the plantation slaves. Instead there was a customary one-year "seasoning" period, usually supervised by a reliable, elderly slave. Common in all the British plantation islands, seasoning possibly came about from the high slave death rates of earlier periods. To expect a new slave to take his place in a veteran estate gang of eighteenth-century St. Kitts would be "murder," observed Dr. Grainger, a local physician.[26] This term had doubtless been similarly appropriate during the previous century, although in earlier times it had been more expedient to disregard it.

Slave importation to the Leeward Islands slowed by the late eighteenth century. By 1788, both St. Kitts and Nevis were importing fewer than 100 per year, and 65 percent of the slaves on the larger island were estimated to be "creole" or native-born.[27] Slave women, although occasionally berated for becoming pregnant and therefore temporarily "useless," were usually encouraged to give birth and thereby increase the slave population, and they were rewarded with baby linens for their infants on some Nevis estates. Higher slave birth rates and increased slave populations, however, bore no guaranteed correlation with one another because of extremely high infant mortality rates. Slave infants clung precariously to life in their first days. In 1807 as many as one-fourth of newborn Jamaican slaves died within two weeks. In Grenada one-third died in the first month.[28]

If a slave child survived infancy on St. Kitts or Nevis, he or she could look forward to a life of indeterminate length but of guaranteed hard labor. By the time children were four or five, they were incorporated into the plantation's "hogmeat gang," a group of children supervised by an older female slave and charged with light weeding chores and gathering livestock feed. At night in the slave quarters the young slaves ate scanty meals of locally cultivated provisions or imported grain, meals probably prepared by their mothers or other female relatives. They were soon acquainted with many "aunts" and "uncles," not necessarily blood relatives but part of a larger network of fictive kin based upon shipmate relationships developed among those who had together survived the passage from Africa. At birth the young slave had automatically become the property of the master who owned the mother. The master was legally responsible for the slave's housing and sustenance, an arrangement that possibly diminished the role of the father in the child's upbringing. Had the child been born in the late eighteenth century on St. Kitts or Nevis, however, he or she may have very well been raised in a two-parent nuclear family, since informal slave "marriages" were encouraged and nominally rewarded by slave owners who recorded these unions in plantation books.[29]

Whether or not their biological parents lived with and cared for them, young slaves soon became socialized into the group as a whole. They learned internal rules and customs of behavior from friends and family, behavior patterns that were, in part, responses to endless captivity. We can be sure, for instance, that young slaves learned and passed on stories and folk tales that they heard at night in the slave quarters. The most prevalent of these tales involved the exploits of the trickster-hero spider Anancy, a character originally derived from West African folklore. Selected from a rich variety of folklore possibilities, the Afro-Caribbean spider stories portrayed a hero whose exploits were considered laudable behavior in a slave society. In most cases the spider hero survived by its cunning and ability to outwit its foes. If it had to, it could sting and kill, thereby surviving "by its wits and its venom."[30]

After their weekday work in the hogmeat gang, the young slaves possibly played with friends or were dispatched to the provision grounds in order to weed or chase birds or livestock from the small vegetable patches. Sunday provided a chance to accompany their parents to market at a nearby plantation or occasionally as far away as Basseterre or Charlestown. At the marketplace, fellow slaves and freedmen offered for cash sale "greens, roots, grass, green beans, cassava, milk, eggs, fresh fish, small stock, fresh butter, fruits of any kind, firewood, and cotton."[31] Just as important as traffic in foodstuffs, the Sunday marketplace offered an opportunity for diversion, a chance for slaves of the towns and plantations to come together to exchange conversation, stories about friends, and bits of gossip. Slave diversions also had a seasonal dimension; Christmas, the most important holiday of the year, came between the planting and harvest seasons. For a brief period in late December, slaves had relative freedom on St. Kitts and Nevis, and costumed performers portrayed fictitious characters and sang from one plantation yard to another.[32] At Christmas the planters rewarded slaves with extra rations of beef or pork. Underlying the Christmas celebration was the continuous possibility that frivolity and mirth could quickly become rebellion. Until the 1820s a "guard of whites" was on duty throughout Nevis at the Christmas season so that slaves' celebration and merriment would not take such a turn.

The Christmas guard on Nevis was a fitting reminder that the public activities of slaves, whether the daily travails on sugar-cane estates or the few ephemeral slave diversions, were all ultimately regulated by the white planter class. Slaves were, after all, legally controlled by the planters, who were in turn responsible for clothing, food, and minimal land for the slaves and technically responsible for their health and welfare. This domination of a large black population by a relatively small planter class was made easier by the white-perpetuated myths of black inferiority and laziness and by continuous reference to the "primitive," "childlike," and even "animal" nature of the slaves.[33] Just as the provision of the physical necessities of life were the responsibility of the Caribbean planter class, the conditions of the slaves' freedom and captivity were also in their hands. Freedom was enjoyed almost exclusively by whites and granted only by whites. And the granting of freedom was occasionally and paradoxically used to weaken the solidarity among enslaved portions of the populace. For instance, when slaves murdered a white servant in Basseterre in 1773, the local assembly offered freedom to any slave supplying information leading to conviction.[34]

Although born into a condition of abject servitude, slaves soon learned resistance to the plantation system. In order to survive during periods of short rations they would occasionally "steal" from plantation foodstores or illegally butcher and eat estate livestock. The cane fields and boiling houses themselves also offered possibilities for extra rations: In the 1830s Kittitian planter Wentworth estimated that up to 20 percent of his annual crop was lost to slaves chewing the juice from the ripe canes.[35] Active destruction of plantation crops and equipment were more malicious forms of resistance. Intentional burning of the cane fields by slaves was punishable by death in the Leeward Islands, although it could sometimes be disguised as part of a field slave's duties, since cane trash was usually burned after harvest to rid the fields of animal and insect pests.

Resistance to slavery was a daily activity, not simply sporadic acts of violence or theft. Passive resistance took many forms: general inefficiency, "laziness," feigned stupidity, wastefulness, slowness, rote behavior toward work. Routine and monotony characterized almost all of the plantation work, and inefficient techniques of production were perpetuated by the planters in order to occupy large labor forces all through the year. Field preparation by animal plowing, for instance, was attempted in a few cases on Nevis but never adopted on a wide scale on either island. Instead, field preparation was by hoe: "In their cultivation of the cane the slaves were entirely without economic incentive. They could be made to work hard and for long hours, but no compulsion could force them to work well."[36]

Incipient resistance may well have taken a number of other forms known only among the slaves themselves. Two such forms were probably satire and mockery of the white planter class. For instance, a number of slaves met every Saturday evening in the Palmetto Point district of St. Kitts and elected their own officials and assemblies in apparent imitation of the white planters.[37] This seemingly harmless activity was nonetheless viewed with suspicion by the island whites, and laws were passed forbidding the imitation of whites by slaves, an apparent response to the slave mockery that could, under certain circumstances, become troublesome.

Before they could resist slavery, slaves had to survive the punishment and cruelty inherent in the system, and survival meant maintaining their health in the face of malnutrition. Food shortages for slaves were common on St. Kitts and Nevis. The marginally fertile and hazard-prone provision grounds were always subject to drought and flood. Late in the eighteenth century on St. Kitts the weekly food allowance was six to eight imported herrings. On Nevis the rations were similar, and some slaves were occasionally reduced to eating insects and rats from the cane fields. The continuous importation of corn and salt fish from British North America in order to supplement local provisions underlined the precarious nature of the slaves' food supply. During the hurricane season in the Caribbean, shipping in the islands was slowed. This was always the "hungry time," when slave malnutrition or outright starvation was evident everywhere. The effects of complete disruption of the shipping trade or of high prices for food caused by international events were fatal for many slaves. In the late 1770s the price of "Indian Corn" from North America increased from three to sixteen shillings per bushel because of the war there. On Nevis the slave population fell from 9,000 to 8,300 between 1778 to 1788:[38] Nevisian planters, unwilling or unable to pay the higher prices for imported corn, apparently had allowed their slaves to die, since they had become too expensive to support. Involved in an enterprise that spanned two hemispheres, the planters of the two islands were wary of international events that disrupted shipping, destabilized markets, and thereby halted orderly flows of goods and profits. The slaves, with absolutely no control over these events, were, however, affected even more by them: their very lives were at stake.

Malnutrition and disease among the slave population were inevitably linked. Slaves had particular susceptibility to "leprosy, yaws, worms, mal d'estomac, guinea worms, and smallpox."[39] And during periods of epidemic, such as those that brought measles, whooping cough, and diphtheria to St. Kitts from 1821 to 1824, slave death rates were even higher than usual. Every plantation had its own hospital or "hot house" for treating sick slaves, and visits by doctors were usually scheduled on a weekly basis. Some estates had their own slave "doctors." John Pinney's driver, Wiltshire, was adept at treating venereal disease. Pinney also had a midwife on his plantation and a houseboy "able to bleed and draw teeth." A naturally healthy slave who could survive the remedies for his illnesses and afflictions might live a long life. Old men who had been faithful workers often acted as watchmen or fed the animals of the plantation yard. Old women had light duties such as caring for the slave children. But a slave of St. Kitts or Nevis was susceptible to malnutrition and disease throughout his or her life, and these ever-present hazards often led to early death.

An unceremonious event for a planter, the death of a slave was cause for elaborate ceremony among his peers. The Moravian missionaries of St. Kitts in 1825 were aghast at the "great disorder and irregularities" attending wake periods of slave funerals.[40] A series of laws throughout the Leewards in the late seventeenth century called for the punishment of slaves celebrating funerals that imitated white death ceremonies, especially after dark.[41] Similarities in slave funeral practices throughout the British Caribbean suggest a common African origin. Incantations and songs accompanying Caribbean slave burials predicted that the dead would eventually meet their kin again in Africa. Slave burials were therefore a response to slavery, at least to that portion that separated Africans from their native land. On the Caribbean islands they were doubtless also diversions from plantation cruelty, routine, and monotony.

The Complexity of a Slave Society

The asymmetrical dualities of the Caribbean plantation system—white versus black, planter versus slave, cash crop versus subsistence, large scale versus small scale, power holder versus power seeker—that were established in the seventeenth century and have persisted into the late twentieth have been modified through time. On St. Kitts and Nevis on the eve of emancipation, the local society was far from a monolithic unit composed solely of white planters and black slaves. A growing number of "colored" freedmen (the offspring of black slave women and white planters and plantation officials) enjoyed relative ease of movement and controlled limited but distinct segments of the two islands' internal economies such as some of the small-scale retailing and manufacturing. Nor were all white people the large-scale sugar-cane planters and their families. In addition, there were "small white" merchants or hucksters, and a growing number of missionaries, all of European origin.

Differentiation among slaves existed as well. In the region in general, according to Peter Wilson,

> Within the slave population, domestic and artisan slaves were ranked above the vast majority, the field slaves. They enjoyed a higher standard of living, and they were enabled to enjoy greater mobility, often being hired out to work for others by their owners. Hence on the basis of occupation slaves were ranked among themselves and enjoyed different life styles.[42]

Occupational stratification among the slaves was linked to financial reward. Mechanics, masons, carpenters, and tailors were rented out by their owners and thereby earned several shillings per day. This enabled them to obtain better food and clothing in comparison with the field slaves for work that was much less exhausting. In the British Caribbean as a whole, an artisan or field slave sometimes earned enough to purchase his own freedom; this usually depended upon access to cash crop production. The practice was widespread in the Windward Islands but all but nonexistent on St. Kitts and Nevis both before and after emancipation.[43]

Within the physical confines of the plantation units, slave boilermen enjoyed the greatest prestige, for plantation profits often depended on their skills. A head boilerman was expected to know "how the cane had been raised and treated, the kind of soil in which it grew . . . the age of the cane, its species, whether it had been topped long or short in the cutting, and whether it had been arrowed, bored, or rat-eaten."[44] Integrating these and related bits of knowledge, the boilerman knew how much lime to add and when to "strike" or cool the bubbling cane juice, expertise crucial to his craft and possibly passed on from father to son. Clement Caines advised his fellow planters of St. Kitts not to dictate to their boilermen, who had learned the painstaking art of sugar production over many years and who were "more perfect in their business than any white man can pretend to be."[45] Slave boilermen were therefore relatively free of the absolute subjugation suffered by field slaves and enjoyed greater personal benefits and rewards. But the comparative kindness with which boilermen were treated by plantation owners and managers was based upon financial motives rather than altruistic sentiment: on her visit to the Leeward islands in the 1770s, Janet Schaw noted that St. Kitts boilermen had been whipped for neglecting their own health "which is indeed the greatest fault they can commit."[46] Apologists for slavery at the time doubtless cited such cases as evidence that there were no lengths to which planters would not go to ensure the health of the working class!

Slave fishermen trolled the inlets, bays, and shoals of both islands. Although less is known of them than of estate slaves, fishermen seem to have formed a slave elite. They were as skilled as any other artisans or craftsmen, and both planters and slaves depended on them for fresh fish. They were assured of a higher quality diet than most and probably sold extra fish for cash; and their exploitation of a special subsistence niche provided a way out from plantation oppression, similar to the slave access to cash crop production in the British Windwards.[47] Probably most important, slave fishermen, by the very nature of their work, were free at least part of the day—physically separated from the islands themselves and from the unending supervision faced by all others. The feasibility of escape was also doubtless a daily temptation for slave fishermen. An observer at the turn of the nineteenth century described Old Road and Dieppe Bay in St. Kitts as trifling settlements, inhabited by "fishermen, and persons of the lower orders of the people," types who were undesirable doubtless because of their position outside the direct jurisdiction of the planter class.[48]

The few towns of the two islands, Charlestown on Nevis, and Basseterre, Sandy Point, and Cayon—besides Old Road and Dieppe Bay—on St. Kitts, were also where a small but growing number of freedmen congregated in the decades before emancipation, working as "servants, fishermen, tradesmen, hucksters, and small shopkeepers."[49] The freedmen population on St. Kitts increased from 1,996 in 1812 to 2,500 in 1826 to 3,000 in 1830. In Nevis the figure increased from 600 in 1812 to 1,700 in 1834. These increases came almost certainly from local manumission rather than immigration from elsewhere.[50] Buying one's own freedom was only one of several ways it could be achieved; others were by legislative acts, by will and deed, by imperial authority, and by applying for it on other islands. On Nevis, John Pinney had long been freeing his oldest slaves in order to avoid paying taxes on them, a practice frowned upon elsewhere in the Caribbean lest it become a welfare "burden" on the local societies.[51]

Colored slaves had been manumitted in a much higher proportion than blacks on St. Kitts and Nevis, although not even colored freedmen had much chance of gaining access to land.[52] As hucksters, fishermen, small merchants, and artisans, the freedmen nevertheless filled important middle-position economic roles in the local economies, and their freedom was a continuous reminder to the slave populations of their own servile status. Freedmen, for instance, could emigrate with impunity to other islands. Some had left Nevis as early as the 1770s, and between 1817 and 1824 manumitted slaves of St. Kitts sailed away to earn higher wages in other places, especially to Trinidad and Demerara.[53]

By 1800 both St. Kitts and Nevis were truly islandwide slave societies. The plantation, to be sure, remained the fundamental socioeconomic unit in both places, although interpersonal relationships among slaves extended well beyond estate boundaries. Gangs of slaves were seasonally transferred from one estate to another, movement that involved making new friends and acquaintances away from home. News of friends, parents, or "aunts and uncles" was doubtless recounted by traveling hucksters or fishermen. And we can be fairly certain that, as a whole, Kittitian and Nevisian slave societies were tied together even more closely than those on Jamaica, where on the eve of emancipation slaves were "all married (in their way) to a husband, or wife" or had other "family connexions, in almost every parish throughout the island."[54] Owing to the small size of St. Kitts and Nevis, visits and contact with kin would have been much easier there than in Jamaica. On these two tiny islands daily or weekly visits surely reinforced a complex islandwide web of kin and friends by the early nineteenth century.

Running Away

Interpersonal ties among slaves on Caribbean islands were, in part, survival responses to the plantation regime. But responses to slavery took many forms, from malingering to suicide to mass revolt. Among the most common was physical escape from the system. As in all West Indian slave communities, slaves escaped from the estates of St. Kitts and Nevis, but Leeward runaways had different physical constraints from those in the larger colonies, such as Jamaica or the Guianas. The confusion and chaos accompanying Anglo-French rivalry over Nevis and St. Kitts in the first century of colonization provided some of the earliest possibilities for the escape of black slaves. A series of laws on the two islands in the early eighteenth century stipulated whipping and fines as punishment for harboring runaways, and a slave owner could ransack the huts of slaves on any plantation if he suspected that one of his escaped slaves was hiding there.

By the beginning of the nineteenth century, slaves occasionally fled from plantations and then returned of their own accord or were sought by fellow "hunters." In 1798 a new plantation overseer on Nevis was "tested" by the field hands who started leaving in small groups of less than ten; then the hunters sent after them ran away as well.[55] Similar periodic absence was common throughout the Caribbean; on Jamaica habitual runaways or absentees were assigned to "vagabond gangs" for special surveillance.[56] Escape was, however, not a playful exercise. White planters lived in constant fear of theft, arson, and murder, activities they habitually associated with all runaway slaves. In the 1830s about thirty maroons led by "Markus, King of the Woods" roamed the forested highlands above the plantation lands of St. Kitts, some having been absent from their estates for as long as six years. They had firearms and occasionally raided lowland plantations.

The longevity of the freedom of Markus's band had to depend upon constant movement in order to avoid capture, since St. Kitts lacked the vast interior expanses of rugged, forested terrain of the larger islands. It is therefore possible that slaves of the smaller islands began to contemplate escape from the islands themselves at an early date. Neighboring islands were also, literally, never out of sight. Besides being able to see each other's islands, slaves of St. Kitts and Nevis could see, on clear days from elevated slopes in the canelands, Montserrat, St. Barthelemy, St. Eustatius, Saba, and St. Martin. These daily reminders of at least the possibility of freedom were not unnoticed by the planters, who made every effort to control the activities of the slave fishermen. As early as 1717, any black man traveling from St. Kitts to Nevis via small boat was liable to be whipped unless accompanied by a "credible white man." Later in the century, St. Kitts slave fishermen were not allowed to go to Nevis unaccompanied to haul their seines.[57]

Insularity at this scale was inevitably associated with ocean travel. The slaves, or their parents or grandparents, had come to St. Kitts and Nevis via ship, slave food arrived by boat, and the financial fortunes of the plantations themselves depended upon close shipping ties with England. Daily plantation activities were thus closely interrelated with going and

coming by sea. Trusted slaves accompanied their masters to other islands
and occasionally as far as England. By 1774, the small-scale interisland
shipping activities in the Leewards were largely controlled by slaves.[58]
This incipient folk sailing tradition, developed within the broader
framework of the Caribbean's plantation slavery system, would paradoxically provide an opportunity for escape from the local plantations after
emancipation. But in 1807, before this occurred, the African slave trade
was abolished, and inter-Caribbean shipping served the planters by allowing them to redistribute slave laborers from one island to another. Most of
this interisland slave trade was from the smaller, worn-out plantation
colonies, including St. Kitts and Nevis, to the larger, "newer" colonies of
Trinidad and Demerara in the southern Caribbean. From 1808 to 1830,
planters on St. Kitts imported 123 slaves from other British colonies and
sent 383 away to the large southern colonies; possibly as many were
carried without record to the southern Caribbean.[59]

Actual escape by boat seems to have become an ever more practical
venture over the years. Many slaves escaped on ships controlled by foreigners, who were exempt from local control.[60] In October 1824, a
Nevisian slave named Branch bribed two local freedmen with two sheep,
one hog, and two dollars to take him to neighboring St. Barthelemy.
Halfway to St. Barts, the two threw Branch overboard, and he was
rescued by a passing fishing boat and returned to Nevis. Branch's exploits
and those of others inspired the bill passed by the Nevis Assembly two
years later calling for punishment and fines "to guard against the admis-
sion of improper persons into this Community—more effectually to
prevent the escape of debtors and fugitive slaves from the Island, and to
relugate Porters, Watermen, and all Fishing and other Boats and
Canoes."[61] In 1826 the British colonial secretary ordered the Barbados
legislature not to repatriate runaway slaves from foreign islands but to
treat them "as alien freedmen."[62] Thus, successful escape and landing on
another British island meant almost guaranteed freedom, a fact not lost on
the slave populations of St. Kitts and Nevis.

Apprenticeship and Riot, 1834–1838

The inevitability of slave emancipation in the British Caribbean was
hastened by the growing influence of antislavery forces in the home
country, the competition for European markets from other tropical areas,
and economic depression in Britain. By 1830, falling sugar prices had led
to low profits on many British Caribbean plantations and heavy financial

loss on many others. One way to cut estate expenses was to free the slaves, thereby eliminating taxes paid on each slave as well as provisioning costs. This strategy dominated the thinking of the planters of Antigua in 1833 as they discussed whether the local slaves should be apprenticed after emancipation or granted outright freedom. Although they would now have to pay wages, most Antigua planters reasoned that profits would be higher with free labor. But freeing labor did not mean freeing land. By keeping close control of Antigua's best land, the planters would maintain control of the ex-slaves, because provision farming on drought-prone Antigua could not sustain a truly free population. The ex-slaves would, very simply, be forced to work for the planters if they were going to eat.

On St. Kitts, Nevis, and in the rest of the British Caribbean except Antigua, the apprenticeship period from 1834 to 1838 bridged the transition from slavery to freedom. This was to be a time of adjustment for all parties concerned, a time of accommodation and mutual understanding. The "freedom" granted in August 1834, however, did not presume that equality existed between ex-master and ex-slave: former slaves were to perform forty-five hours of weekly labor for their former masters in return for wages, clothing, and in some cases land allotments. Legal stipulations and limitations were, in the view of many planters, crucial to this new arrangement, since the estate owners dreaded the possibility of total insurrection by the former slave population.

On August 1, 1834, slavery became apprenticeship. The former slaves on Nevis were "dissatisfied" that they had not been granted outright freedom.[63] On St. Kitts the newly apprenticed populace engaged in a massive work stoppage to resist a lack of complete freedom and "rioted" for almost three weeks.[64] The former slaves knew that total freedom had been granted on Antigua, two planters on St. Kitts had granted complete freedom, and the rumor spread on St. Kitts that although "the king" had actually declared freedom, it was being withheld by the local planters. A majority of the workers left their estates, many withdrawing into the hills. Potential islandwide revolt was imminent, a situation well beyond the control of the local military detachment at Brimstone Hill, which was separated from Basseterre by poor roads.[65]

Governor MacGregor of the Leeward Islands declared martial law on St. Kitts on August 6 and sent a naval force from Antigua. By this time most of the fieldworkers had departed to the hills. British troops and the local militia retaliated by burning huts and, forming a long skirmish line, swept through the forested hills in order to "encourage" striking estate workers to return to the plantations below. Some of those fleeing the estates had apparently joined the maroon leader Markus, by now an accused murderer whose capture was considered vital to the restoration of order. The resistance was over by August 18, when martial law was terminated on St. Kitts. Miraculously, no one was killed during the uprising or executed in reprisal, although several instigators were whipped and five were exiled to Bermuda.[66] The period of apprenticeship then lasted until 1838 on both islands in an atmosphere of relative tranquility.

Deprived of a formerly captured labor force, the planter class of St. Kitts and Nevis sought effective means of controlling the newly apprenticed populace. The two islands' lands, viewed by the planters as a source of continuing wealth and by the former slaves as a potential means of subsistence livelihood, took on added importance. Land law was, however, passed and implemented by the planter-monopolized assemblies so that planter-apprentice competition over land never really occurred. The planters continued to control all land, but either food or access to land for the workers was a condition of British West Indian apprenticeship. On St. Kitts the planters generally decided to allow more food crop cultivation rather than importing food from abroad; ex-slaves cultivated idle canelands to a greater extent than before, some producing extra provisions for sale after their week's work of forty-five hours. On Nevis, planters continued to import much of the workers' food, seeking to maintain control over the laborers by doling out provisions.

Although planters on both islands continued to dominate their local apprentices, a plantation infrastructure and routine developed during slavery was incompatible with freedom or even partial freedom. The stipulated weekly work hours, for instance, did not fit the need for labor stints of twenty-four hours at harvest time, since apprenticeship laws called for work to be performed only between dawn and dusk. "Thus, even in these islands, the ex-slaves, though not completely free, began to appreciate the strength of their bargaining power at a certain time of the year."[67] Former slaves were, however, far from satisfied with the new order of things because they were denied free access to the lands and therefore still dependent on the estate owners. The struggle between planter and slave had reached a milestone in the 1830s but had not come to an end. The nominal freedom of the black apprentices and the continuing control of the local environments by the white planters represented both persistence and change in the old system that neither satisfied nor realigned either faction on St. Kitts and Nevis.

CHAPTER FOUR

The Postslavery Migration Adaptation

. . . near two thousand persons, as is shewn by the Custom House Returns, the greater portion of whom were adult males have emigrated from this Island to Trinidad between the 1st day of August 1838 and the present date; in addition to which it is fully ascertained that a large number of persons, amounting probably to at least One Thousand have been carried away clandestinely from the various outbays of this Island.

Nevis Council Minutes (September 29, 1842)

THE TRIAL of Quick, a black seaman from Trinidad, took place on St. Kitts shortly after full slave emancipation on August 1, 1838. Quick was the captain of the small sailing sloop *Flora,* commissioned by the Trinidad government to carry black freedmen from St. Kitts and Nevis to the southern Caribbean. The charge brought against Quick by St. Kitts planters was "abduction" of an unwed sixteen-year-old girl; Quick defended himself by claiming that he thought her married to a worker who had already agreed to depart via the *Flora.* Not surprisingly, Quick was convicted, sentenced to six months' imprisonment in Basseterre, and fined £30, although the punishment was subsequently lessened after he appealed the verdict to Governor Colebrooke of the Leeward Islands.[1] Quick's case exemplified the hundreds of related incidents on St. Kitts and Nevis after emancipation as the black populace attempted to assert their freedom and the local white planters attempted—ultimately unsuccessfully—to suppress it.

Quick's trial was a single event that reflected a multilevel series of

Caribbean-wide struggles in the aftermath of British slave emancipation. First, island legislatures—all dominated by the planters—adopted new laws and retained many statutes passed during apprenticeship in an attempt to curtail the movements of black men and women of the newly emancipated laboring classes. The ex-slaves, the objects of this legislation, struggled in turn to achieve the economic and social freedom denied them during generations of slavery, including the freedom to circulate within and among the various islands with impunity.

A second struggle involved competition among planters from different British Caribbean colonies that indirectly aided the black freedmen of St. Kitts and Nevis and the other "old islands." As the Leeward Island planters attempted to keep their workers at home, planters of Trinidad and British Guiana were trying to lure the same workers to the large, modern plantations of the southern Caribbean. In later decades, Trinidadian and Guianese estate owners relied upon the Indian subcontinent for thousands of indentured field laborers. But in the first years after slavery, travel back and forth to the southern Caribbean by freedmen of the Leewards—travel encouraged and facilitated by southern planters—was a valuable outlet for black men and women of St. Kitts and Nevis who sought economic independence from the planters of their home islands.

A final postemancipation struggle, that pitting Caribbean planters against the British crown, further aided black peoples of the two islands. The British Parliament and foreign office, under growing antislavery influence in the early nineteenth century, had begun to intervene in cases previously dealt with exclusively by island assemblies. Therefore, at emancipation, imperial decrees, decisions, and ratifications of colonial laws were often designed to protect the black British West Indian populace from their white ruling classes. This included the rescinding of the most punitive and discriminatory laws through which planters of the smaller Caribbean islands attempted to immobilize their newly freed laborers.

The postslavery migration adaptation on St. Kitts and Nevis represented a pivotal continuity with the peoples' past and future. The longings for freedom that had been stifled during slavery were expressed by emigrating to the southern Caribbean. And this experience would be invaluable as a future survival technique. The courageous acts of sailing away on small sailing vessels and overcoming the hazards of the long voyage to Trinidad and back would also be long remembered and played out time and again on the two islands. One and one-half centuries later it is not simply the prospects for economic gain that motivate returning male migrants to invest their earnings in boats, fishpots, and assorted fishing gear. And it is little wonder that throughout the Lesser Antilles there are few activities more prestigious among the local black men than those involved in earning a living on board one of the sailing vessels that travels from island to island.[2]

Establishing the Trinidad Connection

The flow of black laborers from north to south within the British Caribbean had predated emancipation. The interisland slave trade from the Leewards to the southern colonies followed the abolition of the British transatlantic slave traffic in 1807. Several years later freedmen from St. Kitts and Nevis had voluntarily migrated to Trinidad and British Guiana. The modern, steam-powered mills of the large southern colonies required thousands of acres of cane—and a massive workforce—for efficient, profitable sugar production. Both Trinidad and British Guiana were recent British acquisitions, the former from Spain and the latter from the Netherlands. Neither had suffered the environmental degradation wrought by decades of cane cultivation in the "old islands" of the Caribbean, but both needed substantial pools of labor for factory maintenance, fieldwork, and the reorientation of rain forest and mangrove swamps to fields of sugar cane. Coveting what they considered surplus labor in the densely populated Leewards, southern planters began sending worker recruiting agents into the northeastern Caribbean during the time of the apprenticeship system. On free Antigua, planters complained bitterly in 1837 about the planters of Demerara enticing their workers in open boats to Montserrat and then to British Guiana.[3] One agent from British Guiana scoured the Leewards that year for likely emigrants, purchasing the unexpired apprentice contracts for blacks in Tortola, Montserrat, Nevis, and St. Kitts.[4] Southern planters were willing to pay in cash, rum, and food for necessary labor, and they advertised these benefits throughout the British Antilles as full emancipation approached.

The apprehension of Leeward Island planters increased accordingly. Many feared that all of the black workers would leave when apprenticeship ended, just as they had refused to work in St. Kitts in 1834. On July 2, 1838, Lt. Governor MacLeod of St. Kitts spoke to a large group of the island's fieldworkers. He described the prospects of impending freedom, exhorting the workers to be industrious and to work hard and explained that after August 1 written contracts between former masters and slaves would be necessary to specify working conditions and housing arrangements. MacLeod warned especially against emigration, invoking dark references to those recruiting agents who were paid for persuading innocent workers to emigrate, to the high food prices that prevailed elsewhere, and especially to the few workers who had already gone away, and, contrary to their expectations, had been "sold as slaves into strange countries."[5] MacLeod further referred to recently enacted local laws requiring prospective emigrants to give thirty days' notice to their employers before departing and to advise local magistrates of their intent to leave. Those desiring to emigrate would not only have to give notice well in advance but would also have to prove that he or she had no "aged or infirm Father or Mother, Wife, or Infant child, legitimate or illegitimate . . . who may or ought to be dependent on him for support."[6]

Thus, when emancipation occurred in August the newly freed workers suddenly found themselves entangled in a web of immobilizing legal rules. The laws essentially held all former slaves financially liable for all of their kin. And although the restrictive elements of these laws were later disallowed in London, their immediate enactment in the islands, combined with the lengthy travel time for legal briefs to London and back, provided a moderately successful deterrent to massive migration from the two islands in the latter months of 1838.[7] The subsequent rulings advised that the laborers should be allowed to seek the highest wages in order to support their families, whatever the destination. At the same time, the laborers should not avoid indebtedness by moving from one island to the next. Prospective migrants from both St. Kitts and Nevis soon complained that planters took advantage of the latter opinion by filing false debt claims against workers attempting to leave the islands.[8]

At emancipation, labor recruiters from Trinidad and British Guiana were greeted in the Leewards with yet another series of laws, these designed to obstruct the access of southbound vessels to prospective emigrants. These regulations, enacted throughout the Leewards, were all similar to Nevis's Emigration Act of 1838. It called for ship captains, upon arrival, to post a bond of £300 and not to leave seamen (labor recruiters) behind "as a charge on the public." The law allowed foreign vessels to carry away only those laborers who had a proper license from the colonial secretary, proving they had satisfied the many local regulations necessary for prospective emigrants legally to depart.[9] Although most of these restrictions were, again, eventually not allowed by higher authorities, the Leeward Island planters continued legal efforts to limit the loss of their workers to the southern colonies. On September 1, 1842, for instance, Nevis officials issued a proclamation requiring vessels from Trinidad and Demerara "having on board any disorder" to undergo quarantine for thirty days in the Charlestown roadstead.[10]

Planter control of the lands of the two islands at emancipation was similarly restrictive, but it was more successful because it was less subject to disallowance by British law officers. Sugar production was, after all, the business of the islands, and this justified almost total domination of all the lands of the two islands by plantation owners after emancipation. Except for some house plots that were individually owned on St. Kitts and Nevis, the islands in late 1838 remained under the complete control of plantations, "even the mountains, woodlands, and pastures . . . considered as annexed to certain estates."[11] On each plantation, written contracts now specified arrangements between former masters and ex-slaves. The latter were to perform daily estate labor from dawn until dark in return for the following: wages; a cottage (either old slave quarters or new huts built by the workers); access to provision grounds, pasturage grounds, and hillsides for firewood gathering; and free medical care.

In theory the contracts benefited both owners and workers, but they were weighted heavily in favor of the planters who owned the lands. Without land, the former slave had little incentive. His wages could be revoked if he was accused of malingering, and he could be summarily ejected from his cottage for not rendering proper estate labor of sufficient duration.[12] Though viewed with disfavor by London, eviction of black workers from estate-owned cottages on St. Kitts persisted throughout the nineteenth century and into the twentieth. Eviction, however, was only one of the repressive postemancipation laws on St. Kitts and Nevis that controlled not only emigration but also individual mobility from place to place on the islands themselves. Others were the "vagrancy acts," which, like most rules controlling emigration, were subsequently disallowed. They nevertheless severely hindered workers' movements in the first months after emancipation. On St. Kitts, vagrants found guilty of "trespassing or encroachment" on another's (planter's) land could be punished by a maximum fine of £50 and six months' imprisonment, sentences rarely carried out in their entirety but inhibiting to workers' traveling from one estate to another to seek better wages.[13] Lighter sentences were more common, but they were so often imposed for trivial "offenses" as to make one wonder if emancipation had come about at all:

> Penny Markham, under 2d clause of Vagrancy Act, crossing a rattoon piece on the Walk estate, having been previously warned not to do so on a former occasion, there being no public path through the same piece. Informer, the Hon. W.W. Rawlins.
> Date, 29th August, 1838.
> Punishment, 14 days' labour in penal gang.[14]

Hundreds of such cases occurred on St. Kitts and Nevis in the first months after emancipation. From August 22 to November 28, 1838, in the windward portion of St. Kitts alone, fifty-two laborers were convicted for trespass or absence from work.[15] The activities of dock workers and porters were tightly controlled as well in order to prevent crowds from gathering at docksides and resultant mass migration in small boats. Each year men working near island piers and quays were issued special badges, and badgeless "loiterers" were subject to fines, thirty days' imprisonment, or both. Improperly displayed badges were also decreed as offensive, punishable acts. These trespassing and vagrancy laws, and others, had been in effect on St. Kitts since 1834 but never ratified in London.[16] In the end, however, the repressive efforts to curtail human movement would be futile. Legal disallowance in London was only partly responsible; the planters' efforts to restrain the black workers created the eventual effect of driving many of them away.

Some Nevisians fled across the channel to St. Kitts for higher wages. St. Kitts, larger and more fertile, was—at least economically—better off at emancipation. In comparison, Nevisian planters, on their small stony island, were financially much harder pressed than they had been during slavery, and they paid some of the lowest postslavery wages in the British Caribbean. In 1842, "first-class" fieldworkers on Nevis received only sixpence as a daily wage whereas on St. Kitts they earned ninepence.[17] A few emigrants also went to St. Kitts from Anguilla, which had been devastated by a hurricane in 1842. St. Kitts also received runaway slaves from nearby French and Dutch colonies that had not yet abolished slavery. Laborers from the tiny islands nearby seeking escape from social repression or ecological hazard could at least survive on St. Kitts. Compared with other Leeward islands, St. Kitts's wages seemed reasonable, and laborers were said to be able to cultivate provision crops in rotation with sugar cane on "as much land as they wish."[18]

None of the Leewards, however, could compete with the attractions offered in the southern Caribbean, where "one could earn as much in an hour in Trinidad as a day in Tortola."[19] So by late 1840, after the most blatantly discriminatory sections of the vagrancy and emigration laws had been abolished, hundreds of black Kittitians and Nevisians were leaving for the southern Caribbean legally and illegally via small boats and large. Although attracted by high wages at their destination, they were also impelled to leave because of dissatisfaction with conditions at home, where many of the characteristics of slavery had extended into emancipation. Lt. Gov. C.J. Cunningham stated in 1840:

> I am sorry to believe that the peasantry are emigrating from this Island in considerable numbers. . . . having made personal enquiries from many of the most intelligent of the Emigrants, as to the reasons for leaving their homes all assign the same cause—the uncertainty of the tenure by which they hold their houses and grounds.[20]

Trinidad and British Guiana planters paid cash bounties for foreign laborers delivered to their colonies, a system designed to counterbalance Leeward planters' legal efforts to curb emigration. Bounties were paid to ship captains for passengers' "rates of passage and maintenance on board" the vessel, and payments increased with distance, providing incentive for seamen to roam throughout the Caribbean seeking laborers to bring south (Figure 4). For instance, in 1840 a ship captain bringing laborers to Trinidad received $5 for each one imported from Grenada; $8 from St. Vincent; $14 from St. Kitts, Nevis, Montserrat, and Antigua; and $25 from the Bahamas.[21] The Trinidad government sponsored and funded the bounty system until 1846, although the scheme had been forbidden in London two years earlier. Individual planters also commissioned ship captains to bring laborers. Planters in British Guiana were not allowed to tap their colonial treasury, but they pooled funds in a private immigration society. The Guiana society expended more than $250,000 in a nine-month period in 1840–41, thereby netting almost 3,000 West Indian immigrants, the majority from Barbados.[22]

The immigration bounties financed a widespread network of recruiting agents who, like Quick, traveled from island to island in order to entice workers to leave. The agents were hounded by local police, legislated against by island assemblies, and condemned by endless planter pejoratives. Governor Cunningham of St. Kitts was horrified over the activities of "sordid agents" who persuaded heads of families to leave and thereby sever "sacred domestic ties."[23] Nevis planters expressed similarly new-

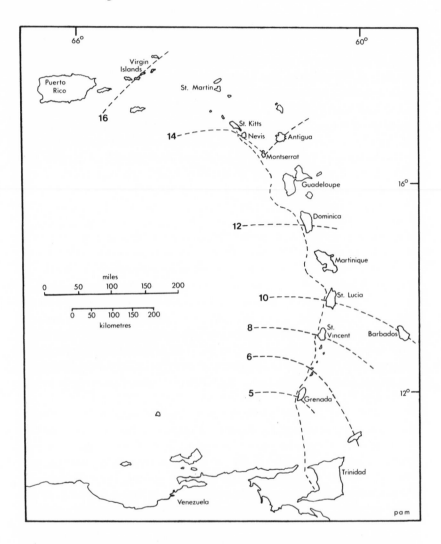

Figure 4. Hypothesized postemancipation sailing route between the Leewards and Trinidad. The numbers represent dollar amounts paid in Trinidad for "immigrants of African descent" imported in 1840. Data from P.P. 1840/xxxiv/363, "Copy of circular despatch . . . relative to immigration into Trinidad." With permission from Bonham C. Richardson, "Freedom and Migration in the Leeward Caribbean, 1838-48," *Journal of Historical Geography* (1980.) Copyright by Academic Press Inc. (London) Ltd.

found concern about the sanctity of local black family life and its potential dissolution at the hands of foreign recruiters. Two agents from British Guiana, Thomas Day and Benjamin Storey, had persuaded sixty to seventy young Nevisians to leave with them in September 1838. The most effective recruiters were the islanders themselves, black men and women informally commissioned by southern planters to enlist workers. In January 1839, native residents of Nevis were circulating among the working populace of that island promising high wages and large food allowances to those bound for Guiana.[24] Across the channel on St. Kitts returning local migrants from the southern Caribbean acted as "decoys," their recruiting activities designed "to unsettle and lead away others."[25] In their anxiety over losing their heretofore captive workforce, Leeward planters found themselves condemning both emigration and return: a black laborer who left thereby violated his sacred family ties; when he returned he was a troublemaker.

The unofficial, occasionally illegal, and oscillating nature of this migration at both ends permits only an estimate of the numbers actually travelling from St. Kitts and Nevis to the southern Caribbean after amancipation. Table 4 shows the "official" migration to the southern colonies over a decade spanning the years immediately before and after full British slave emancipation. The data for Trinidad are limited only to those persons imported at public expense, and they are almost certainly much lower than the actual number who made the voyage. Individual Trinidad estate owners brought thousands more from northerly islands, many to the port of San Fernando in the heart of western Trinidad's sugar-cane region. In July 1841, Trinidad's agent-general, Thomas Johnston, estimated that 8,000 people, twice the official number, had already come from the smaller islands to Trinidad.[26] By September of the following year four sailing vessels were carrying Nevisians to Trinidad, then returning for more after each trip. Nevisian planters estimated that, by that time, almost 3,000 workers had emigrated from the island, one-third of those illegally.[27] Official records show that only half that many had emigrated from Nevis. Of course, some of those leaving had probably been counted twice or more as they traveled back and forth from the Leewards to Trinidad.

Awareness of the quantitative discrepancies between official and unofficial migration estimates from St. Kitts and Nevis helps in understanding the qualitative nature of the voyages themselves. The British foreign office, exercising a watchful eye over West Indian planters for practices akin to those of slavery, had sanctioned Trinidad's bounty-induced immigration program for a brief period only under certain conditions: on board the immigrant vessels, males could outnumber females by only a three-to-two ratio, sufficient food and fresh water had to be provided for all passengers, and overcrowding was prohibited. On the actual voyages, however, overcrowding was the rule, not the exception. Local ship captains, anxious to earn bounties offered by estate owners, packed prospective laborers on board their sailing boats. Unofficial migrants to Trinidad were therefore often not enumerated in the official records.[28] The semi-clandestine nature of much of the migration thereby compounded the danger of the undertaking. And the danger was not only from sailing open

Table 4. Official Migration to Trinidad and British Guiana from St. Kitts and Nevis, 1835–1845

	To Trinidad					To British Guiana			
	From St. Kitts		From Nevis		From All West Indies	From St. Kitts	From Nevis	From All West Indies
	M	F	M	F				
1835	—	—	—	—	—	—	157	157
1836	—	—	—	—	—	356	65	981
1837	—	—	—	—	—	—	—	1,411
1838	—	—	—	—	—	46	40	967
1839	31	1	40	9	692	—	—	37
1840	131	130	126	97	1,106	—	—	871
1841	57	56	244	261	1,719	47	—	2,791
1842	71	38	419	338	1,956	21	32	484
1843	150	100	226	230	2,075	—	—	37
1844	55	45	174	141	1,708	—	—	—
1845	6	5	127	9	990	—	—	722
Subtotal	501	375	1,356	1,085	—	—	—	—
Total	876		2,441		10,246	470	294	8,458

Note: Dashes indicate no data avilable.
Sources: Hall, Five of the Leewards, 41, citing C.O. 7/84 of Aug. 5, 1846; P.P. 1847/XXXIX, Free Emigrants from the West Indies and Mauritius, 2–3; The Reports . . . of Her Majesty's Colonial Possessions: Transmitted with the Blue Books for the Year 1845 (London: W. Clowes and Sons, 1847), 93. With permission from Bonham C. Richardson, "Freedom and Migration in the Leeward Caribbean, 1838–48," Journal of Historical Geography (1980.) Copyright by Academic Press Inc. (London) Ltd.

waters in crowded boats. Kittitians and Nevisians often boarded boats from Trinidad at night in remote, secluded, and dangerous bays and inlets around the two islands to avoid detection by island authorities.

Colonial immigration officials maintained no records of this early labor migration by vessel type, although it seems certain that sailing craft carried all of the unofficial migrants. Steamships, only recent arrivals in the Caribbean, were used to a limited extent to transport workers. By the early 1840s the British Royal Mail Steam Packet Company included St. Kitts in its circuit linking Europe, North America, and the West Indies.[29] Two years later the government of British Guiana dispatched the steamer *Venezuela* to round up laborers in several West Indian islands. The ship was greeted with ill will by the local government officials at various islands, and in several cases potential emigrants were served with falsified bad debt summonses, preventing their departure. When the *Venezuela* arrived at St. Kitts it was threatened with seizure by local authorities under a clause of the island's emigration act.[30]

The preponderance of the migration to the southern Caribbean was, however, accomplished on small sailing sloops and schooners, boats constructed both before and after emancipation. They were commanded by black men like Quick who had learned the art of sailing during slavery, when their cargoes consisted of interisland produce and livestock or transshipments of raw sugar to a colony's main harbor. The light sailing boats had for decades carried goods and people in the protected waters off Trinidad's western coast, and all of the colonies saw an increase in these vessels at emancipation. Some were built with local lumber and some with "Bermuda cedar." Their capacity ratings ranged from twenty to fifty tons, and they could cover the ninety miles of open water between Grenada and Trinidad in fifteen hours.[31] By the early 1840s a brisk sailing traffic in these vessels carried crews, goods, and passengers from island to island across the Caribbean. In 1840, 132 small sailing vessels from other British colonies, averaging thirty tons apiece, called at Nevis; 111 came the next year and 134 the year after. In those same three years, St. Kitts saw, respectively, 245, 138, and 242 sailing vessels, averaging five men in each of their crews.[32] Though calling at all of the islands, the common focal point of this small boat traffic was Trinidad. The large southern island could be reached within a few days by sailing vessel from any of the Lesser Antilles. The route to Trinidad was partly protected from the direct force of Atlantic gales and winds, since it was on the leeward side of the islands. Planters of British Guiana, on the other hand, could not always count on flotillas of small sailboats periodically to replenish local labor supplies. The mudflats of the South American colony were 300 miles farther than Trinidad, and sailing to the Guianas involved combatting both the northeast trade winds and the easterly equatorial current.

The image emerging from the evidence of these voyages is that of a sailing adventure involving thousands of small islanders in the years after slavery, among them thousands of black Kittitians and Nevisians, mainly male but many female. Their emigration was a symbolic assertion of freedom, an act that involved danger and the courage to overcome it. Boarding a vessel at night required bravery in the face of possible punishment by local island officials. It was even more difficult leaving homes and loved ones, parting invariably performed with reluctance.[33] The passage itself was at once spiritually exhilarating and physically dangerous. It took several days and nights to sail the 500 miles to Trinidad, an odyssey involving the risks of action by hostile colonial officials along the way, unmarked rocks and shoals, navigation without the benefit of charts or compasses in crowded open boats, and the omnipresent risk of death by drowning. Upon returning home from Trinidad in mid-1845, a number of Nevisians recounted stories of comrades' deaths.[34] Their causes were unspecified, but it seems certain that the voyages themselves accounted for many. Once in Trinidad, an emigrant was under the control of foreign planters and overseers, and he had to assert his individuality and acuity to find the most remunerative jobs. But even if he prospered in Trinidad he was still a stranger there, and after earning enough cash he usually returned home, once more braving the hazards of the interisland passage. By successfully emigrating and returning, a black man or woman from St. Kitts or Nevis had secured the freedom and independence prescribed by emancipation and had established himself or herself as one of those special people who had worked abroad. The dress of these people in "fashionable array, with a gawdy display of tinsel ornaments" were reminders to acquaintances and kinsmen of their success away from home and the boldness they had displayed in getting there—signals not lost on the community staying behind.[35]

The work in Trinidad was hard but relatively high-paying field labor—cane harvesting and then weeding in the off-season. It is therefore most likely that the labor migrants from St. Kitts and Nevis were among those who had been counted as field laborers and inferior laborers at emancipation. Of the 15,667 slaves on St. Kitts at emancipation, 11,350 fell into these two categories; on Nevis, 4,636 of the 7,225 slaves had been counted as field or inferior laborers.[36] In other words, the early migration experience was color and class selective, monopolized by those from among the black "lower classes."

Some of the migrants doubtless stayed on in Trinidad, but the majority seem to have returned, at least temporarily. The comparison of the St. Kitts and Nevis census figures in July 1838 and June 1844, in fact, show population increase rather than decline, suggesting that most of the migrants had come back. Between 1838 and 1844, St. Kitts's population grew from 21,578 to 23,177, while Nevis's increased dramatically from 7,470 to 9,571.[37] The data for 1844 must be regarded as only rough population estimates, and later colonial census takers were very skeptical about their validity, but these figures are roughly supported by colonial observers who noted considerable return migration almost as soon as the exodus began. By 1842, "many" Kittitian travelers had returned from Trinidad and British Guiana.[38] By Christmas of the following year some of the laborers had come back to Nevis, purchasing cottages with money they had earned abroad.[39] By January 1845, a "considerable number" of Nevisians were back.[40]

While in Trinidad, the workers from Nevis, St. Kitts, and the other "old islands" provided necessary labor but were unreliably mobile, drifting from estate to estate and rarely settling in one place. Unlike their black Trinidadian counterparts, who had begun to establish independent settlements on the fringes of the large sugar-cane estates, the small islanders rarely purchased or cultivated land. Some of the immigrants had paid their own passages south and would stay to perform work by the task only as long as planters offered high wages.[41] And, as free men and women, they could choose to withdraw their labor under unsuitable conditions just as they had at home. Thus in July 1844, when Trinidadian planters lowered wages, large numbers of migrants responded by returning home.[42] Those sailing back to St. Kitts and Nevis had prospered in a relative sense and had also successfully resisted planter oppression on both ends of their journeys by exercising their mobility—by emigrating and then by going home again.

The British Sugar Duties Act of 1846, which removed West Indian price preferences, affected both planters' profits and freedmen's wages throughout the region. On St. Kitts and Nevis, sugar prices fell by almost 20 percent between 1845 and 1848, and wages were reduced by half. Trinidad planters lowered wages, too.[43] The Trinidad estate owners began to realize that the solution to their labor shortage would lie in importing thousands of indentured workers from India, immigration that would last until the early twentieth century. Low wages and a more crowded labor market in Trinidad thus stemmed the tide of massive emigration there from the Lesser Antilles in the late 1840s and sent even more small islanders home. By February 1848, only 2,641 of the "old islanders" remained of the 11,339 who had been imported in the preceding decade, and stricter surveillance over their back-and-forth movements was considered desirable but acknowledged as next to impossible.[44]

The black migrants of St. Kitts, Nevis, and the other small islands had departed only temporarily. Trinidad was now a part of their world, and they would return from time to time as the need arose. By 1845, for instance, blacks from the eastern villages of St. Kitts routinely bartered their garden provisions by sailing south to the Windwards and Trinidad.[45] In St. Kitts and Nevis, planters still monopolized the island lands and would continue to do so throughout the nineteenth century. Their black workers would accordingly continue to ameliorate their own economic or ecological uncertainties at home by periodically traveling back and forth to the southern islands. For the black freedmen of St. Kitts and Nevis, a migration adaptation rooted in slavery and realized in freedom had established a vital connection with the world outside.

Migration and Demography in the Nineteenth Century

The populations of St. Kitts and Nevis increased steadily throughout the rest of the century (Table 5). Sex imbalances in all cases reflected the prevalence of male emigration from the islands during this period, a cause and effect invariably reiterated by colonial administrators and clerks attempting to analyze the population figures they forwarded to London. Static population data recorded at predetermined intervals could not, however, adequately represent a highly mobile population, and population mobility often rendered these reports admittedly inaccurate. Migration from and return to St. Kitts and Nevis was the despair of nineteenth-century colonial record keepers. A good example is the forlorn conclusion reached by the St. Kitts census takers in 1855 as they attempted to reconcile their findings with the figures of eleven years earlier:

We have good reason to believe that errors, by which the amount of the population was materially enhanced, did occur in 1844, and that the mode in which the enumerations were then made afforded no opportunity for corrections. We are also aware that some of the labouring population have left this island, allured by mercenary emissaries to neighbouring colonies, under promise of higher wages, and although many have returned, we have no clue by which we can trace the number of departures and returns.[46]

Neither were the census data uniform from one decade to the next. The racial composition of the population was not always included with colony census figures, although blacks always predominated numerically. In 1891 the white population of St. Kitts was 2,343, up from 1,612 at the 1812 census. On Nevis the white population had fallen from 260 in 1861 to 182 in 1891.

Table 5. Population of St. Kitts and Nevis, 1844–1891

	St. Kitts			Nevis		
	M	F	Total	M	F	Total
1844	10,523	12,654	23,177	4,418	5,153	9,571
1855	9,525	11,216	20,741	—	—	—
1861	11,437	13,003	24,440	4,734	5,088	9,822
1871	13,259	14,910	28,169	5,433	6,247	11,680
1881	13,706	15,431	29,137	5,436	6,248	11,684
1891	14,410	16,466	30,876	5,945	7,142	13,087

Note: No census was taken on Nevis in 1855.
Sources: P.P. 1845/XXXI/331; St. Kitts *Blue Books* of 1844, 1854, 1864, 1871, 1881; Nevis *Blue Books* of 1862, 1872, 1881; Leeward Islands *Blue Book* 1893.

One check on human population increase in the two islands in the nineteenth century was disease. In 1860, diphtheria killed 165 on St. Kitts.[47] Seven years earlier, during an eighteen-month period from 1853 to 1855, cholera raged through St. Kitts and Nevis as part of a regional epidemic. On St. Kitts, 3,920 died, a fact that helps to explain the population decrease there between 1844 and 1855. Cholera had appeared first on Nevis in the autumn of 1853, where it was mainly confined to the laboring classes.[48] In all, 891 Nevisians eventually died of the disease. St. Kitts officials waited apprehensively. The first death from cholera on St. Kitts was reported in Basseterre on November 6, 1854. Dr. Thomas Cooper, a cholera specialist from Barbados, was then summoned. He remained on St. Kitts until the last cholera death occurred in St. Paul's village on January 31, 1855.

Cooper's subsequent report on the St. Kitts cholera epidemic was an exhaustive description of death and burial.[49] It was also an eloquent testimony to the futility of attempting to enforce quarantine in the mid-nineteenth-century Caribbean; the small sailing boats carrying passengers back and forth from place to place had ample opportunity to transmit disease to each island many times over. Cholera had first appeared on Barbados and St. Vincent in 1850. Four years later it ravaged Trinidad, where 5 to 6 percent died, of a population of 75,000. When the disease hit Nevis, officials on St. Kitts strictly monitored small-craft traffic between the two islands. It was to no avail, and colonial officers on St. Kitts could take little consolation in the fact that quarantine was usually unsuccessful in the other islands as well. Quarantine regulations, such as the one prohibiting communication between St. Kitts and Dominica, Guadeloupe, and St. Martin in 1865 and mandated recurrently throughout the islands in the nineteenth century, provided little or no control over the spread of disease.

Even without periodic disease epidemics death rates were high on the two islands, especially on St. Kitts, where occasionally the number of "natural" deaths exceeded births, for example, in 1872 when 1,316 people died and 1,293 were born.[50] Infant mortality was particularly high. From 1863 to 1865, a three-year period during which 2,614 persons died on St. Kitts, 1,187 were less than a year old.[51] High infant mortality was especially prevalent in the black laboring population, which had stillborn rates of 10 percent and even higher.[52] Poor sanitation and nutrition were the likely causes, but colonial administrators insisted that adequate if not exemplary medical facilities were available to the working class and their children. In seeking periodically to explain high death rates and high infant mortality rates, officials usually cited black improvidence—the propensity of the black workers to "squander" their money on inconsequential clothing and baubles to the eventual detriment of their families' health.

The high mortality during the cholera epidemic was used by the planters of both islands to attempt to justify importing more laborers. Ever since emancipation they had sought to stabilize or enlarge the resident workforces, not only by attempting to curb emigration but also by trying to attract labor from elsewhere. In February 1841, the Nevis Assembly had adopted a resolution to import "liberated Africans" in order to swell the island's labor force.[53] The Nevisian planters were referring to the Africans recently freed by the British navy from slave vessels bound for Cuba and Brazil. Some of the Africans were brought directly to Caribbean ports, and many were settled in West Africa, then sent to the British West Indies as workers during the 1840s. The larger colonies of British Guiana, Trinidad, and Jamaica together received more than 9,000 of the Africans.[54] Smaller islands received fewer. St. Kitts and Nevis together imported only 455 free African immigrants in the nineteenth century, all of them going to the larger island.[55] The Africans, though initially unfamiliar with their surroundings and the local language, normally became assimilated with the native black population quickly. Ninety-seven laborers from Sierra Leone arrived on St. Kitts in April 1849. They were indentured under annual contracts and provided "comparatively steady continuous labour" in comparison with their native counterparts.[56]

A contingent of English laborers arriving on St. Kitts in 1845 had not fared nearly as well. Almost as soon as they appeared they became fatigued by the subtropical heat and generally succumbed to "fevers" and "strong drink." Within months, a spokesman for the immigrant group had sent a petition to London asking to be returned, a pathetically worded statement complaining of the miseries of tropical climate and disease.[57] No more British were imported as laborers, although St. Kitts continued to receive a trickle of immigrants from nearby islands. Among the more than 20,000 Kittitians counted in the census of 1855, 194 had been born in Anguilla, 179 in St. Martin, and 129 in Nevis.[58]

Indentured immigration from Portuguese Madeira provided the largest number of non-African workers to St. Kitts and Nevis in the nineteenth century. From 1847 to 1870, 1,180 Madeirans arrived, almost all on St. Kitts.[59] The planters on the larger island had adopted a bounty system to import Portuguese workers. Transatlantic vessel captains received payment upon delivery. The British government tolerated the system only after stipulating that a local official visit the ship upon its arrival in order to ascertain whether or not the voyage had been satisfactory, to explain indenture terms to the newly arrived, and to ensure that "genuine" signatures had been voluntarily affixed to indenture contracts. British authorities remained skeptical of the system, suggesting that a bewildered newcomer who spoke no English would hardly be in a position to determine whether he or she was being treated fairly or not.[60]

As Mediterraneans, who were linguistically alien to the region, the Portuguese newcomers identified with neither their fellow black plantation workers nor the ruling white planter elite. A few Madeirans introduced to Nevis in 1847 died shortly thereafter.[61] Two years later, on St. Kitts, Portuguese immigrants were considered adequate and reliable field laborers. When their indenture contracts expired, however, the Madeirans tended to open small retail shops in the plantation villages and capital towns.[62] The stereotype of the Portuguese shopkeeper of the Caribbean, so common on Trinidad and British Guiana, where Madeirans had been imported in much larger numbers, was also true for St. Kitts and Nevis. By 1870 the Portuguese merchants had achieved not only a measure of prosperity on St. Kitts but were accorded a degree of social prestige. According to Governor Cairns in 1869, "Nine-tenths of our respectable and well-to-do shopkeepers are immigrants who have served out their indentures here."[63] Not all the Portuguese remained in the Leewards; some preferred to emigrate to the southern Caribbean.[64]

A few Indian "coolie" (the term invariably used in colonial reports) migrants were indentured on St. Kitts and Nevis in the nineteenth century while tens of thousands of Indians were being taken to the southern Caribbean. Today, in the late twentieth century, the only noticeable vestige of this immigration on the two islands is a few Indian families in the Cotton Ground village area of Nevis, north of Charlestown. In 1861, 337 Indians were brought to St. Kitts. Twenty-two died during their indenture and 63 left for Trinidad and Guiana when their contracts expired.[65] On March 30, 1874, 315 Indians came to Nevis. During their indenture period on Nevis many were homesick and lonely, and some broke their contracts in order to emigrate to Trinidad. The others were offered reindenture contracts after their five-year periods had expired, but they chose to remain on Nevis as free laborers.[66]

While the planters on the two islands experimented with small groups of imported laborers from near and far, the native black populace continued to toil on estates and to respond periodically to changing local conditions by emigration in small but varying numbers, mainly to Trinidad and then usually back home. Their movements were occasionally responses to local economic conditions such as low wage levels or failed provision grounds. In some cases emigrations followed recurring environmental calamities that directly affected laborers' livelihoods and survival. Both islands suffered a devastating earthquake in February 1843 that was particularly destructive on Nevis, where several sugar mills and all of the public buildings in Charlestown were demolished.[67] Drought, always possible in the Leewards, was so intense in 1863 that a "day of fast and humiliation" was observed on Nevis.[68] Almost every building in Basseterre burned down on July 3, 1867, eventually bringing contributions of food and clothing from England and also from neighboring islands.[69] In 1871 a hurricane passed through St. Kitts destroying not only the sugar-cane crop but also avocado and breadfruit trees.[70] Heavy rains and subsequent flooding caused several deaths by drowning on St Kitts in January 1880.[71]

Whatever the reason, emigration continued, and it was as poorly recorded in the latter half of the nineteenth century as in the years immediately following emancipation. Small boats leaving Nevis in 1845 with fewer than thirty passengers on board were not required to file reports with customs officers, confounding any effort to quantify departures.[72] Ten years later emigrants were leaving St. Kitts "crowded together in small vessels . . . destitute of all necessary arrangements for carrying passengers."[73] The back-and-forth movement from the islands was usually routine and often led to a state of local population equilibrium, at least in the eyes of colonial administrators: "many of the labourers who migrate to Trinidad and other places, return, after a time, to Nevis; the population, therefore, is not likely to be materially thinned by this cause."[74] As in earlier days, the movement was usually on the small sailing vessels. Increased steamship service in the West Indies in the 1870s and 1880s allowed for travel to Trinidad, or at least part of the way, by black laborers from the two islands as steamer deck passengers.[75]

Emigration was not always temporary. In each decade dozens, if not hundreds, left St. Kitts and Nevis permanently. "Permanent" and "temporary" are, however, theoretical categories, better suited to social scientists' pigeonholes than they are to the motivations and desires of a mobile human populace. Doubtless many who departed the two islands in the nineteenth century and established homes and families elsewhere maintained some kind of contact with those left behind. In any case, net birth and death data from both islands from the decade of the 1870s, when compared with population figures at either end of the decade, provide a measure of "permanent" migration during that period. From 1871 to 1880 on St. Kitts, births exceeded deaths by 1,959, whereas, population increased by only 968 (Table 5), leaving a net population "loss" of 991. On Nevis the natural increase of the population was 2,173 and the census increase 184, suggesting a population loss of 1,989.[76]

This is not to suggest that the 1870s were "representative" of the late nineteenth century on the two islands. Each decade, each year, and each season presented its own problems and opportunities. The 1870s, for instance, were years of relative prosperity on Trinidad, and the promise of good markets and high wages lured more workers than usual to the southern island. In 1876, 181 left Nevis, followed by 342 the following year, and 206 in 1880.[77] In 1879 the governments of both St. Kitts and Nevis passed laws against the emigration of "unauthorized workers," although these rules had even less effect than they had forty years earlier.[78]

Trinidad now offered a greater variety of jobs, and small islanders gravitated to Port of Spain and San Fernando more than in the earlier decades when their labors had usually been confined to the sugar-cane plantations. As early as 1851, 80 percent of the 10,800 residents on Trinidad from the other British Caribbean colonies lived in the two urban districts rather than in the country areas where the sugar estates were located.[79] By 1881, "other" British West Indians on Trinidad numbered over 24,000, probably as much a reflection of improving modes of travel as a desire of small islanders to settle permanently there. Low-cost steamship connections allowed fieldworkers from the Windwards to cut cane in western Trinidad then to return home, where the cost of living was lower, after the harvest season. But more often, visiting West Indians filled industrial and skilled jobs on Trinidad—as mechanics, blacksmiths, carpenters, tailors, and masons. Some remained on the large southern island. Many others worked for a period and then returned home. They were part of the large "floating" West Indian population on Trinidad, emigrating from their home islands and then returning as their fathers and mothers had in the past.[80]

A growing variety of Caribbean destinations, other than Trinidad, also began to attract migrating Kittitians and Nevisians in the years after slavery. The insular British colonies between the Leewards and Trinidad were places with which they were familiar, and job possibilities there were occasionally exploited. In late 1850, a few Nevisians left the windward area of their own island to work on St. Vincent before returning.[81] In the following decades, dozens of Kittitian and Nevisian workers traveled for temporary jobs on Dominica.[82] And as time went on, workers from both islands began to discover work possibilities in "foreign" islands of the Caribbean. About 200 Kittitians traveled to Danish St. Croix in 1864 after drought had desiccated the sugar-cane crop at home.[83] By the last quarter of the nineteenth century, men from both islands had found their way to the Dominican Republic to work in the cane fields.[84]

Plantations, Provisions, and Subsistence

Although planters owned the land on both islands throughout the nineteenth century, distinct differences developed between the land and labor systems of St. Kitts and Nevis shortly after emancipation. Nevis had always been considered less fertile than St. Kitts. Estate owners on the smaller, stonier, and steeper colony were not only uncompetitive in postemancipation wages but even found it difficult to raise cash to pay their workers. Therefore, in 1847, Nevisian planters introduced the metairie method of sugar-cane production. In this system, owners allocated portions of land to freedmen, who planted and cultivated the cane for a percentage—one-third to one-half—of the crop's value. Planters continued to control land, vehicles, and processing machinery. Although profits were lower than planters would have liked, and both parties disputed cane tonnage and the sharing of proceeds, metairie allowed planters to postpone paying workers until the crop was sold. Metairie, common in the Windwards, was considered only a temporary state of affairs by the Nevis estate owners, an arrangement to carry them through economic depression. When prices rose again, planters would reinstitute more efficient and profitable wage labor.[85]

The metairie system gave Nevisians a greater personal stake in local land use than their counterparts had on St. Kitts. Black peasants of the smaller island did not hold titles to the land they worked, but their greater access to the land inevitably led to a degree of control over what was planted. Nevisian peasants usually planted larger acreages in food crops than did Kittitians. Such planting was, of course, dependent on cane prices and subject to the landowners' ultimate approval. In the early 1860s, for instance, planters from Barbados purchased several Nevisian plantations and imparted "new energy to sugar cane cultivation."[86] Even at this time, however, about one-third of the cultivated lands on Nevis was in food crops; of a reported 6,300 cultivated acres on Nevis in 1864, 4,000 were planted in cane, 100 in cotton, and the remainder in "potatoes, beans and peas, maize, and arrowroot."[87] On Nevis, metairie had provided at least a slight measure of control over local resources, certainly more than the black estate workers of St. Kitts had; in 1857 this sharecropping mode was cited as responsible for the "advanced" condition of the Nevisian peasantry over those on neighboring islands.[88]

The wages of freedmen on St. Kitts, on the other hand, were tied directly to fluctuating cane prices. Although Kittitian estate lowlands were occasionally planted in food crops during the nineteenth century, they never were for long. Higher sugar prices would bring back cane, and the Kittitian estate workers' provision grounds would be relegated to marginal plots on the slopes and around their huts. In general, the rural blacks of the larger island inhabited houses on the estate grounds, where they could occasionally grow their own food in rotation with cane or, after working hours, on subsistence grounds, as their parents had during slavery. Unlike the Nevis blacks, where a quasi-independent peasantry was beginning to emerge under the metairie system, St. Kitts blacks always faced the interposition of the white planter class between them and the land, and they were therefore continuously obliged to negotiate and bargain for the "privileges" of pasturing livestock, planting provisions, or gathering firewood.[89]

The white planters or their representatives lacked the personal continuity with the land that the black workers had, because estates on St. Kitts and Nevis often changed hands in the nineteenth century. By 1845 some St. Kitts plantations had come under the control of several English merchant shipowners, who brought goods from Britain and returned with sugar from their estates, harvesting and processing the crop on their arrival whether it was ripe or not.[90] Plantations on both islands were controlled and operated in a variety of ways. Of the 137 estates on St. Kitts in 1856, 58 belonged to resident owners, 22 were run by lessees, and the remaining 57 belonged to absentee owners, the majority of the latter representing mercantile houses in Britain.[91] Estates remained small on both islands, a single plantation rarely more than 300 acres. It was difficult for such small land units to compete with the large plantations of the southern Caribbean, especially in light of fluctuating sugar prices. It therefore became increasingly important for the local plantations, if they were to survive economically under a single owner, to be controlled by "men possessed or having command of capital."[92] Small plantation size also led to a degree of consolidation and, by the 1880s, a growing tendency for 2 or 3 adjoining plantations on St. Kitts to be worked as a single unit.[93]

Sugar cane remained the single cash crop of both St. Kitts and Nevis throughout the century, although the colonial *Blue Books* reflect an experiment with cotton in the 1850s and 1860s.[94] Crop identity was unchanging, but technology—especially on St. Kitts—had changed considerably by the end of the century. Sugar-cane planters introduced cultivation equipment to St. Kitts shortly after emancipation. Workers could no longer be forced to prepare and weed plantation lands, so planters compensated with horse-drawn plows, harrows, and weeding machines. By 1860, estates on St. Kitts required only one-fourth of the cultivation labor needed during slavery, but the substitution of machines reinforced a seasonal regimen for the island's black populace in the production of raw sugar: gangs of cane cutters were still needed at harvest time.[95] Nevis's stony terrain was less suited for field machinery, although animal-drawn plows and other implements had been introduced there by the 1860s.[96] During the nineteenth century, St. Kitts planters converted almost completely to steampower for milling; the sugar factories were largely brick or iron buildings from which tall smokestacks emitted noxious fumes and smoke during the grinding season.[97] Planters on the smaller island, however, lacked the capital for renovation and modernization in cane processing, and retained antiquated methods. At the end of the century all but one of St. Kitts's sixty-three sugar factories were powered by steam. Of Nevis's fifty-two mills, fifteen continued to be windpowered.[98] Neither island's planters could afford the kinds of technical advances necessary to compete with sugar produced in the larger West Indian areas. In the latter half of the nineteenth century a superior grade of sugar was produced throughout British Guiana and Trinidad using vacuum-pan boiling techniques. In contrast, only one estate on St. Kitts and Nevis combined had a vacuum pan by 1900.[99]

Leeward planters had introduced field machinery to the islands with an element of bitterness. Expenses for such equipment could have been saved with a "reliable" workforce. Even in the relatively prosperous years, such as the 1870s, colonial authorities insisted that things would be better if only the blacks would offer their labor more regularly rather than absenting themselves for protracted periods of time and leaving their work when the pay did not suit them. Some freedmen occasionally withdrew to the margins of the forest in order to raise livestock and tend provision grounds.[100]

The villages of Nevisian workers were usually on or near plantations, the huts invariably on poor land—in drainage ghauts, or lowlands, or the steeper slopes.[101] On St. Kitts, black workers inhabited small houses on the plantation grounds and in 1861 there were about 5,500 workers' dwellings, which were

> generally speaking wooden erections, about 14 feet square, consisting of one or at the utmost two rooms. A European lady lately compared them to bathing machines with the wheels off; a comparison scarcely complimentary to the latter. These houses rest on posts or blocks of wood, a foot or two from the ground itself. . . . The furniture of their houses consists generally of a sack stuffed with grass for a bed, sometimes a bedstead, two or

three boxes which serve at once for wardrobes and chairs, and a looking glass.[102]

Black families of seven or eight slept crowded together in these small houses. The families were ordinarily not bound together by formal Christian marriage, the lack of marriage being an "evil" and "deplorable" state in the eyes of colonial officials, who found in low marriage rates a facile explanation for high mortality and morbidity rates. Black households and families, deprived of their own land, were dependent on a combination of wages earned locally, money brought home from abroad, and small-scale provision farming on the estate lands. Maintaining at least partial control over all three sources of livelihood at the same time was crucial to long-term survival. Both local wages and foreign jobs were subject to planter control and foreign market prices. The marginal provision grounds were subject to hurricane and drought damage as well as to intermittent taxes.[103] If one element of livelihood failed, another might pull an individual or family through hard times. This method of survival was often incompatible with the labor needs of the planters, who interpreted sporadic turnouts for wage work in the cane fields as "laziness" and "unreliability."

The precariousness of black livelihood and survival was compounded by a continuing dependency on food importation to supplement local subsistence elements. In general, black laborers ate only two meals per day. The dietary staples were homegrown vegetables and imported fish and bread products, and black fieldworkers often drank cane juice or rum in the fields in order to curb fatigue or exhaustion.[104] The imported food—flour, dried fish, and pork—was principally from North America, imported in bulk. As always, a food chain stretching to the fishing banks of North America invited disruption by intervening events. In 1863 the American Civil War threatened to terminate the importation of staple foods to the two islands, leading to alarmed reactions about a possible state of "comparative starvation."[105]

Local fishing in the nineteenth century in the surrounding waters provided, as in slavery days, a nearby source of protein varying in abundance from season to season. In any given year there were 70 to 100 small fishing boats in the waters of St. Kitts and an estimated 125 in Nevis.[106] Native shipwrights occasionally built small sloops and schooners in the relatively sheltered, quiet littorals of the two islands. And although long-distance sailing was less well-known in the Leewards than on Trinidad or the Grenadines, a man with a boat on St. Kitts or Nevis was always better off socially and economically than one without. Boatmen were free of estate domination and planter-decreed wages. On Nevis the freedom enjoyed by native boatmen was at once the source of envy by the black peasantry and frustration in the eyes of white planters and colonial agents. In 1856 the president of Nevis, Frederick Seymour, stated, "A boat here makes a man independent. The power which it gives him of earning money far beyond his present wants render the boatmen generally about the laziest and least worthy portion of the population."[107]

Satisfying "present wants" kept most black freedmen fully occupied, and any extra earnings from a laboring stint abroad that could be laid aside for future contingencies was as important as leaving one's economic options open. But a migrant returning with coins he had earned abroad faced a dilemma. There were no savings banks on either island until the 1860s, and even then they were not widely used by native black workers, possibly because of a bank failure on Trinidad in 1847 that had wiped out workers' small savings accounts.[108] Investment in small land plots on St. Kitts and Nevis for future security would have been a reasonable option, but the possibilities for this were, of course, extremely limited because of the planters' refusal to sell the land. Yet money was necessary for the purchase of household articles, foodstuffs, clothing, and small farming implements. Returning migrants and others hid coins in and around their houses, a device that led to murders on Nevis in 1855.[109]

Most migrants and other cash earners invested heavily in livestock, both in the types of small animals that they or their parents had owned during slavery as well as in cattle and horses. By 1856, "every family" on Nevis was said to own "at least one cow," a probable exaggeration but a characteristic that caused parts of the island to begin to look overgrazed.[110] The peasants' animals were usually tethered during the day then turned loose to feed at night—in towns as well as country areas. Both islands passed a series of impoundment and animal trespass acts during the century with little effect in controlling animals' activities or numbers. A livestock census on about half of the St. Kitts estates in the early 1860s enumerated a remarkably high number of animals—581 horses, 131 asses, 1,063 horned cattle, 1,193 sheep, 2,366 goats, and 2,902 swine.[111] Livestock were not only sources of milk, meat, and cash; horses and donkeys on both islands provided a certain independence. Their owners were able to invest in wagons and dray carts and become petty carters for individuals and estates, hauling equipment or hogsheads of sugar to town and thereby earning a living outside the cane fields. Not all of the black peasants were able to afford such a strategy as a way out from the plantation regime. The practice was, however, widespread enough to draw occasional comment from nineteenth-century observers. In a few cases black freedmen were known to deprive themselves and their families of food in order to save money for draft animals and carts and thereby to gain a partial economic independence from the island's plantation system.[112]

The livelihood of blacks on St. Kitts and Nevis in the nineteenth century was only partly based on local resources; survival strategies were responses to both conditions at home and varying prospects abroad, all of which were subject to hazard and change. As Kittitians and Nevisians extended their livelihood spaces by migrating part of the time to other Caribbean islands after slavery, they did so as mobile individuals rather than as emissaries of a well-defined, land-based culture. They had no real physical refuge to which they could repair to escape pressures and uncertainty from abroad; even their own "village" lands were beyond their control. Neither could they rely on a well-defined cultural organization at home to coordinate and implement their periodic sojourns abroad. Political, social, and economic control of the home islands was in the hands of the white planters. The goal of black Kittitians and Nevisians was survival, and they had little to aid them in their quest save for their own courage and abilities. Economic depression in the last two decades of the century led to desperate conditions on St. Kitts and Nevis in particular and the British Caribbean in general and sorely tested their survival instincts.

Depression and Riot, 1884–1900

Since the Sugar Duties Act of 1846, British West Indian planters had struggled back to a position of relative prosperity by the 1870s. The duties on sugar in London had generally favored West Indian muscovado sugar as opposed to the semirefined product imported from other areas that had more modern milling facilities. During the same period, growing competition for the British consumption and refining market came from sugar beets cultivated in western Europe. A system of intergovernmental tariffs, generally referred to as the "bounty system," inspired European farmers to improve beet-sugar content. Bounties also profited refiners and generally lowered the price of sugar. West Indian interests clamored to no avail for countervailing British duties against French and German beet sugar. By the decade of the 1880s, West Indian sugar exports to Britain decreased, but the island sugar producers maintained relatively high levels of production owing partly to a European crop failure. But in 1884 an enormous quantity of cheap German beet sugar was sent to Britain. The effects were immediate and financially ruinous for many West Indian planters. During 1884 the price of muscovado sugar fell from twenty shillings per 100 pounds to thirteen. In the Caribbean islands fields were abandoned, mills ceased grinding, and planters and merchants alike suffered economic ruin.[113]

St. Kitts and Nevis were partially spared because most of their sugar was now destined for the United States. Local sugar was loaded onto American steamships that called at St. Kitts, the final Caribbean stop going north to the United States from South America. The Leeward planters now saw their destiny linked to that of North America. Europe was a distant and unreliable market, and the United States was nearby.[114] The British West Indian colonies and the United States signed a trade agreement in 1891, but it lasted only four years. In 1895 the United States awarded preferential sugar duties to Brazil, the Dominican Republic, Puerto Rico, and Cuba. Further preferences to Cuba in 1903 and American territorial status for Puerto Rico in 1901 essentially closed the American market to British West Indian sugar. By 1910, British Caribbean sugar "had been virtually eliminated from the American market."[115]

Even after the American duty preference went to other areas, St. Kitts and Nevis continued to export some muscovado sugar regularly to the United States, but the two islands, as well as the rest of the British Caribbean, suffered acute economic depression. Faced with job layoffs and lowered wages, the black workers of the two islands responded by emigrating just as they and their parents had in the past; although emigration had been occurring regularly, many more workers began to leave as the depression increased in severity, and the local estates had difficulty finding reliable workers.[116] Workers emigrated, as usual, to Trinidad; some few traveled to Bermuda; and a growing number headed for the Dominican Republic, whose sugar-cane industry had profited from both American duty preference and capital investment. Men from Nevis traveled to Venezuela to work in the gold mines.[117] A few of the more prosperous Kittitians and Nevisians took advantage of intermittent steamer passage to the United States. Thousands of West Indians had emigrated to the East Coast of the United States during the nineteenth century, but only a tiny number were from Nevis and St. Kitts.[118] By

1894, however, a noticeable colony of "enterprising and thrifty" West Indians had developed—mainly in New York and Boston—that included a few Kittitians.[119]

Emigration, however, failed to relieve local distress that persisted on St. Kitts and Nevis through the decade and beyond. One observer reported, "the mass of the people here are in a deplorable state of starvation, which I regret to say is daily increasing. Generally speaking it's no exaggeration to remark that hale strong men and women are now daily seen begging their bread, most willing to work but unable to procure same."[120] Pressed to the limit, the black workers' frustration and despair flared into violence in February 1896. The local incident, beginning what would later be called the "Portuguese riots," was predictably concerned with workers' wages. A rise in muscovado sugar prices had not been accompanied by a corresponding wage increase, and wages were already severely depressed. On Sunday, February 16, demands for higher wages became disorders on the Pond and Needsmust estates, northeast of Basseterre. At the Stone Fort Estate near Old Road, workers set fire to the cane fields, directing their anger toward a wealthy ex-indentured Portuguese landowner and storeowner with a reputation as an oppressive miser. Disorder sprang up on other estates, and cane fires occurred on both islands. On the following day, crowds of black workers from outlying districts invaded Basseterre and were joined by striking boatmen and dock workers, the resultant throng smashing street lights and looting "Portuguese" shops. The H.M.S. *Cordelia* then arrived from Antigua, landing a force of eighty six bluejackets, some in Basseterre and some in Old Road. The British marines had to fix bayonets to control the surging crowds. At the height of the uprising, the bluejackets shot two young men dead and wounded seven others. Warned of impending riot on Nevis, a detachment of marines then went to Charlestown in order to prevent similar violence.[121]

After the 1896 disturbances, the two islands were relatively peaceful but uneasy. Economic depression and repression continued, as it did throughout the British Caribbean, and British soldiers and native police were called upon to quell a series of West Indian disturbances during these years. Dominica had riots in 1893 and 1898, Montserrat in 1898, British Guiana in 1896 and 1903, Trinidad in 1903, and Jamaica in 1902.[122] The particular incidents differed, although the ultimate cause was the same. West Indian peasantries, their economic options limited by severe economic depression, turned to violence because more conventional adaptations were impossible.

It is difficult to imagine more dismal conditions than those facing the black folk of St. Kitts and Nevis at the end of the nineteenth century. Economic desperation was nevertheless compounded by environmental hazard at century's end. The two islands were damaged by hurricanes in 1898 and 1899. The first, causing widespread destruction on Barbados and St. Vincent, was rather mild in the Leewards. Hurricane-force winds overturned several boats on Nevis, drowning their passengers, on September 12, 1898.[123] The second was far worse. On August 7, 1899, a hurricane that had devastated Montserrat similarly pounded Nevis, killing an unknown number of people and literally blowing some peasant houses away. Crops and buildings were also destroyed on St. Kitts. Relief from England and other West Indian islands was sent in the form of money, food, clothing, and lumber, bringing slight relief to the two islands.[124]

The first decades of the twentieth century would see a lessening of economic stresses afflicting the black people of the two islands because of emigration to Bermuda, the Dominican Republic, and the United States. The latter months of 1899, however, could have hardly been more difficult on St. Kitts and Nevis, owing to grim economic and environmental circumstances. For the black working class of the two islands, the nineteenth century, begun in slavery, had ended in despair.

CHAPTER FIVE

To Bermuda and
Santo Domingo, and
Back Again

The exodus of labourers to Santo Domingo has begun. Year by year, the people of the labouring class are brought face to face with this necessity. On the afternoon of Wednesday . . . four schooners—"WARSPITE," "MURIEL," "BETSY R," and "EAGLE"—sailed out of our roadstead, each heavily laden with its cargo of human freight.

The Union Messenger
(St. Kitts) November 7, 1923

Deep economic depression persisted into the twentieth century. The marginal sugar-cane plantations of the small British Caribbean islands suffered from competition from American-financed estates of the region. Black laborers from the small British islands, subsisting on starvation wages as they had since the 1880s, anxiously sought extraisland livelihood outlets. Many were attracted to jobs created elsewhere by United States capital. Jamaicans, Barbadians, and Windward islanders went to work on the Panama Canal. Others traveled seasonally to harvest sugar cane in Cuba. In the first few years of the twentieth century, Kittitians and Nevisians went temporarily to work in Bermuda. Many middle-class families of the two islands began to emigrate permanently to the eastern United States. In the first three decades of the century, thousands of laborers from St. Kitts and Nevis spent seasonal cane-cutting sojourns in the Dominican Republic, sailing back and forth each year from their home islands to Hispaniola. Laborers' families on both islands came to depend heavily on wages remitted and brought home from Santo Domingo. The precariousness of this dependency on migration as livelihood became all too clear in the 1930s. World depression abruptly halted most of the laboring traffic to Hispaniola, and black workers of the two islands again found themselves restricted to starvation wages, unemployment, and environmental hazard on their tiny islands.

According to many British West Indian estate owners at the turn of the century, competition from German beet sugar and a fickle United States trade policy were to blame for depression in the British Caribbean. But the planters needed only to survey conditions on their own islands to find many of the reasons for stagnation. Especially on the smaller islands the soil was worn out, and throughout the British colonies the declining sugar profits that often supported absentee owners were needed as reinvestment capital to replace antiquated equipment. Caribbean cane sugar was still a lucrative investment but only on modern, efficient, large-scale terms, such as in the Greater Antilles, where United States capital investment was creating enormous, industrial plantations. This competition finally doomed the traditional, individually owned estates of the British Leewards. These small land units, whose owners had been struggling against large-scale competitors of Trinidad and British Guiana throughout the nineteenth century, could no longer survive against economies of scale.

British Caribbean islands could compete successfully for the international sugar market only by revamping their outdated insular infrastructures. The financial success of the large central sugar factories of the Caribbean in the late nineteenth century—in Cuba, St. Lucia, Trinidad, and the French Antilles—was not unnoticed by the Royal Commission of 1897 that investigated Caribbean economic conditions. The commission recommended, among other things, government loans for the construction of central sugar-cane factories on several of the islands. These recommendations were not immediately taken up, and to make matters even worse in the Leewards at century's end, British grants-in-aid for public services, including education and hospitals, were substantially reduced.[1]

Depression had hit hardest, as it always does, on the smallest Caribbean islands. Larger British territories—Trinidad with cacao and asphalt; British Guiana with rice, forest industries, and gold; and Jamaica with coffee, dyewoods, and an incipient banana industry—had non–sugar-cane activities that could sustain economic productivity and absorb excess labor. But for the black working classes of St. Kitts and Nevis, "depression" meant much more than unfavorable economic indexes and low wages. Because of the reliance on imported food and the lack of wage-earning and large-scale subsistence alternatives found in the larger places, economic depression accompanied by low hand-to-mouth wages again brought workers of both islands to the verge of starvation. Responses to this situation were theoretically numerous, but in a practical sense they were limited. Large-scale land seizure by the laborers on St. Kitts, for instance, would have certainly led to violent confrontation between the planter and worker classes, thereby provoking the arrival of a British gunboat as in 1896. For many—if not most—of the black workers, continued labor emigration was the only practical alternative to poverty and starvation. A way out would be to travel to where American capital, indirectly creating depression at home, offered jobs elsewhere.

United States investment in the West Indies had adversely affected the sugar-cane colonies of the British Caribbean in at least two ways. First, preferential American treatment for sugar from Cuba and the Dominican Republic—both of which had a solid foundation of United States money—and the United States' annexation of Puerto Rico had essentially driven British West Indian sugar from the United States market. Second, American investments provided nearby work opportunities for the British island's best laborers. American capital attracting British West Indian labor was not new. Jamaicans by the thousands had already traveled to work in the banana lands of eastern Costa Rica, and steamers were beginning to haul thousands of Jamaicans and Barbadians to Central America for construction work on the Panama Canal.

The lack of direct shipping routes between the Leewards and Central America limited travel opportunities for emigrants from St. Kitts and Nevis. The few old men of St. Kitts and Nevis who worked on the Panama Canal recall traveling to Jamaica on sailing craft before proceeding to Panama via steam vessels. Thus, few Kittitians and Nevisians went to Panama; of almost 20,000 British West Indians who died in the Canal Zone from 1906 to 1923, only 112 were from St. Kitts and Nevis.[2] Similarly circuitous and irregular routes restricted emigration by men from the two islands to the American-operated banana plantations in Costa Rica. In October 1910, D.C. Laws, Jr., a recruiting agent of the United Fruit Company, visited Basseterre. He gave cash advances to some of the men around town, and he took workers with him to Costa Rica via the company steamer *Alderney*. Laws was, however, less than fully successful in his mission to St. Kitts. Many men were wary because there was no direct return route from Costa Rica to the Leewards and no reliable means of remitting wages from Central America to families left home.[3]

Just as travel to Central America was inhibited by indirect shipping routes, proximity and regular steamer lines directed black labor emigrants from St. Kitts and Nevis to Bermuda, Cuba, and the Dominican Republic in the first decades of the twentieth century. Dockyard and military construction in Bermuda attracted hundreds of Kittitians and Nevisians, who subsequently remitted thousands of British pounds back to the two islands. And thousands of seasonal cane harvesters from the two islands traveled annually via steamers and sailing schooners to Cuba and, especially, to the Dominican Republic until the depression years. Wages brought home or mailed brought relief to families left behind. Dockyard wages from Bermuda and American dollars earned by men in the cane fields of Santo Domingo allowed parents, wives, and children on St. Kitts and Nevis to buy imported food, clothing, and building material.

By the early twentieth century, the two islands had taken diverging paths in local land use. St. Kitts remained a sugar-cane island, and Nevis concentrated on cotton and provision crops, an extension of the differences emerging after slavery. Similarities between the two islands, however—their common insularity, environmental uncertainty, and the prospects of much higher wages abroad—continued to send hundreds of Kittitians and Nevisians away to work every year.

The Dockyards of Bermuda, 1900–1906

Regularly scheduled steamship service from St. Kitts and Nevis to Bermuda and then to Canada was established in 1899. The route was essentially a mail service between eastern Canada and the several British Leewards and Windwards via Bermuda, but the shipping agreement also provided second-class and deck passage from one island to another.[4] This was an improvement over the irregular steamer service from the Basseterre roadstead to Bermuda that had been available for several years. Bermuda was one of the places to which black West Indians had traveled in the depression of the 1890s to seek work, but Bermudian employers were reluctant to hire black West Indian immigrants, and in 1894 "dozens" of them, mainly from Jamaica, were in a "pitiable . . . almost starving condition."[5]

At the turn of the century, however, thousands of short-lived laboring jobs suddenly became available in Bermuda. A floating dry dock, constructed in England and towed across the Atlantic, was installed in the main harbor at Hamilton. The British government also called for improvements of Bermuda's fortifications and military barracks. Large numbers of mechanics and laborers were thus required for a relatively brief

A Kittitian fisherman mending his net. *Photo by Caroline Quillian, used by permission of R.C. Goodwin and Associates.*

A fisherman selling part of his catch on Pinney's Beach, Nevis. *Photo by Cyd Heymann, used by permission of R.C. Goodwin and Associates.*

112

Goats and garbage near Ft. Charles, Nevis. *Photo by the author.*

The result of overgrazing in eastern Nevis, where forest originally stood. *Photo by the author.*

Charlestown and Nevis Peak from the public pier. *Photo by the author.*

The main square in Charlestown, Nevis. *Photo by the author.*

Nevisian vendors and produce assembled at the Charlestown pier for the trip to St. Kitts. *Photo by Cyd Heymann, used by permission of R.C. Goodwin and Associates.*

Offloading Nevisian provisions at the Treasury pier, St. Kitts. *Photo by Cyd Heymann, used by permission of R.C. Goodwin and Associates.*

A village settlement on the eastern side of St. Kitts. *Photo by the author.*

A wooden vessel, probably like those that sailed to Trinidad after emancipation, under construction in St. Kitts. *Photo by the author.*

Members of the "Canary Birds," a string band from Nevis. *Photo by Cyd Heymann, used by permission of R.C. Goodwin and Associates.*

Mechanical sugar-cane loaders on St. Kitts. *Photo by the author.*

but intensive labor effort. News of jobs in Bermuda spread quickly through the plantation villages of St. Kitts and Nevis. For many, the greatest problem was affording the passage: a second-class ticket to Bermuda cost $40. This would call for borrowing money or selling one's belongings, but in light of conditions at home the possible reward of relatively high-paying work was worth the risk of arriving penniless in a foreign colony.[6]

Hundreds of West Indian blacks responded to the call. Arriving as deck or second-class steamer passengers, mainly from the Leeward Islands, an estimated 1,600 were in Bermuda by April 1901, half of these having arrived during the previous three years.[7] More black workers from the Caribbean—795 in 1901, 597 in 1902, 308 in 1903, 731 in 1904—arrived to work in Bermuda in the next four years.[8] The harbor construction labor they undertook was arduous, involving heavy work in and around the water. Gangs of young black laborers excavated mud and silt at the waterside with shovels, and they subsequently laid pilings to support the dock facilities. Men and equipment were continuously lightered around the waters of Hamilton's harbor for five years on this project, a large-scale undertaking accomplished by black laborers mainly from St. Kitts and Nevis. Some workers from the two islands had had no previous training for this work, since their plantation labor backgrounds had acquainted them only with the cutlass and hoe, but others had carpentry and mechanical skills from work in the sugar factories at home and abroad. Most important, each laborer was suitably underspecialized so that he could undertake a variety of possible jobs. This personal underspecialization, mobility, and a high degree of adaptability—traits that had served his father and grandfather well during periodic work sojourns to Trinidad—now benefited a young black laboring immigrant in Bermuda and would serve his own offspring at different work destinations well into the future.

English dock contractors required a rigorous medical examination of the men applying for dock construction work. Those failing the examinations usually drifted into carpentry, masonry, or other forms of semi-skilled labor. They were paid lower wages than at the docks but still earned much more than they would have had they remained at home.[9] Ten to 20 percent of the West Indian labor migrants were women, who worked for European Bermudian families as cooks and maids. Scores of West Indians left Bermuda each year, but more immigrated than emigrated annually until 1904. In that year black West Indians numbered slightly more than

3,000 in Bermuda, a sizable minority in the Atlantic colony whose native population was only 17,535 in 1901.[10]

Dockyard workers earned twenty-four shillings a week in silver British currency. From these wages they paid for their subsistence, Bermudian fish and vegetables produced locally, and flour and meat imported from North America, and they established savings accounts for their eventual passage back home or passage to a subsequent work destination. In addition, they purchased postal money orders and sent more than £40,000 to their families in the West Indies from 1901 through 1905.

It is from comparative remittance data, not the estimates of Bermudian immigration officials, that we know that "West Indian" migration to the Bermuda dockyards in the first decade of the twentieth century was essentially a migration of Kittitians and Nevisians (Table 6). The immigration officer at Hamilton made no distinction among islands of origin for the Caribbean labor migrants, referring to them collectively as "colored West Indians." Of the roughly £40,000 remitted to the West Indies from the Bermuda post office from 1901 to 1905, however, almost £30,000 ended up in St. Kitts and Nevis. And on the streets of Hamilton, native Bermudians referred to the newly arrived black workers from the West Indies collectively (and scornfully) as "de gentleman an' de leddy from Sain' Kitts."[11]

Table 6. Postal Money Order Remittances
From Bermuda to St. Kitts and Nevis, 1901–1907

	Total to "West Indies," Including St. Kitts and Nevis	*St. Kitts*	*Nevis*	*Total to St. Kitts and Nevis*
1901	8,780	6,505	326	6,831
1902	9,381	5,992	326	6,318
1903	8,437	5,679	543	6,222
1904	9,341	5,852	906	6,758
1905	4,429	2,886	645	3,531
1906	1,587	957	143	1,100
1907	991	634	63	697

Note: All figures are British pounds.
Sources: Annual Reports for Bermuda, 1901–7; Leeward Islands, *Blue Books,* 1901–2 through 1907–8.

The remittance figures in Table 6 suggest that the overwhelming majority of the emigrants to Bermuda from the two islands were from St. Kitts. But the disparity in remittances between the two islands probably is a reflection of the nature of the interisland mail service between Nevis and St. Kitts at the time. Most mail to the two islands from abroad was brought to Basseterre by steamer then sent to Nevis by sailing vessel. The latter voyage was unreliable, however, owing to occasional stormy weather or lack of winds, and Nevisians, already accustomed to traveling back and forth to St. Kitts on small sailing sloops, often used the Basseterre postal facilities instead of their own.

On both islands postal remittances from Bermuda brought relief from the depression of the 1890s. Families could purchase food and replace worn clothing, household utensils, and tools. The money orders arrived by steamer, and the appearance of one of the Bermudian steamers, especially at Christmas time, was marked by exuberance at the Basseterre roadstead:

> Since the arrival of the Canadian steamship *Orinoco* on Thursday last, the Post Master and his assistants have been busily engaged in paying out Money from Bermuda. We are informed that upwards of £1,000 have been received in Post Office Orders and Registered Letters from relatives resident in the "little Eldorado," and our folks have been gladdened by the welcome aid for the necessaries of the Xmas season. Trade is a bit livelier in consequence thereof, and merchants . . . are hoping for a brighter season than was anticipated. We are also informed that a good many of the necessaries for the Xmas table arrived by freight. We are pleased to note this good trait in our people: "old folks at home are never forgotten."[12]

Christmas postal orders and gifts were only part of the benefits derived from Bermuda. By 1905 dock workers were also remitting English bank notes and United States greenbacks, as paper currency was being more widely circulated on the small Atlantic island. And the hundreds of West Indians leaving Bermuda each year to travel home, at least temporarily, doubtless included many Kittitians and Nevisians personally carrying money and gifts for family and friends.

The colonial officials at Bermuda regarded the influx of West Indian labor as a necessary evil, at best a temporary state of affairs to be tolerated only until the completion of dock construction. As early as 1901 the Bermuda colonial secretary warned of the "difficulty" and "danger" that would inevitably follow the completion of the harbor works when the itinerant laborers were then to be "thrown out of employment."[13] In the same year, the Bermuda government issued published warnings to the populace of St. Kitts and Nevis that no further work was available in Bermuda. Surplus labor there would be a "burden" on the government. But published notices did little to curb the flow of labor migrants from St. Kitts and Nevis to Bermuda; the success of those who had already emigrated, demonstrated by the regular remittance payments home, was ample evidence that leaving for Bermuda was better than staying behind.[14] Warnings of a saturated labor market in Bermuda were therefore ignored by Kittitians and Nevisians, who continued to travel there via steamer steerage.

The next year, in 1902, stricter measures were taken to reduce the numbers of immigrants from St. Kitts, Nevis, and other West Indian islands. New arrivals at Hamilton had to deposit £10 with the colonial officials, a deposit refundable upon exit from Bermuda. This rule was also relatively unsuccessful; immigrants were met upon their arrival by their relatives or friends who paid the entry deposit for them, an "ingenious" circumvention of the new regulation according to the Bermudian immigration officials.[15] During the following year, the Bermuda government imposed even more stringent measures to keep Kittitians and Nevisians out by periodically instructing ticket agents in Basseterre to disallow second-class steamer passage for Bermuda.[16]

Even after West Indian laborers had successfully entered Bermuda and found dockyard work, they encountered economic and racial discrimination from the contractors themselves. In late 1901 the managers of the dock construction project reduced wages from twenty-four to twenty-one shillings per week, provoking a strike among the West Indian workers.[17] Management countered by hiring Argentine Italians, who had been imported as strikebreakers; declining dock construction work for even higher wages than the West Indians had been receiving they subsequently drifted into other jobs.[18] Although the twenty-four-shilling wage and West Indian jobs were soon restored, the dockyard incident had racial overtones that were common and symptomatic of the feeling toward itinerant blacks: "The negro is always at a discount and employers of labour would rather have Italians and pay them more, than satisfy the demands of the West Indian labourer for a wage which will assist him in meeting the demands of a growing civilization."[19]

The completion of the dock project in 1906 and the termination of military construction the year before eventually "solved" most of the problem of excess West Indian labor in the eyes of Bermudian officials. In 1905, 492 West Indians left Bermuda, followed by 617 in 1906, and 389 in

1907.[20] Jobs were no longer available, reflected by the decrease in remittances from Bermuda after 1904 (Table 6). A residual contingent of Kittitians and Nevisians had, however, secured permanent work in Bermuda, and they stayed on after most others had emigrated. Although now living away from St. Kitts and Nevis, these new residents of Bermuda maintained close contact with their home islands by regularly remitting sums of money through the post office for decades.

The Bermuda dockyard experience was both a reflection of past migration experience and a preview of similar circumstances that would face Kittitians and Nevisians in the future. Ever-deteriorating economic conditions at home had sent workers abroad who were attracted by higher wages elsewhere. The welcome in Bermuda was far from warm. Black West Indians had traded one hostile set of colonial administrators for another and in Bermuda found themselves considered an economic necessity but a social nuisance. Through ingenuity, doggedness, individual adaptability, and economic underspecialization they had effectively exploited in Bermuda a remote and short-lived wage source for all it was worth. They accomplished this exploitation despite the attempts of colonial authorities on either end to curb prematurely the flow of migrants for the Atlantic colony before the actual completion of the Hamilton dock project. Sensing the temporary nature of their work even while they were in Bermuda, they were alert to job possibilities elsewhere. So when the exodus from Bermuda began in 1905, black workers from St. Kitts and Nevis went to subsequent work destinations in the United States and Canada, and many returned home for brief visits before moving on to labor in the cane fields of Cuba and the Dominican Republic.

The Cane Fields of the Dominican Republic, 1900–1930

On October 28, 1901, the same day that the Canadian steamer *Erna* carried 30 local passengers from the St. Kitts roadstead bound for Bermuda, the sailing schooner *Maid of the Mist* took 160 to work in the Dominican Republic.[21] Seasonal cane harvesters had already been traveling to Santo Domingo and Cuba from the British Leewards during the last quarter of the nineteenth century, and in the first decades of the twentieth, the large Spanish-speaking territories of the West Indies were to become second homes—during the January to July harvest period—for thousands of men from the British Caribbean. Men from St. Kitts and Nevis traveled to both Cuba and the Dominican Republic, but Santo Domingo was closer, and the overwhelming majority of Kittitians and Nevisians went there. Today, in the late twentieth century, shopkeepers, professionals, and schoolchildren of Basseterre and Charlestown all recall their fathers' and grandfathers' reminiscenses of the "La Romana" days, stories of the immense American-owned cane plantation in the southeastern portion of the Dominican Republic.

From the seventeenth to the nineteenth centuries, while the British and French Caribbean islands developed and deteriorated, the eastern half of Hispaniola had become an economic backwater. Repeated invasion by the Haitians across the mountains from the west, brief recolonization by Spain in the 1860s, and general political instability had rendered the Dominican Republic even more vulnerable to outside control by the late nineteenth century. The sugar industry of the Dominican Republic was then stimulated in about 1880 by the investments of Cuban planters fleeing the ravages of a recent war; shortly thereafter American capital was attracted to Dominican cane plantations. American interest in the Dominican Republic grew by the turn of the century as Puerto Rico was acquired and the Panama Canal begun, and as the Caribbean in general took on greater strategic importance for the United States. By 1900 the Dominican Republic's National Bank and railroad construction were managed by the San Domingo Improvement Company of New York, "which for some years had carried on varied and sometimes questionable financial operations in the Dominican Republic."[22] In 1911 the La Romana sugar estate, a branch of the American-owned South Porto Rico Sugar Company, was carved out of forests of the Dominican Republic in the southern coastal plain, and by 1925 it covered a sprawling 144,000 acres. This was the largest among fourteen Dominican estates that were owned outright or controlled by Americans in 1925, together covering 366,000 acres (more than 570 square miles), mainly in the lightly settled part of the country.[23] The American military occupation from 1916 to 1924 had created order in the Dominican land tenure system by establishing a land court, a system of recording titles, and by imposing a land tax. Critics of the United States asserted that this not only created order but also facilitated American takeover of the country's sugar-cane industry.

U.S. sugar-cane plantations in Santo Domingo involved extensive forest clearance and the construction of plantation settlements and towns. The estates and their communities were usually built by American engineers with imported machinery and construction techniques and were therefore more closely related to American business interests than to the country in which they were located. The cane was processed at large central grinding factories. Hand harvesting of cane was accomplished by thousands of Haitians and British West Indians, who were imported and then sent home again each year. Like the managers, towns, and machinery of the Dominican sugar plantations, the British West Indian workforce was also foreign, and it included the migrant laborers from St. Kitts and Nevis.

Travel back and forth from the Leewards to the Dominican Republic from 1900 into the 1930s was seasonal and by both steamship and sailing schooners (Figure 5). The voyages involved occasional stopovers at intervening islands both going and coming, and the individual departures and returns and numbers of people on board each vessel were therefore poorly recorded. British officials kept track of overall emigration and immigration from St. Kitts and Nevis starting in 1914. The data (Table 7), which include all known persons, including foreigners and inhabitants of other islands, who officially left and entered St. Kitts and Nevis, are undoubtedly incomplete because they did not account for informal, unscheduled departures and returns on sailing vessels. Nevertheless, the figures in Table 7 suggest the magnitude of the annual labor circulation to the Dominican Republic and back. Roughly 10 percent of the two islands' inhabitants left and returned annually. This was a selective 10 percent— young and middleaged and usually men—who were absent from their home islands six months of the year.

The cane harvest at the Santo Domingo estates began in January, and the annual exodus to Hispaniola from St. Kitts and Nevis usually began in November and December.[24] Local newspapers printed circulars and published notices about boats leaving for the Dominican Republic, and unofficial news dissemination about boat departures diffused quickly through the island villages. Both kinds of notices attracted young black workers from the two islands, predominantly those from rural areas, who were completely dependent on local estate wages and marginal provision farms. The Basseterre treasury building pier was the congregation point for blacks from St. Kitts, Nevis, and also often from Montserrat, Dominica, and Antigua, many of whom had hitched rides on fishing vessels to St. Kitts. They made up a talkative, gesturing gang of young workers, with white cotton shirts, dark trousers, and broad-brimmed felt hats. Many carried the family's only suitcase. Others stowed their belongings in duffel bags. All were confident in their own individual ability to work, and they knew

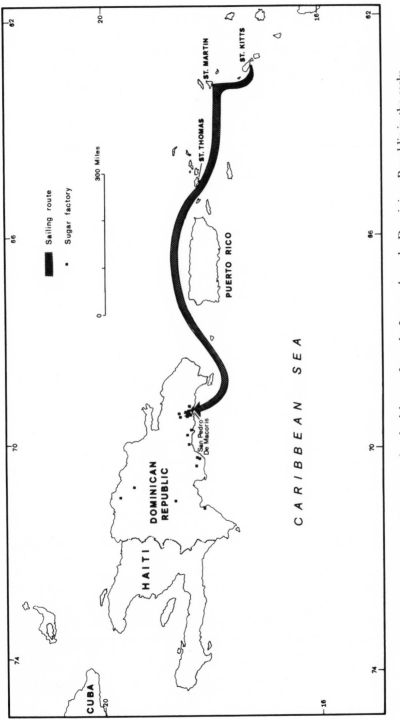

Figure 5. The sailing route taken by laborers from the Leewards to the Dominican Republic in the early twentieth century. Information from personal interviews; Knight, *Americans in Santo Domingo,* 139.

Table 7. Emigration from and Immigration to St. Kitts
and Nevis, 1914–1939

Year	Emigration	Immigration	Year	Emigration	Immigration
1914	2,752	2,873	1927	3,043	2,773
1915	2,990	3,061	1928	3,877	3,280
1916	2,966	3,145	1929	4,685	4,325
1917	3,623	3,447	1930	3,426	3,647
1918	4,099	3,338	1931	2,996	2,870
1919	4,815	4,700	1932	2,830	2,800
1920	5,589	4,602	1933	2,720	2,301
1921	4,985	4,057	1934	2,423	2,443
1922	—[a]	—[a]	1935	3,018	2,701
1923	3,224	2,261	1936	3,143	2,481
1924	3,664	2,763	1937	2,403	2,481
1925	3,447	2,651	1938	3,907	2,851
1926	3,567	2,829	1939	4,465	4,356

[a]No data available.
Sources: Leeward Islands, Blue Books, 1914–15 through 1919–20 and 1920
through 1939.

that if they were given a chance they would earn three or four times more money in Santo Domingo than they would if they stayed home.

In the earlier years of the annual emigration, the voyages were mainly on wooden sailing schooners not unlike those that had carried the workers' grandparents to Trinidad and back after emancipation. Steamer travel was more common after 1920. Whether by schooner or steamer the voyages were usually punctuated by intermediate stops in Anguilla, St. Martin, and the Virgin Islands to pick up additional laborers and also food and water. Agents representing United States plantations in the Dominican Republic, acknowledging the potential danger in thousands of cane cutters traveling back and forth across the Caribbean each year in hazard-prone sailboats, asserted in 1912 that all laborers would thereafter be transported by steamship and none admitted to the country by sailing craft.[25] But sailing schooners, partly subsidized by the sugar interests themselves, continued to bring workers: E.S. Bridgewater of Birdrock, St. Kitts, recalled traveling to the Dominican Republic via sailing vessel in 1919. He was one of 235 men and 6 women on a schooner so crowded that he occupied the same place on the vessel for eight days. All of the travelers carried their own rations of bread and cheese. Passage for the travelers to Santo Domingo was "free," since the vessel's captain received six dollars for each worker he delivered at San Pedro de Macorís, the main town in the Dominican sugarcane district.

Upon arrival at San Pedro de Macorís, vessels were inspected and cleared by immigration authorities, and the passengers were vaccinated before they were assembled and lined up on the dock. Then native Dominicans representing each estate selected and grouped workers for their plantations, inspecting potential cane-cutters' hands to ensure that they were sufficiently calloused for hard fieldwork. After mutual agreement on wages between workers and estate representatives, the laborers were taken by trains and steamships from Macorís to their respective estates. In the late afternoon the workers arrived at the plantations, where they were assigned quarters and issued machetes and oblong badges, the latter identifying them as assigned to a particular estate. Each worker was then given fifty cents in order to purchase rations at the company store.

On any given Santo Domingo estate Kittitians and Nevisians were essentially undifferentiated black laboring cogs in an agro-industrial operation. The grinding mill at La Romana was erected in 1918, and its capacity was doubled in 1925 by moving machinery from Puerto Rico.[26] The huge sugar mills towered over the landscape, which by this time was an unbroken field of cane, tens of thousands of acres in extent intersected by railroad tracks that brought the harvested crop to the factories. Most men worked six days per week as canecutters; this paid a weekly wage of U.S. $20–$30 (paid in United States currency), as opposed to as little as U.S. $12 per month in St. Kitts. Wages were lower for the odd jobs of cleaning up, carpentry, and livestock-tending around the plantation nucleus and settlement. The few women who made the annual migration worked as cooks and maids for the estate officials and occasionally in the workers' barracks. Field and factory overseers were usually Dominicans, and management positions were held by young white American men.

The relative isolation of the foreign-owned sugar-cane plantations facilitated control over the mass of seasonal cane cutters, who were separated both geographically and socially from the rural inhabitants of the Dominican Republic and who actually outnumbered their native counterparts in the estate districts. Former seasonal migrants to Santo Domingo from St. Kitts and Nevis recall that black workers occasionally drifted away from the estates, finding other work in the countryside. This was not easy. They had been admitted to the country on six-month work permits, and immigration authorities soon deported them if they overstayed. They were conspicuous by their dark skin and unfamiliarity with Spanish, and they were almost universally disliked and insulted by the Dominicans with whom they came into contact. Even when they did abandon the estates, their absence from plantation labor forces was easily remedied by estate managers, who simply brought in more British West Indians who were eager for work. When a labor shortage arose at La Romana during the 1927 harvest, for instance, the company's steamer *Romanita* was dispatched to the British Windward Islands and made three successive trips, returning each time with hundreds of laborers.

Although cane cutters' wages were high by Leeward Island standards, they were the lowest within the Santo Domingo cane industry, and migrant workers complained continuously of inhumane treatment on the sugar estates. These charges often centered around the alleged brutality of local overseers and primitive housing conditions for the itinerant laborers. Work conditions and compensation were particularly poor on six Italian-owned plantations in the Dominican Republic. On these plantations, workers' habitations were flimsy and run-down, and injured workers received no compensation.[27] Neither did the Italians send injured workers home as the Americans did. The British government did provide a minimal consular presence for the migrants who were, after all, British subjects. A British vice-consulate office was established in San Pedro de Macorís in 1910. By 1913 the migrating workers' legal positions were further formalized by a law requiring passports and birth certificates for travel.[28] The status, legal and otherwise, of an individual black West Indian in Santo Domingo was nevertheless always tenuous. He was essentially powerless and at the lowest rung of an industrial social order in a foreign country, and a token British diplomatic presence in the Dominican canelands provided little recourse for action against a local citizen or estate official. In the mid-1920s, for instance, the British consular agent at San Pedro de Macorís was himself an executive at the La Romana estate.

The cane cutters were housed in elongated wooden *cuartels* or *barrancones*, usually 200 to 300 feet long and 20 feet wide. These buildings were divided into small rooms, most with dirt floors, that each housed four workers. The barracks life was spartan, if not impoverished, but it provided a respite from long days of cutting cane. Women migrant workers often tended communal cooking fires, where the rations of flour, beans, fresh vegetables, and occasionally chicken and fish were prepared.

In an essentially all-male barracks setting, a natural camaraderie developed. Those who were most literate wrote letters home for others in the evenings. Informal scratch-band music provided diversion after a day's work. Workers' friendships extended beyond their own home islands as black men from all over the Lesser Antilles became acquainted with one another. A letter published in the *Union Messenger* of St. Kitts stated, "Here by virtue of numbers the Kittitians come first, and in order, the Antiguans, Nevisians, Montserratians, Virgin Islanders, natives of Dominica, Windward Islanders, and Turks Islanders."[29] Interisland stereotypes were developed. Anguillans, for instance, were universally considered the "best savers." The home islands provided the basis for stories, anecdotes, and an informal comparison of similarities and differences that existed among the small insular colonies of the British Caribbean. Men from St. Kitts and Nevis learned secondhand for example, of the prevalence of drought in Antigua or of stevedore wage levels in St. Vincent, although they themselves had never been to either place. An incipient pan-Caribbean identity was thus formed around the campfires of the cane plantations in Santo Domingo. Through a shared work experience and difficult living conditions, circumstances arising partially from the necessity to escape similar economic predicaments on all of their home islands, the black labor migrants from throughout the British Caribbean developed a feeling of mutual solidarity.

Unlike the "free" voyage at the beginning of the harvest season, the trip home was paid for by migrants themselves. The annual voyage home, after the July or August crop was in, gave British West Indians occasional chances actually to visit the other islands. Some accompanied their new friends home. Often, men from Antigua, Montserrat, and the Windwards were dropped off in Basseterre before proceeding to their respective islands on fishing schooners. Almost all the men returned with sums of cash, although most had regularly remitted their earned U.S. currency through postal money orders. From 1910 to 1930, thousands of pounds worth of U.S. currency was sent to St. Kitts and Nevis, much of it from the Dominican Republic. In the peak year, 1918, £13,000 worth of U.S. money came to the two islands through the post office. Possibly more came from savings accounts maintained by the migrant workers in Santo Domingo.[30]

Not all of the cash earned was on hand when the men returned to St. Kitts and Nevis because they had often bought at least one set of new clothes. Their "fancy clothes and gold teeth" were unmistakable symbols that they had emigrated, returned, and prospered in the interim. Returning veterans of the Santo Domingo canelands preferred each other's company during the months back at home, recounting mutual travel and work experiences and self-consciously using Spanish terms here and there, lest nonmigrants forget that they had traveled far. Upon return, family reunions were happy occasions, not least because the return of men invariably meant brief prosperity. The tempo of life on St. Kitts and Nevis had thereby become geared to the presence or absence of migrating men. From January to July, during the men's absence, the mothers, wives, and children hoped for help through the mail. When the men returned, however, local authorities dreaded the inevitable "unemployment" problem. Burglary rates were also invariably higher when the men were home. Theft was more common on St. Kitts than Nevis: on the smaller island men had access to provision lands during the off-season; on the larger island alternatives to ephemeral estate work were almost nonexistent.[31]

Migration back and forth from the British Leewards to Hispaniola was always subject to government control and possible sanctions at either end. Officials in the Dominican Republic imposed varying and changing rules about health certificates, deposit money, and immigrants' credentials that were only partially effective in regulating the flow of workers into the country from year to year. By arriving on a preferred ship or after working for several seasons on an estate in Santo Domingo, the migrants could often circumvent existing rules and find work. Similar constraints at home impeded a free emigration, taxing further the persistence of the potential emigrants. The loss of the Leeward Islands' best workers year after year to Santo Domingo often left the cane fields of the British islands to be tilled by women and grandparents. A series of investigations of working conditions in the Dominican Republic by British agents resulted in a law enacted in 1924 ostensibly designed to keep home and thus "protect" the workers of St. Kitts, Nevis, and other British islands. According to local newspaper reports, these actions were ploys to keep laborers captives of the two islands' estate owners.[32] The law, reminiscent of those at emancipation, was never enthusiastically enforced by local officials and was virtually ignored by the laborers. It therefore had only limited impact on the flow of people from island to island.

World economic depression, combined with more stringent rules enforced by Dominican immigration agents, finally curtailed the annual ebb and flow of cane cutters from the small British islands. In 1929 the Dominican Republic severely restricted immigration of black workers from the English-speaking islands.[33] Men from St. Kitts and Nevis who

130

had stayed in the Dominican Republic were being deported by the early 1930s. In 1935, an article in the *Union Messenger* stated, ". . . conditions on the outside are becoming increasingly difficult . . . now under the new policy of extreme nationalism—a result of post war rivalries, West Indians are no longer wanted and those who escape being hounded out have a thin time in making two ends meet."[34]

The restrictions were incapable of stopping all movement from St. Kitts and Nevis (Table 7), and infrequent seasonal migration continued to the Dominican Republic. But the greater part of the mass migration to San Pedro de Macorís, and thousands of the dollars that the annual exodus brought to St. Kitts and Nevis each year, had been cut back by 1930. As in the Bermuda dockyards in 1905, black British West Indians were no longer necessary in the Dominican Republic. Another source of livelihood had essentially been eliminated.

Emigration to the United States

Scheduled steamship connections from the Leewards to Bermuda facilitated travel not only to that small island but also to the eastern seaboard of North America. When the Bermuda dockyard project ended in 1905, and earlier, many unemployed West Indians traveled on via steamer steerage to the East Coast of the United States, most to New York but some to eastern Canada. At their destination, some joined friends and relatives who had emigrated earlier. Prospective emigrants to the United States were required to deposit a U.S. $30 bond as well as their ticket purchase, a substantial sum of money for a West Indian laborer.[35] Travel cost and the deposit requirement in the early part of the century as well as in later years appears to have allowed only comparatively prosperous West Indians to emigrate to North America.[36]

Human migration to the United States from Nevis and St. Kitts in the first decades of the twentieth century ran into the thousands. This figure cannot be verified, because emigration data by destination were not kept by colonial authorities in the Leeward Islands; and immigration figures for the United States were not compiled by island of origin. Table 8 shows aggregate population figures for the two islands from the censuses of 1901, 1911, and 1921, along with summed annual birth and death data for intervening decades. The nearly 10,000 Kittitians and more than 5,000 Nevisians seemingly "lost" from 1901 to 1921 had emigrated to several destinations. Perhaps as many as 1,000 had stayed on in Bermuda, and

Table 8. Population and Loss from Emigration on St. Kitts and Nevis, 1901–1921

	St. Kitts			Nevis		
	M	F	Total	M	F	Total
1901 census	12,977	16,805	29,782	5,605	7,169	12,774
Natural increase 1901–11[a]	—	—	1,694	—	—	2,496
1911 Census	10,969	15,314	26,283	5,521	7,424	12,945
Net loss, 1901–11	—	—	(5,193)	—	—	(2,325)
Natural increase, 1912–20[a]	—	—	720	—	—	1,485
1921 census	9,115	13,300	22,415	4,678	6,891	11,569
Net loss, 1912–20	—	—	(4,588)	—	—	(2,861)

[a]Births minus deaths.
Source: Leeward Islands, *Blue Books,* 1901–2 to 1922.

2,000 or so could have drifted away to other islands during the back-and-forth travel to the Dominican Republic. This leaves possibly 12,000 unaccounted for who might have emigrated to the United States from St. Kitts and Nevis, a remarkably high percentage of the 80,000 "Negro Immigrant Aliens" who migrated from the West Indies to the United States from 1901 to 1921.[37] But amost certainly 12,000 is too high a figure: census takers probably missed many of the labor migrants who were temporarily absent and therefore not available to be counted. The 1911 census was conducted on December 31, for instance, when the majority of the cane harvesters would already have departed for Santo Domingo.

Ben Croft of Sandy Point, St. Kitts, traveled to New York in 1915 and stayed for fifty-five years before returning home.[38] His mother had gone to New York five years earlier. His father, a shipwright, had accompanied her, but he disliked New York and immediately returned. Croft remembers waiting several days at Ellis Island, where he was checked for disease and parasites and also given a literacy examination. Potential migrants to the United States had already been warned of severe North American immigration laws leading to the probable deportation of anyone who could not pass various examinations and tests.[39] But many entered the

United States illegally, a fact further weakening the already poorly quantified movement of West Indians to North America during this period.[40]

Migration from St. Kitts and Nevis to the United States in the early twentieth century was qualitatively different from the contemporaneous interisland labor movements in at least two ways. First, the majority of Kittitians and Nevisians traveling to the United States probably stayed there permanently.[41] Not all, however, stayed on; between 1908 and 1937, nearly 30 percent of all black aliens legally entering the United States departed again.[42] Second, the movement to North America was class selective, involving a disproportionate number of light-skinned middle-class artisans, tradesmen, and shopkeepers. As early as 1903 a Basseterre newspaper lamented "the continual exodus of our respectable people to the States and Canada."[43] Richard Frucht reported the same class selection exerted on Nevis early in the century. Among the Nevisians traveling to the United States, the great majority were of the middle class, "from merchant, estate manager, and overseer families."[44] The middle-class migration from St. Kitts and Nevis to North America appears to have been typical of the Caribbean at this time. In 1909, during a drought in Antigua, the laborers were leaving for the Canal Zone and some for work on the Mexican railroads, whereas the "middle-class young men and women" were going to the United States and Canada.[45]

The colored middle class of St. Kitts and Nevis had not joined the annual exodus of cane cutters bound for Santo Domingo, where the hard manual labor was appropriate for the mass of "low-class" blacks but not for the lighter-skinned storeowners and clerks, whose interests were more closely aligned with the colonial British.[46] Economic depression had nevertheless affected all nonwhite peoples of the small British islands with small respect for their color or class. Thus the middle classes of St. Kitts and Nevis had little alternative to emigration to the United States at this time. Unable to maintain their economic and social positions at home and unwilling to perform the lowly tasks necessary for survival, including the ignoble traveling back and forth to harvest cane in the Dominican Republic, they left for North America by the thousands.

Most Kittitian migrants went to New York, principally to Harlem. An early group of Nevisians emigrated to Boston, and then a sizable number settled in New Haven, Connecticut, during the second decade of the century. Regardless of their particular residential locales, colored Kittitians and Nevisians found themselves viewed as members of an undifferentiated Negro population by the white majority in the United States.

The menial jobs available to them—as maids, janitors, porters, unskilled laborers—were relatively high-paying by West Indian standards but work they would never have considered performing on their home islands. Letters home to St. Kitts and Nevis warned potential emigrants to the United States of the racial discrimination and advised friends and family members that they would have to "stoop and conquer" if they planned to come.[47]

Although forced to accept what they considered denigrating jobs that provided little inherent distinction from "low-class" West Indians and United States blacks, the lighter-skinned immigrants continued to practice a Caribbean color caste system. Club memberships, marriages, friendships, and social aspirations among newly arrived West Indians were based heavily on skin color in the near-absence of the economic differentiation that had helped to clarify social distinctions in the Caribbean.[48] West Indians maintained their own identities and separation from local blacks. West Indians from particular islands formed literary clubs, mutual aid societies, and athletic associations, all of which reinforced ethnic separation from U.S. blacks. In 1924 the team representing St. Kitts won the championship of the New York County Cricket League that was composed of teams of recent immigrants to New York from all over the Antilles.[49]

Recent West Indian immigrants also kept track of developments back home, an ongoing involvement from afar that futher differentiated them from the U.S. blacks. Considerable sums of U.S. currency were remitted to St. Kitts and Nevis from the New York area. Kittitians and Nevisians in the United States also followed Caribbean economic and social conditions closely through West Indian newspapers in New York and letters from home. In June 1924, when a severe tightening of U.S. immigration law was about to close another migration destination for West Indians, a crowd of Kittitians, Nevisians, and other West Indians gathered in Harlem. With another large-scale migration outlet closed, their friends and relatives back home would continue to suffer conditions that they themselves had so recently escaped. The object of the Harlem rally was to denounce British policies in West Indian islands which were said to perpetuate conditions of "slavery."[50]

The U.S. immigrant quota law that became effective on July 1, 1924, shut yet another door. The first comprehensive U.S. immigration act had been passed in 1882, and each one of the seven more since that date had been more restrictive than the one before. The 1924 act limited emigrants

134

from the British West Indies to 200 per year. A flood of West Indian immigrants came in that year to beat the deadline: 10,630 "Negro Immigrant Aliens" arrived from the Caribbean in 1924, and only 308 the year after.[51] The closing of the United States as a viable migration alternative created despondence in both the West Indies and among the recent immigrants. During the following depression decade many newly arrived West Indians were to be denied U.S. unemployment relief and repatriated to their home islands, worsening an already "desperate" situation there.[52] Following the few Kittitians and Nevisians who had gone to eastern Canada in the early twentieth century appeared to be a similarly fruitless migration strategy. Although Canada's laws were not as restrictive as those in the United States, Canadian immigration officers officially discouraged black immigrants.[53]

Land Consolidation on St. Kitts and Fragmentation on Nevis

The migrants to Bermuda and Santo Domingo from St. Kitts and Nevis at the turn of the century were predominantly rural dwellers. At home they inhabited clusters of thatched-roof wooden shacks on land owned by a neighboring plantation. The rural landscapes of the two islands had changed little from postemancipation days. The tiny village garden plots had to be protected from scavenging chickens and goats, and transportation into Charlestown or Basseterre was by foot, donkey, and occasionally by bicycle. By the 1920s a veneer of modernization came to rural areas of both islands in the form of cheap motorized bus routes. Rough, locally built, wooden bus bodies were fitted over truck frames brought from England. The resulting vehicles provided inelegant but cheap and quick travel into town and back home again.[54]

Such "modernization" or "development" for St. Kitts and Nevis has always been similarly incremental and ultimately under colonial control, just as any real changes in local land use has come about, directly or indirectly, from economic decisions made abroad. Such decisions early in the twentieth century led to widely differing uses of land on the two islands. By this time Nevis was losing its sugar industry to more widespread cotton cultivation, which in turn gave way to small-scale production of more foodstuffs. The smaller island therefore became "derelict," "worn out," and a "relic," terms used by European observers and colonial administrators who equated an island's success with the sugar profits it could provide. On St. Kitts, however, a British-owned sugar factory was erected outside Basseterre in 1911 that eventually consolidated St. Kitts's sugar-cane industry into a more "efficient" operation.

The establishment of the St. Kitts central sugar factory was a response to economic depression and the diffuse nature of the island's sugar industry. During the last two decades of the nineteenth century many of the St. Kitts sugar estates had changed owners and been consolidated, but the industry was still not competitive. In 1901, St. Kitts had fifty-four estates in operation, most producing muscovado sugar in their antiquated steam factories that retrieved as little as 50 percent of the potential sugar that came to the mill.[55] The low profitability because of low sugar production led to the formation of the St. Kitts (Basseterre) Sugar Factory Ltd. A public stock company registered in London, its equity was jointly held by two British sugar companies and individual stockholders, the majority of the latter being resident St. Kitts estate owners.[56] Besides providing the modern—85 to 90 percent efficient—cane crushers and boilers housed in new buildings, the company laid out a light railway system thereby linking the factory with the canelands on both sides of the island. Rail sidings were built on the estates, which in turn provided cane contracts for the factory. By 1926 the railway completely encircled the island.

Consolidation and control of the St. Kitts canelands by the sugar factory company and its railway had replaced the redundancy of individual estates and mills. The London-based company, with access to international capital markets, had also resuscitated the St. Kitts sugar-cane infrastructure the way local estate owners never could. A local planter class, however, remained in control of the lands themselves, control that was passing more and more into the hands of Basseterre merchants, notably J. W. Thurston and Co. and S. L. Horsford and Co., who had bought up "fully half" of the island's canelands from absentee planters by 1923.[57] Direct metropolitan corporate control over planting, harvesting, transportation, and processing of St. Kitts sugar cane had been necessary for "efficiency," but it meant even fewer local jobs for resident black workers. Economic centralization had not freed new lands for subsistence purposes but had instead reduced employment opportunities. And instead of having direct contact with local proprietors and factory managers, many workers now had to deal with corporate impersonality over matters of jobs, wages, and working conditions. Consolidation of the St. Kitts sugar-cane industry from 1911 to 1926 had profited English corporations, reinforced land control by a local plantocracy, and called upon black Kittitians to bear the dual burden of both nineteenth-century inequality and twentieth-century efficiency.

The land-use differences between St. Kitts and Nevis that had begun in the nineteenth century became pronounced in the first decades of the twentieth. Of the 126 small estates on Nevis in 1901, 57 were still based on a metairie system.[58] Sea-island cotton had become the smaller island's main cash crop by 1920. Both St. Kitts and Nevis plantation owners were encouraged by high prices to plant cotton after 1900, and each island had three cotton gins by 1908. Cotton was rotated with cane and planted as a first crop on many St. Kitts estates. On Nevis, cotton acreage replaced sugar cane and increased steadily from 300 acres in 1903 to 1,000 in 1905, 1,200 in 1908, 2,000 in 1911, and 3,000 in 1918. By 1933, however, cotton acreage for the two islands together was below 400 because of a series of environmental and economic reverses that hit Nevis particularly hard. Outbreaks of pink bollworm had become very troublesome, and on August 28, 1924, a hurricane again hit Nevis, killing four people, destroying 600 peasant houses, and reducing cotton lint yields to twenty-eight pounds per acre, the lowest on record.[59] Three years later a price decline of "crisis" proportions eliminated most hope for a truly viable cash crop economy on Nevis.[60]

Increasing cotton acreage on Nevis had obviously called for corresponding decreases in sugar cane. As the Basseterre factory extended its control over St. Kitts, sugar-cane planters from northern and western Nevis began shipping canes across the channel for milling. Their transportation costs were high, and Nevisian planters barely profited from the more efficient milling. The relic milling equipment on Nevis, formerly merely inefficient, was now obsolete and useless. Much of the machinery was dismantled and sold abroad in the 1920s, and for a short time the smaller island specialized in a molasses trade derived from muscovado sugar. This short-lived Nevisian specialty was one of the final gasps from an aging industry using outdated equipment. For example, old machinery and parts from both islands were brought together at Cane Garden estate in the Gingerlands district of Nevis for a molasses plant, but the explosion of a secondhand boiler soon terminated the operation.[61]

Without either the land area or equipment to sustain a sugar-cane industry and with much of its land scarred by cotton-induced sheet erosion, Nevis was, by the 1920s and 1930s, seriously lagging in export agriculture. In the absence of outside investors competing for the island's land, house plots and farming acreage finally came under the control of the black Nevisians themselves. White planters sold their estates to colored speculators who, in turn, sold off small land plots. These sales were sporadic, informal, and poorly recorded. In the 1920s, for instance, when part of Round Hill Estate was partitioned into small plots, the buyers were cautioned to have their land surveyed and registered, advice they did not always follow.[62] Despite the informality of these land sales on Nevis, they marked an important discontinuity in land tenure. Black slaves and their descendants had been working white planters' lands on Nevis for three centuries; now the land was becoming theirs. Some Nevisian estates became "settlement schemes" for small landowners following a recommendation of the 1897 commission. By 1929 there were 292 landholdings of less than ten acres each on Nevis; five years later there were 363, compared with only 11 on St. Kitts.[63] On Nevis, money earned abroad could now be invested in local land plots, where returning labor migrants could settle and farm before passing the land on to their children.

High environmental as well as monetary costs had been paid for decontrol of Nevis's lands by the plantocracy. One report after another in the early twentieth century described Nevis as a tired, worn-out island, a place providing everywhere stark evidence of past prosperity but present poverty.[64] Much of this overall assessment can be attributed to an ethnocentric view by planters and expatriates, equating the ragged diversity of subsistence agriculture with decline. At the same time, environmental conditions seem to have deteriorated more and more. The denudation of wooded areas on the island's higher slopes had led to noticeably serious "wash" erosion by 1904, and the decades of cotton clear-cropping thereafter did the same.[65] The steady environmental deterioration was not aided by the ongoing climatic perturbations, such as the 1924 hurricane. In 1930 a severe and prolonged drought afflicted the Leewards. On St. Kitts, planters laid off workers, and the colonial government provided roadwork as wage relief. Similar roadwork on Nevis supplemented cash advances to peasant subsistence farmers whose crops failed on their desiccated provision grounds.[66]

Land tenure differences on the two islands were reflected in both the quality and quantity of crop output. Sugar cane and a few provisions on St. Kitts stood in sharp contrast to the corn, eddoes, yams, potatoes, arrowroot, and beans on Nevis. While becoming less attractive to expatriate investors, Nevis had become more self-sufficient in foodstuffs, a fact that

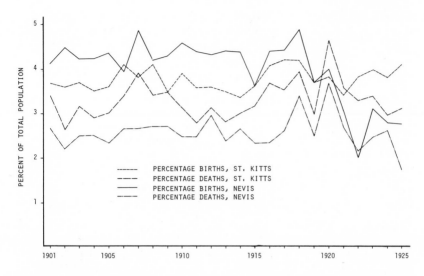

Figure 6. Birth and death rates on St. Kitts and Nevis, 1901–1925. Data from colonial censuses, annual *Blue Books*.

may throw light on possible major nutritional differences between the two islands at the time. The common people of both islands suffered greatly in the early twentieth century, as they had in the nineteenth, but "desperate" and "starving" were always routine descriptions for St. Kitts, less so for Nevis. By 1938 high infant mortality rates on St. Kitts, as opposed to Nevis, were attributed to a lack of available land on the larger island, where cane employment supported the populace for only five months of each year with little recourse to subsistence cropping for the remainder.[67] Figure 6 displays birth and death figures for the two islands from 1901 to 1925. The data are not age specific so one cannot safely infer that the consistently lower death rate for Nevis was because of higher infant mortality on St. Kitts. And the peculiar drop in Nevisian birth rates in the early 1920s occurs at the time when Nevisian peasants were beginning to assume control over their own land parcels and thereby in a better position to produce their own food. An obvious problem exists in calculating birth and death percentages during a period when thousands of cane cutters were circulating back and forth to the Dominican Republic and thousands more were emigrating to North America. Reservations about data reliability and interpretations notwithstanding, higher Nevisian birth rates in most years and lower Nevisian death rates in all years led to substantially higher natural population increases than on St. Kitts in the early twentieth century (Table 8), increases probably related closely to a homegrown, and therefore more dependable, food supply on the smaller island.

Depression and Riot in the 1930s

St. Kitts's precarious dependency upon extraisland food supplies, combined with a sharp decrease in outside job opportunities, again developed into desperation for the island's black working class in the depression decade. The volume of labor circulation to Santo Domingo and elsewhere had dropped considerably, and remittances in United States currency earned in the Dominican Republic declined even more dramatically. Not only had the "outside money" dwindled sharply, but now there were more mouths to feed on a reduced island income, since many of the men could no longer emigrate seasonally. The many laborers deported from Cuba and the Dominican Republic continued to worsen matters; on August 3, 1932, a sailing schooner brought back to Basseterre 109 deported workers from the Dominican Republic, an event that was becoming more and more frequent and swelling the ranks of the unemployed on both islands.[68]

Laborers returning to Nevis resorted to a subsistence adaptation on settlement-scheme lands and other rented and owned plots. On St. Kitts, the consolidation of the sugar-cane industry, under the indirect control of the Basseterre factory, had stifled any hope for the development of a peasant agricultural sector and had even reduced the narrow zone of subsistence agriculture halfway up the mountain slopes. Overall modernization in the island's cane industry had included the widespread use of artificial fertilizers, the replacement of draft oxen by tractors and trucks, and the adoption of contour plowing. These "improvements" pushed cane cultivation higher into hillside areas formerly cultivated in rootcrops, vegetables, and bananas by estate workers. Total sugar tonnage on St. Kitts rose from 15,563 in 1925 to 18,680 in 1930 to 28,491 in 1935, partly because of improved technique but also because of the conversion of subsistence acreage to cane acreage. Kittitian workers could not simply rent farm plots higher in the mountains. As in the 1840s these highest areas were all still estate-owned and "jealously preserved" by forest rangers, who prohibited provision cropping so that highland forest devastation would not lead to soil erosion on the sugar-cane plantations below.[69] Even despite prohibitions against hillside provision farming on St. Kitts, the need for food in the 1930s led to more intense small-scale subsistence cultivation on steep slopes and a noticeable increase in soil erosion.[70]

The St. Kitts Workers' League complained that increased cane acreage reduced subsistence possibilities for estate laborers.[71] Small-scale and semiorganized workers' strikes had occurred on St. Kitts as early as 1905.[72] In the following decade a group of returning labor migrants attempted to form a union, but this was forbidden by local statutes. In 1921 the *Union Messenger* became the first working-class newspaper for the two islands, and workers' dissatisfactions could now be openly and regularly aired. Labor discontent and strikes in the 1920s from Jamaica to Trinidad were reported routinely in the *Union Messenger*. But it was in the depression decade of the 1930s, when emigration outlets diminished and local conditions worsened, that laborers' groups, especially on St. Kitts, developed into an active, although loosely organized, force. In 1932, West Indian labor leaders Albert Marryshow of Grenada and Arthur Cipriani of Trinidad, visited St. Kitts and met with groups of workers. Their message: black West Indians everywhere were being suppressed by expatriate planters, and effective labor organization was the only effective response. Incipient labor organization was also reinforced by an increasing class consciousness, an awareness of pan-Caribbean labor discontent, and a heightened sense of negritude in not only a West Indian, but a world, context. The *Union Messenger* of 1935 covered battle-by-battle accounts of the Italo-Ethiopian war accompanied by lengthy local editorial commentary of how this was but one more example of the ongoing suppression of blacks throughout the world by European colonialism.

On January 28, 1935, labor discontent became violence. Workers' groups had asked for a guaranteed bonus for the 1935 crop, similar to one they had received in the previous year. An extra cash bonus would ameliorate the grim economic circumstances on the island, and it seemed little to ask of a sugar industry that had paid out an annual average dividend of £17,000 from 1929 to 1934 and had added £40,000 profits to its reserves during the same period—tidy sums during a depression.[73] When the workers' demands were refused, an angry crowd assembled at Buckley's Estate, west of Basseterre, and marched together for six miles through the town to Lodge Estate, on the eastern side of the island, where they beat the proprietor, let livestock loose, and stoned the estate buildings. The arriving police read the Riot Act to the crowd, which failed to disperse. Then the police opened fire on the rioters, killing three and wounding eight. This quelled the riot, although a strike against the estates and factory lasted into the following day.[74]

The St. Kitts disturbance was the first in a series of work stoppages and labor protests throughout the British Caribbean. In the same year, sugar workers in British Guiana, coal workers in St. Lucia, and laborers in St. Vincent struck. In 1937 the oil field strike at Fyzabad in southern Trinidad spread to become general work stoppages in Barbados, British Guiana, and St. Lucia, as well as in Trinidad. British colonial authorities reinforced local police with army units, and order was restored after a considerable loss in life and property. Out of the West Indian riot and chaos of the 1930s, which was a response to economic repression worsened by depression, labor unions and movements had developed in all of the British Caribbean colonies.

The cutoff of emigration outlets for laborers of the smallest islands was a fundamental cause of West Indian unrest. Particularly on St. Kitts, the role of returning emigrants was crucial in "explaining" the riots of January 1935. Colonial investigators acknowledged, though distorted, the emigration factor, attributing the disturbances to "returned Santo Domingo malcontents" rather than to dismal local economic circumstances that had traditionally been improved through emigrants' working abroad.[75] Distortions aside, the official report of the St. Kitts disturbances accorded major importance to the returning labor migrants:

> Basseterre, St. Kitts, has always been the port where labourers from other islands are collected to be transshipped in the labour schooners to Santo Domingo and other "Spanish" sugar islands, and at the end of the season are set down again at the same port to await other vessels on to their homes. Many of them either remain in Basseterre for weeks waiting for ships, or even take up permanent residence there. Thus there is always a bad crowd of "loafers" in that town.[76]

Deportation from the Dominican Republic back to the British Leewards continued apace during the 1930s, bringing home workers, swelling the ranks of the unemployed, and improving the prospects for further indolence and "loafing" by the working class. Despite the downplaying of local economic miseries by colonial authorities in accounting for riots in St. Kitts and elsewhere, the official report of the Buckley's riots had underlined a key point: the multi-island origins of the rioting men. Three months after the 1935 labor riots, a typical schooner, one among many, arrived in Basseterre with laborers deported from Santo Domingo. The returning men numbered 30 from St. Kitts, 5 from Nevis, 2 from Anguilla, 2 from Tortola, 6 from Antigua, 3 from Montserrat, and 7 from St. Martin.[77]

But migrating men could no longer return to La Romana at the first of the year. Faced with deteriorating economic circumstances at home, they responded with force and an incipient organization that they had developed abroad. Men from a variety of British West Indian islands had emigrated together, worked Santo Domingo cane fields together, and in some cases been deported as shipmates together. The camaraderie among male workers that had developed in the Dominican Republic was now channeled into strikes and political actions in an attempt to ameliorate conditions created by oppression and starvation at home.

Incipient labor organization and mass labor action on St. Kitts and Nevis, though heightened in the 1930s, was afflicted with an inherent weakness: the periodic necessary migration of young black laborers—the potential core of any truly aggressive labor movement. Although a greater awareness of the world and political organization on the part of the workers accompanied the disturbances of the 1930s, a more fundamental reason for their occurrence and the same as that underlying the disturbance of 1896 was simply that extraisland labor outlets were closed and more workers were therefore home to vent their frustration. In the intervening years, when the men traveled back and forth to Bermuda and Santo Domingo, conditions at home were similarly oppressive and impoverished, but outside sources of livelihood compensated, and—more important for potential labor organization—the most aggressive laborers traveled away each year thereby inhibiting the local, long-term coalescence of a critical mass of laborers for a truly unified political organization. This had also been the case in the nineteenth century when men and women from St. Kitts and Nevis traveled to Trinidad, not as an organized group, but as individuals determined to better conditions for themselves and their families. In later years, after the depression decade, emigration outlets farther afield would similarly detract from group organization in St. Kitts and Nevis.

In the first decades of the twentieth century the Caribbean as a whole had been selectively "modernized," a process that called for enormous capital investment and consolidation on some islands and abandonment of others. Caught in the middle, the laborers of the small islands of the British West Indies adapted to economic change and environmental uncertainty as they had ever since emancipation: they had migrated, by now a learned survival strategy.

CHAPTER SIX

Journey to the Metropoles

Like the unrest of the 1890s, the British Caribbean labor disturbances in the 1930s inspired several colonial reports dealing with West Indian social and economic despair. One was based upon an extended Caribbean fact-finding tour by Major G. Browne, the labour advisor to the British secretary of state. Browne visited the Leewards in 1937, noting the sugar-cane monoculture of St. Kitts standing in stark contrast with the worn-out look of Nevis. According to Browne, the populace of both islands seemed healthy enough, although the infant mortality rate was 189 per 1,000 live births, and there was a worrisome dependence on imported food. On St. Kitts, sugar estate workers received only slightly more than one shilling per day. The meagerness of the pay was acknowledged by the planters, who nevertheless attributed their own high profits to good weather over the previous several years. Why not increase wages? This would be economically unsound according to the planters because there was always the "possibility" of drought in the Leewards that would depreciate cane yields and profits. Browne also noted in passing that it was customary throughout the Lesser Antilles for working-class men to travel away for higher wages. In earlier years this migration had been mainly to Santo Domingo. Larger numbers of migrants were now headed for the oil refinery on Aruba, although the informal, unsupervised nature of this movement made quantifying this traffic in migrating men next to impossible.[1]

The oil refinery jobs in Aruba and Curaçao were important for a few Kittitians and Nevisians but relatively short-lived. Of even shorter duration were jobs with the U.S. armed forces in Antigua and Trinidad during World War II. By war's end the black laboring classes of St. Kitts and Nevis, and the rest of the Commonwealth Caribbean had, in very general terms, returned to pent-up impoverishment. The overcrowdedness of the Lesser Antilles suggested possible resettlement schemes in the larger mainland colonies of British Guiana and British Honduras, and Caribbean colonial officials were hopeful that new emigration outlets would eventually relieve population stress in the islands (Table 9).

Table 9. Population of St. Kitts and Nevis, 1946–1970

	St. Kitts			Nevis		
	M	F	Total	M	F	Total
1946	13,581	16,237	29,818	5,062	6,326	11,388
1960	17,913	20,200	38,113	5,653	7,117	12,770
1970	15,917	17,820	33,737	5,127	6,020	11,147

Sources: *West Indian Census 1946*, II, Part F, Table 2; *Census of St. Kitts, Nevis, Anguilla, 7th April 1960*, II, 16, 20; *1970 Population Census of the Commonwealth Caribbean*, III, 146–53.

Subtle yet distinct changes during the war years had, however, heightened the aspirations of the black laboring class of the British Caribbean. Returning men from U.S. military bases spoke with familiarity of the relaxed, approachable, and free-spending American soldiers whom they had befriended. A few West Indian soldiers fought in European campaigns and then returned. The presence of German submarines—one was reported to have landed on Nevis—in the Caribbean sea had created a sense of West Indian war involvement and had heightened patriotic fervor throughout the British islands.[2] Men from the islands had worked away, not only in Caribbean islands, but also in farm and factory jobs in the United States, returning with money to build better houses and small island shops. By war's end, British West Indian Airways provided light aircraft travel among most of the Leewards and Windwards, including St. Kitts. In short, the war had opened a window on the world, at least the North Atlantic world, which black West Indians now saw in a more familiar, inviting, and accessible light.

More convenient travel facilities, poverty and overcrowding at home, and the need for postwar reconstruction labor in the United Kingdom then led to the British Caribbean population exodus to Britain. This lasted from about 1950 into the 1960s and involved roughly a quarter of a million West Indian migrants. From 1955 through 1964 almost 15,000 from St. Kitts, Nevis, and Anguilla traveled to England. Emigration to the United Kingdom, especially in 1960–62, eased growing population pressures at home. The restrictions of Britain's Commonwealth Immigrants Act in 1962, however, redirected the emigration stream from St. Kitts and Nevis to the

146

U.S. Virgin Islands until similarly restrictive acts also curtailed travel to St. Thomas and St. Croix.

Unlike much of the back-and-forth travel of earlier years, Kittitian and Nevisian emigration to the United Kingdom and the Virgin Islands has been "permanent." Long travel distances, commitment to full-time urban employment, and the establishment of homes and families in metropolitan countries or their territories have sometimes broken bonds with the home islands. At the same time this long-distance migration provides a continuity with the earlier emigration tradition of St. Kitts and Nevis because the people of the two islands continue to depend on those who have gone away.

A continuity of sorts with earlier migration days persists through the experience of the recent migrants themselves. A Kittitian or Nevisian arriving in London or New York by jet aircraft today is subjected, in very general terms, to the same kinds of immigration restrictions greeting the early steerage travelers to Bermuda or the schooner passengers to Santo Domingo. West Indian immigrants, once established abroad, moreover, tend to stick together for mutual support in alien lands, stressing their Caribbean identities in the face of discrimination from numerically dominant host populations. And metropolitan patterns of domination and control over the islands themselves continue to make life hard and precarious for those who have remained on St. Kitts and Nevis. A prime example is currency devaluation and inflation, together striking hard at the local islanders, whose cash earnings and remittances purchase imported food, clothing, and building materials. In September 1949 the British pound was devalued from U.S. $4.03 to U.S. $2.80. This meant that any given amount of Caribbean colonial currency, which was tied to British sterling, immediately purchased 30 percent less food imported from the United States. In 1967 the pound was further devalued to U.S. $2.40. Four years later the pound was allowed to float against international currencies, and it dropped to roughly $1.60 during 1976. In July 1976, the Commonwealth states of the Leeward Islands pegged the Eastern Caribbean dollar to the United States dollar, the latter subsequently falling sharply against the British pound. In the past thirty years, the local currency earned by Kittitians and Nevisians has thus plummeted to slightly more than one-third of its 1949 value. In international monetary arrangements, as in other ways, the small islander of the West Indies has reaped few of the rewards and many of the losses by virtue of his association with the North Atlantic world. And, in the face of this dependency, a strategy of migration as livelihood is—as it has always been—often less risky than staying at home.

Caribbean Destinations before, during, and after World War II

There is a shopkeeper in Old Road Town in St. Kitts who recalls when she traveled to Curaçao in 1929 with her children in order to meet her husband. He had already gone to Curaçao and found a position as a mechanic at the Royal Dutch Shell oil refinery there. She worked in Curaçao as a seamstress, moved on to Aruba with her husband in 1950, then traveled to Trinidad after his death and finally back to St. Kitts. With the money she accumulated on the other islands together with remittances from her two sons, she maintains a modest "cake shop" with small jars of sweets for the village children as well as imported canned milk, crackers, and soft drinks. She and scores of people like her on St. Kitts and Nevis went to the Netherlands Antilles during and after the world depression. Most of them eventually returned and opened shops at home, having prospered in the Dutch islands and saved their earnings for their eventual return.

The Shell plant on Curaçao began refining Venezuelan oil from Lake Maracaibo in 1918, the Lago refinery on Aruba doing the same eleven years later. The two islands were wage sources for British West Indian labor migrants until the late 1950s, when refinery distilling units were centralized and crude oil transportation and processing operations stream-lined. Technological change in the refineries rendered British subjects "redundant" and eventually sent almost all of them home. Until then, however, refinery and housing construction, building and plant mainte-nance, and service jobs on the two Dutch islands had called for thousands of black laborers from the British islands, who became welders, brick-layers, firemen, handymen, and oil barge captains. The boom years for British West Indian laborers on Aruba and Curaçao were during World War II and shortly thereafter. In the peak year, 1948, the two refineries together employed 5,459 workers from the British West Indies. Most laborers came from the southern islands; just as the British Leewards had earlier supplied most Dominican cane cutters, the majority of the refinery workers on the Dutch islands were from Grenada, St. Vincent, and the Grenadines. Of the 3,370 men working at the Lago refinery in Aruba in 1948, for instance, 1,607 were from Grenada and St. Vincent. In the same year, only 82 Kittitians and 40 Nevisians worked at the same refinery.[3]

A few of the returnees to St. Kitts and Nevis from Santo Domingo in

1935 had moved on to Curaçao. Their travel route was north to St. Martin then south to Curaçao via steamer. In 1938, recruiting agents from Curaçao sought men with carpentry and masonry experience in the Leewards. Unrecruited "free agents" from St. Kitts and Nevis without special qualifications were also traveling to Aruba and Curaçao by this time. The latter usually joined a milling throng of unemployed West Indians, many of whom were unsuccessful in finding work and were subsequently deported to their home islands.[4] Some men from St. Kitts and Nevis found jobs on the Dutch islands and stayed fifteen to twenty years before being laid off. Personal contacts and family ties often were as important as special skills in landing refinery jobs. Reliable and hard-working men returning home for visits were often asked by refinery foremen to bring other dependable workers back with them. They then returned with brothers, nephews, cousins, or sons. Similarly, young men from St. Kitts and Nevis often traveled to Aruba or Curaçao, being joined by their wives after becoming established. Their wives then worked as domestics for the families of refinery executives.

Single men from the British islands occupied rented quarters from the oil companies in the Netherlands Antilles. They also renewed contacts there with fellow workers from the other British Caribbean colonies, some of whom they had known in the Santo Domingo days. Pursuing political developments in their home islands *in absentia,* migrant men organized themselves into trade unions, and young political leaders, such as Eric Gairy of Grenada, received their first political training there.[5] But the Dutch authorities were not sympathetic to the organized demands of the foreign workers. In March 1947, Grenada's Albert Marryshow visited Aruba in his capacity as president of the Caribbean Labour Congress, an organization composed of workers from throughout the region. Accused of labor agitation, Marryshow was unceremoniously expelled from Aruba.

U.S. military bases in the Caribbean in World War II employed more British West Indians than did the refineries of the Dutch Antilles, but for a shorter time. In 1940 the United States took over bases on several British Caribbean islands in return for fifty naval destroyers sent to Britain. Jobs on the U.S. bases—the extension of air base runways, the fortification of harbors, the construction of military barracks, and jobs as messengers, laundry workers, cooks, and maids—attracted tens of thousands of West Indians. The principal U.S. bases were on Trinidad, where the construction and servicing of naval and air corps installations called for thousands of laborers. A U.S. air base on Antigua, Coolidge Field, employed many

Leeward islanders, and military-related jobs on St. Thomas in the Virgin Islands attracted 400 laborers from St. Kitts in 1944.[6]

No records were kept of emigration of Kittitians and Nevisians to particular U.S. military bases, but data from the final Leeward Islands *Blue Book,* published in 1945, suggests that the war had a happy economic impact on the two islands. Local newspapers had hinted darkly that a disruption of interisland boat traffic would lead to local starvation, but this did not occur. Instead, a lively traffic in goods and people, indirectly financed by U.S. currency paid to local workers who had migrated away, created a brief period of slight prosperity. In 1945, 7,473 people left St. Kitts and Nevis and 7,247 returned; in the same year the equivalent of £21,985 in U.S. dollars was remitted to St. Kitts and Nevis through the post office. Some of the money came from families living in the United States, and some came from itinerant farm workers there. But much of it was the "Yankee dollar" paid by American paymasters in Trinidad and the other West Indian bases. Migrating Kittitians and Nevisians also found work in Trinidad outside the U.S. installations, and in 1945 they sent home £1,767 worth of Trinidad currency.[7]

The German submarine campaign did threaten Caribbean shipping early in the war, and in 1942 the "coasting schooners" of the Lesser Antilles were organized into a pool in order to help safeguard the movement of people and produce among the islands. Some of the schooners were by this time fitted with auxiliary diesel engines, but they were still a crowded and dangerous means of travel from the Leewards south to Trinidad. Officials in Trinidad had attempted to exclude "small islanders" in 1938 by requiring a £50 deposit on arrival from each visitor from the Windwards and Leewards.[8] This recurring immigration restriction was, however, removed for those employed by the Americans. The U.S. armed forces employed 24,000 men from Trinidad and the smaller islands in 1942–43, and another 5,000 were hired by subcontractors working for the American military.[9] This infusion of money into the Trinidadian economy of course led to other local work and higher levels of disposable income which, as it always had, indirectly aided people throughout the Lesser Antilles.

Exodus to Great Britain

Neither war money nor the earnings from Aruba and Curaçao altered the essential impoverishment of the working classes of the British Caribbean. At war's end, the plight of British West Indians remained the same as before the war: too few jobs, too many people, landlessness, recurring environmental problems, and associated human ills. Widespread malnutrition and disease hit hardest at the region's poorest people. Observers proclaimed that resettlement and emigration outlets for inhabitants of the West Indian islands were "now more than ever needed."[10] One of the worst examples of rural poverty in the Caribbean could be seen in the plantation villages on St. Kitts. The wooden shacks of the island's sugar-cane workers, as in previous centuries, were packed together along the ghauts and littorals below the cane fields. Many such settlements had no form of sanitation, a condition creating stench in the dry periods and enhancing the prospects for sickness and death among the local populace.[11] The pound's sudden devaluation in 1949 intensified distress throughout St. Kitts and Nevis. The leader of the St. Kitts–Nevis Trades and Labour Union, Robert Bradshaw, deplored the "disaster of devaluation . . . forced upon the colony" and urged the cane workers to plant more food.[12]

As British subjects, Kittitians and Nevisians could travel with British passports without restrictions to the mother country, and it was eventual large-scale emigration to England that ameliorated the postwar economic desperation in the Caribbean. A few West Indian soldiers had traveled to Europe during the war, and earlier a very small number of black dock workers had inhabited coastal towns in Great Britain. The wave of Caribbean laborers who began to come to England in the late 1940s was of a different order. In June 1948, the S.S. *Empire Windrush* arrived carrying 492 passengers, mostly Jamaicans but also some from the smaller islands. The *Windrush* was eventually followed by many ships bringing semiskilled black workers, mainly men, who took up work in London and in the towns and cities of England's industrial heartland.[13]

In the early 1950s a few relatively prosperous Kittitians and Nevisians booked individual steamer and aircraft passage to England. There they established an initial social foundation and network for the thousands who would follow from 1955 until 1962, when the United Kingdom essentially banned further Caribbean immigration. The numbers of emigrants from St. Kitts and Nevis to the United Kingdom are, at best, estimates, because local records of emigration from the two islands included those leaving from Anguilla. Also, the government of the United Kingdom had no statutory powers to collect immigration data from the various colonies until the passage of the Commonwealth Immigrants Act in 1962. The records of travel agents in Basseterre, however, suggest that during the decade beginning in 1955 almost 15,000 left for England from the three islands.[14]

Both individuals and families traveled from St. Kitts and Nevis to Great Britain, and no clear distinction can be made between the type who left and the type who stayed home. In very general terms, migrants to Great Britain were better educated than those staying, and the emigrants were principally skilled and semiskilled workers. From St. Kitts, mechanics, welders, carpenters, and masons—tradesmen with marketable skills—predominated among those leaving. Many had been trained at the central sugar factory, which lost many of its personnel. Nevisian migrants were often young adults from households subsisting on agricultural labor and provision farming.

The migrants left from Basseterre on steamers and chartered aircraft. Italian and Spanish ships that had taken Mediterranean migrants to Venezuela on their outward voyages offered half fares for West Indian women and quarter fares for children, ensuring the steamer lines of passenger revenue on their return trips. The Spanish ships eventually docked at Southampton. The final European destination of the Italian lines was usually Genoa, from which black West Indians traveled by train to London. In the last years of the emigration to Great Britain, chartered aircraft regularly took planeloads of seventy and more from St. Kitts to Shannon, Ireland, on an exhausting journey via Newfoundland. From Shannon the migrants traveled to London via boat and train.

The peak years of the emigration to Great Britain, 1960 to 1962, were momentous and exciting times in Basseterre. Radio advertisements, newspapers, and leaflets publicized the low cost of special transatlantic journeys. Letters home and to the newspapers from those who had gone ahead described Gander, Newfoundland's airport, London's lights, and European winters in breathless detail. Families and individuals from as far as Antigua and Montserrat occasionally came to the Basseterre roadstead to make connections to Europe. Steel bands played at the airport, lending a festive air to the departures, and they played nightly on the ocean voyages for West Indian passengers. Entire families from Nevis came across the channel to see a son or daughter depart. Those leaving for England were attired in their Sunday best—suits and ties and church dresses. They carried with them their travel tickets, new passports, and their belongings in suitcases, parcels, and baskets. Black Kittitians and Nevisians, along with other West Indians, were going "home" to England, where regular employment and higher living standards were available for those willing to work hard.

For many it was an event marked by sadness as well. The departure of loved ones was at least a temporary loss. Families could be eventually reunited in Great Britain, but many friends sensed that they would never see each other again. Entire villages sometimes turned out to see friends, family members, and neighbors leave, departures described in local newspapers.[15]

Emigration for many from St. Kitts and Nevis involved selling off what little they owned. Many of the poorer blacks on St. Kitts sold their houses for as little as E.C. $800 for passage for themselves and their families and a bit of extra money to get started in England. Nevisians often borrowed money from individuals or banks, using their house plots and provision grounds as collateral. Those with several head of livestock sold them for extra cash. Others from both islands would have joined the emigrants but had no means of paying for the trip.

In the early years of the exodus to England men from the two islands tended to travel alone. Their first stop in Great Britain was almost always with a brother, cousin, or friend who had gone earlier and rented a room or flat. The resultant barracks-type living was "temporary," but it often lasted for several months or even years. By saving on rent and working at one or more jobs, black men could then send money home to enable wives and children to join them and also to support parents left behind. In any case, in England Kittitians and Nevisians tended to seek one another out, forming ill-defined "neighborhoods" as part of a larger West Indian immigrant population. Many Kittitians went to the Paddington district of London. Several Nevisians settled in Bedford, north of London, where they worked in a turbine factory and a brickyard. Immigrants from both islands were eventually scattered throughout the poorer districts of London and the industrial cities of the Midlands.

New arrivals from St. Kitts and Nevis found confusion and complexity characteristic of their new home. The contrasts between the tiny home islands and industrial England were awesome. The immigrants marveled at the lights, the noise, and London's endless expanse. Here they were "all mixed up" with immigrants from throughout the Commonwealth, who mingled together in parks and walkways. But the gray tenements, the damp chill of northern Europe, soot and coal dust, and the punctuality expected at work were depressing. The poverty they had left was at least marked by familiarity.

Amidst Great Britain's urban chaos, Kittitians and Nevisians, however, soon learned the rules of industrial England's socioeconomic order. Here they were considered "Jamaicans," undifferentiated black faces that had poured out of the immigrant boats. On the job they faced racial slurs, layoffs, and permanency only in the most menial positions that most whites would not take. Their rooms and flats were in chilly brick buildings in the poorest British neighborhoods, where they faced personal insult and housing discrimination. Their expectations of a fond welcome by fellow Britons had turned to alienation, a feeling that has been noted time and again by social scientists dealing with Britain's blacks.[16] In a matter of months after their triumphant departures from home, Kittitians and Nevisians had usually become disappointed and resigned.

By the 1960s the sudden influx of black West Indians to Great Britain had created suspicion and resentment among that country's white populace. The British government sought an easing of immigration restrictions in Canada and the United States to accommodate immigrants from the Commonwealth Caribbean, claiming that the British labor market was no longer able to absorb the influx. In early 1960, thousands of West Indians were unemployed in Britain.[17] Citing these unemployment figures, the British Parliament in 1962 passed the Commonwealth Immigrants Act, which became law on July 1 of that year. Passed after particularly heated and acrimonious debate, the act eliminated the free flow of Commonwealth immigrants into the country. Those already resident in the United Kingdom could stay and also bring their husbands, wives, and children under sixteen. All others were essentially barred.[18] The immigration bill had been introduced into Parliament in October 1961. When the bill passed in April 1962, Kittitians, Nevisians, and others who had planned eventually to leave for England suddenly had only months to prepare for departure in order to arrive before July. Slightly more than 100,000 West Indians rushed to the United Kingdom in 1961 and the first half of 1962, an exodus from the Caribbean inspired by the discussion over and introduction of the new immigration law.

The exodus to England had profound repercussions on the West Indian islands themselves, especially on the smallest ones. Individuals staying home could depend partially on remittances from family members in England, but so many of the able-bodied had left that insular economies suffered. In 1961, St. Kitts planters imported twelve mechanical loaders to help handle the sugar-cane harvest. The trade-union-dominated government, seeing their position weakened by the emigration of their constituency, was in no position to dispute the move. In 1960, 200 Barbadian cane cutters were brought to St. Kitts to help reap the crop, and in 1961, 200 St. Lucians were imported.[19] The last muscovado mill on Nevis expired in 1958. Poor soil and low outputs on the smaller island were now combined with a loss of skilled personnel. So many had left both islands that some jobs went unfilled. Employers complained that the most competent workers had gone, leaving "second and even third raters" to carry on the island's business.[20]

Table 10. Postal Money Order Remittances in Eastern Caribbean Dollars to St. Kitts and Nevis, 1962–1975

	To St. Kitts		To Nevis		To both
	From U.S.	*From U.K.*	*From U.S.*	*From U.K.*	*From U.S.V.I.*
1962	168,555	778,487	77,809	365,317	98,211
1963	210,476	685,894	83,542	332,376	132,218
1964	274,471	688,801	93,808	332,103	179,955
1965	259,835	687,288	59,873	341,591	155,034
1966	250,803	606,742	40,175	284,875	136,589
1967	202,200	513,619	30,846	272,594	100,562
1968	159,384	528,361	21,778	248,928	52,254
1969	73,557	507,342	14,530	239,120	53,014
1970	77,531	473,976	13,341	250,721	48,8?4
1971	81,102	477,571	10,537	250,732	53,738
1972	65,061	586,535	5,072	314,296	40,650
1973	23,218	753,025	3,680	366,993	—[a]
1974	5,885	954,893	509	416,649	—[a]
1975	2,606	1,041,757	234	542,601	—[a]

Note: The E.C. dollar was worth roughly U.S. $0.60 in 1962, $0.50 in 1967, and $0.37 in 1976.
[a]No data available.
Source: Data courtesy of the General Post Office, Basseterre. Data from the U.S. Virgin Islands are from "Digest of Statistics no. 9, Jan-Dec, 1973," Table 13.

Family members staying behind, however, prospered in a relative sense. They now received regular remittances through the mail. For 1957–59 the average annual sums sent to individuals on St. Kitts and Nevis via the post office were over E.C. $1,300,000.[21] Much of this money financed further emigration. The postal remittance system, revived during the exodus to Great Britain, has provided a steady and reliable source of sterling and dollar currency for those staying behind ever since (Table 10). Possibly even more money arrives through the banks; the sum is so high that the St. Kitts–Nevis government has recently imposed a 1 percent tax on all currency exchanges on the two islands.

The massive emigration to Great Britain was different from the earlier movements of Kittitians and Nevisians in several important ways. First, the emigration was not along the West Indian periphery of the North Atlantic world but directed toward England, whose resident white populace had heretofore considered economic problems involving the empire's darker races as distant colonial problems. Second, it represented a greater volume of migration from St. Kitts and Nevis than ever before. Third, the movement appears to have been permanent, for most who left the West Indies stayed in Great Britain and have never returned. And although remittances to the home islands still maintain links with those who stayed at home, Kittitians and Nevisians and other West Indians who went to England, and especially their children, seem to be, more and more, "black Britons." The longer they stay in Great Britain the more they rely on their own nuclear families for support and identity and the less they have in common with those in the Caribbean.[22] Many West Indians now residing in England say that they would prefer eventual return to their native lands, a return migration that may be perpetrated by future and unforeseen political events.

Emigration to North America and the Virgin Islands

Besides laboring on U.S. military bases in the Caribbean during World War II, a few men from St. Kitts and Nevis also spent work sojourns in fields and factories in the mainland United States. They were part of a wartime West Indian work contingent of an estimated 50,000, principally Jamaicans but also those from the smaller British colonies. Men from St. Kitts and Nevis recall a transient, all-male barracks life but with good pay, most of which they sent home. Their work destinations included cane and citrus fields in Florida, fruit and vegetable lands in Wisconsin and Michigan, and tobacco farms in Connecticut.

Contract farm labor in the United States continued to employ a limited number of Kittitians and Nevisians in the 1950s, although the chances for permanent emigration there were slight. The U.S. Immigration and Nationality Act of 1952 imposed an annual quota of no more than 100 immigrants from each British West Indian territory. While 250,000 black West Indians were traveling to Great Britain in the 1950s under an open immigration policy, half that many from all areas of the West Indies were entering the United States.[23] The movement was redirected in 1965, when the U.S. Immigration and Nationality Act was amended to abolish the national origins system. The act has since generally favored immigration from Latin America and the West Indies, maintaining 120,000 annual immigration visas for citizens of the Western Hemisphere. The resultant "new" immigration from the independent states of the Commonwealth Caribbean to the United States has in fact established a continuity with the movements earlier in this century. And the pre-existing ethnic structure of the United States has provided black West Indian immigrants with opportunities for "upward occupational mobility," not as available in the United Kingdom.[24]

For potential immigrants from St. Kitts and Nevis, however, recent U.S. immigration quota changes have made little difference. As an Associated State (a British dependency in U.S. eyes), St. Kitts and Nevis was allotted an annual quota of only 200 by the United States; in late 1976 an amendment raised the figure to 600. St. Kitts immigration data show that only 127 people from the two islands were "permanent emigrants" to the United States from 1967 through 1975.[25] This figure does not take into account illegal immigration, a phenomenon that has possibly increased in response to increasingly stringent immigration laws in the United States and elsewhere.

From 1967 through 1975, 276 Kittitians and Nevisians emigrated permanently to Canada. Since 1955 a few young women have taken part in a program sponsored by the Canadian and West Indian governments, whereby they are employed as housemaids in Canada and can pursue their educations and then apply for Canadian citizenship.[26] Childless women aged twenty-one to thirty-five are eligible candidates. For West Indians in general, Canadian immigration requirements were eased in 1962. Earlier rules had discriminated against immigrants of non-European origin, and Canada continues to maintain high "occupational skill" standards for those not admitted as relatives of Canadian citizens. The few migrants from St. Kitts and Nevis, including university students, have usually traveled to the English-speaking areas of Ontario, mainly to Toronto.

While the recent volume of migration to the United States and Canada has been relatively small from St. Kitts and Nevis, the U.S. Virgin Islands of St. Thomas and St. Croix have been vital sources of wages for both permanent and temporary migrants from the two islands. Because of their proximity, the Virgin Islands have long been migration destinations from the closest British colonies. Kittitian workers traveled to Danish St. Croix as early as the 1860s. Early in the twentieth century, men and women from the British Virgin Islands worked as gardeners and maids on St. Thomas and St. Croix. Many of the hundreds from St. Kitts and Nevis and the other Leewards who traveled to the Virgin Islands during World War II attempted to remain thereafter. In late 1945 and into 1946 the U.S. Immigration Service deported 700 illegal British aliens to Tortola. That island then became a staging ground for attempted clandestine reentry to St. Thomas and St. Croix. In late 1949, small sailing craft from Tortola were routinely bringing illegal immigrants to the U.S. islands, and some men were reported swimming the channel from Tortola to St. John.[27]

In the 1950s seasonal cane-cutting crews traveled from the British Leewards via boats and planes to St. Croix to harvest cane for the Virgin Islands Corporation. They arrived at the first of the year, lived in temporary barracks while working the cane fields, and left in midsummer. The sudden influx during World War II of hundreds of "down islanders," followed by the seasonal, all-male cane-cutting gangs, established British Leeward islanders—mainly Antiguans, Kittitians, and Nevisians—as a distinct, visible, and transient minority within the ethnic fabric of the Virgin Islands. Their seasonal presence in the 1950s formed stereotypes still maintained on St. Thomas and St. Croix. The itinerant cane harvesters performed jobs that few locals would accept. Although they had limited contact with the local populace, they acquired reputations as quarrelsome, heavy-drinking women chasers. The last cane crop on St. Croix was harvested in 1963.

The islands' economies were becoming more closely bound up with that of the mainland United States in the 1960s. Economic prosperity transformed St. Thomas into a tourist resort, while St. Croix became a tourist and industrial center. Island tourism and "development" called for cheap labor, and workers from the British islands were again invited to enter the Virgin Islands more freely. British islanders were allowed to come, find a job, obtain a "clearance order" from the local employment agency that no local citizen was available for the work, and arrange for their prospective employers to petition the immigration department on their behalf. After one year of working on St. Thomas or St. Croix the alien workers then had to leave temporarily, usually to Tortola, and then return to become certified once more as an alien work "visitor."[28]

In light of Britain's 1962 Commonwealth Immigrants Act, the Virgin Islands had become more accessible at an opportune time for Kittitians and

Nevisians, who sought work on St. Thomas and St. Croix by the hundreds. Many were returnees, veterans of the cane-cutting gangs, who now earned higher pay as unskilled or semiskilled workers on construction crews building houses, offices, condominiums, and tourist hotels. They were joined by other, younger migrants—both male and female—who rushed to the Virgin Islands for work. The Virgin Islands' alien population, always an unreliable estimate, more than doubled within the decade. From 7,000 in 1964 the numbers grew to 13,000 (8,000 in St. Croix and 5,000 in St. Thomas) in 1967, and 16,000 in 1969.[29] The British islanders were mainly from the Leewards, with probably a greater number from St. Kitts and Nevis than any other area. In mid-1975, an estimated 10,700 British "down islanders" were on St. Thomas and St. Croix, a figure reduced from years past by a series of immigration sanctions and rules. Of this number, 4,060 were from St. Kitts, Nevis, and Anguilla.[30]

Job seekers usually flew from St. Kitts and Nevis to the Virgin Islands. Upon arrival they found work as general construction workers, domestic and commercial maids, waiters, gardeners, and in a host of other unskilled wage positions. Male laborers drifted from one job to another, finding work when and where they could. A young man from one of St. Kitts's windward villages recalled traveling to Tortola by boat in 1969, then on to St. Thomas, where he lived with his cousin until he was deported in 1971. During his twenty-two months on St. Thomas he worked as a mason, waiter, rental car mechanic, and dynamiter on a construction crew. When he could save money he sent it to his parents on St. Kitts via bank drafts in U.S. currency. He quickly learned not to send money via postal remittance forms, since these were cashed at fixed exchange rates at the Basseterre post office, and a much more favorable rate of exchange was available at any bank (Table 10).

The rush to the Virgin Islands further depleted St. Kitts and Nevis of young adults. Cane-harvesting crews at home were often hastily assembled gangs of men whose median age was forty-five and older. Hillside provision farms on St. Kitts, formerly intensively cultivated, were occasionally abandoned, since parents and children could now purchase imported food with imported money. Housing and other construction in the Charlestown vicinity of Nevis boomed noticeably, financed partly by money remitted from St. Thomas and St. Croix. Nevisian provision gardens, abandoned for a season or two, were destroyed by an ever-growing island livestock population. Individual travel back and forth to the Virgin Islands from St. Kitts and Nevis, usually via scheduled light aircraft, was now routine. In 1964, 3,939 trips were undertaken by Kittians and Nevisians to the Virgin Islands. This figure increased to 6,822 in 1967 and to 9,103 in 1969.[31] Always fewer returned than had gone, thereby increasing the population of the host islands and reducing the ranks at home. A growing dependence on American money from U.S. territories led to imported American cultural trappings at home. Transistor radios, tennis shoes, Virgin Islands T-shirts, black power slogans, American slang, Coca-Cola, and potato chips all went home along with the cash necessary for the purchase of imported food. The young men and women remaining on St. Kitts and Nevis spoke of places in the Virgin Islands from previous visits, and they often discussed among themselves whether they too would leave for work.

There were drawbacks in making such a decision. The American territories were known, as they are today among Leeward Islanders, as tawdry, distasteful, and "fast" places, where young men and women from the Commonwealth territories—on foreign islands and outside the immediate circle of family and friends—often fell prey to drugs and violence. Once on St. Thomas or St. Croix the "down islanders" were viewed with disdain by everyone else, and they occupied the lowest economic positions and inhabited the poorest housing. In Charlotte Amalie and Christiansted, entire blocks of substandard housing for immigrant West Indians were served with a single spigot and limited sanitary facilities. On St. Croix, small clusters of hastily built clapboard shacks accommodated the immigrant laborers. And rents of U.S. $60 per month for a single unfurnished room took a high percentage of an immigrant worker's cash income.

High rents, the lowest island wages, and subservient economic positions were guaranteed for the Caribbean immigrants, since their legal status in the Virgin Islands was temporary at best, illegal at worst, and always uncertain and subject to change. The majority of immigrants resided there in a tenuous "bonded" legal status, their presence dependent solely on government renewal through individual employers. A bonded immigrant automatically became an "overstay" if his job was terminated, so he was at the mercy of his employer in a system that was often abused. In 1968 a "temporary alien" category was created for some of the foreign workers. This allowed aliens to remain an extra six months to look for work after their job was terminated. A "permanent resident alien" on the other hand had obtained resident status and could apply for American citizenship after a waiting period. All workers in the Virgin Islands were subject to income tax, but foreigners received limited tax benefits, and the family members they supported at home could not be counted as tax deductions. Faced with a mystifying system of immigration categories, certificates, entry cards, validation periods, and allied paperwork, all of which were subject to change, the foreign worker often found himself suddenly an illegal alien and subject to deportation.

The transience and powerlessness of migrant Kittitians and Nevisians as laborers in the U.S. Virgin Islands in the 1960s had conditioned both their attitudes toward work there and local peoples' attitudes toward them. Reminded almost daily of their temporary status through official and unofficial means, migrants from St. Kitts and Nevis resorted to short-term wage-earning strategies. They took jobs others shunned and often performed labor beyond formal job descriptions, thereby depressing the local job market. As in earlier times and in other places, labor migrants from St. Kitts and Nevis moved from job to job on St. Thomas and St. Croix if higher wages were offered. This mobile job-hopping strategy, combined with and because of their migrant status, caused British Leeward Islanders to be dubbed "garots" by local Thomians and Crucians. This pejorative term referred to the garot bird that flies from place to place, stripping each locale of food before it moves on. Local Virgin Islanders embellished their dislike of the alien migrants in their midst by ascribing a number of vulgar and crude behavioral characteristics to the short-term "garots" from St. Kitts, Nevis, and elsewhere.[32]

Local cries about "garot"-induced crime rates and job competition increased as economic recession replaced the boom of the early 1960s. The welcome for part-time labor migrants had soured. By the early 1970s, immigration authorities on St. Thomas and St. Croix intensified their routine searches for "illegals" in an ongoing cat-and-mouse game.[33] In March 1975, immigration sanctions were tightened in the Virgin Islands. By 1978 the number of immigrants from the "British West Indies" residing in the U.S. Virgin Islands had dropped to slightly more than 7,000, down 30 percent from 1974–75.[34] An estimated 1,200 Kittitians and Nevisians were sent home. And although St. Kitts and Nevis continued to depend heavily on remittances from St. Thomas and St. Croix, the U.S. Virgin Islands had proved to be an ephemeral wage source as had so many other Caribbean locales in years past.

Some of the emigration from St. Kitts and Nevis to the Virgin Islands appears to have been permanent. Proximity to and assimilation in the Virgin Islands have often blurred distinctions between temporary and part-time movements there by Kittitians and Nevisians. Some Thomians and Crucians are themselves descended from British islanders who emigrated there earlier, and intermarriage has occurred in recent years among black natives and British islanders. Children born to transient immigrant workers in the Virgin Islands are automatically eligible for U.S. citizenship. The prejudice associated with the "garot" stereotype still holds in the Virgin Islands, although in some cases ethnic rivalries have become less distinct. Most people now residing on St. Kitts and Nevis have family or friends living in the Virgin Islands, which creates a loose interpersonal network that is maintained by the mobility of individuals who travel back and forth across the northeastern Caribbean.

Land Use on St. Kitts and Nevis

By 1938 the ecological contrasts between St. Kitts and Nevis that began at emancipation and intensified in the early twentieth century had been etched into the landscapes of the two home islands. St. Kitts represented a sugar-cane monoculture. Nevis mixed estate-grown cane and individually produced cotton with large areas of subsistence crops.[35] Each year hundreds of Nevisian men crossed the channel to help bring in the cane crop, and then they returned to their own farming communities from July to January. The contrasting land use between the two islands was held partly responsible for stereotyped attitudes and work habits. An article in the *Union Messenger* declared,

> In the case of Nevis we find the small peasant finding his way to St. Kitts to work as an agricultural labourer . . . to augment his capital. . . . It is admitted by many planters here that the Nevis labourer is a better labourer. Is not some of the effectiveness of the Nevis labourer due to his sense of responsibility being more developed as a small land holder, as compared with the generations of landless St. Kitts labourers?[36]

Time and again the working-class newspaper of St. Kitts echoed this same message in the 1930s; more land for local subsistence agriculture would ease the desperation of the St. Kitts plantation workers, and the resulting prosperous peasantry would eventually benefit everyone—planter and laborer alike. The planters were unmoved. Buoyed by the record profits resulting from the combination of central-milling efficiency, low workers' wages, and several years of ideal weather, they had no intention of releasing valuable cane acreage to peasant cultivators. Estate owners retorted that the intermediate slopes above the cane areas had always been available for small-scale gardening. In fact, contended the planters, the precipitous slopes had been "naturally selected" by the plantation workers in preference to the lowland areas.[37] The argument was absurd because the planters owned the islands' lands all the way to the summit and often evicted small producers when excessive soil erosion resulted from highland gardening.

Slope farming of provisions had indeed led to noticeable soil erosion in the intermediate elevations of St. Kitts by 1945. Gullies formed near the heads of the island's drainage ghauts, and although this was not viewed as a calamitous event, planters were warned that more food cropping would lead inevitably to erosion and thus reduce cane acreage and yields.[38] In response, St. Kitts planters further restricted the workers' use of the intermediate elevations; provision cultivation became tightly controlled, and the government and private estates employed rangers to guard against deforestation and clandestine charcoal production in the mountains.[39]

Hurricane rains in both islands led to sheet erosion. In September 1949, rains washed large banks of loamy soil into Basseterre and blocked the highway with soil residue in several areas of the St. Kitts perimeter highway.[40] Nevisian soil erosion was even worse. Torrential rains and high winds there removed soil that had been cleared by small-scale farmers for cotton planting. Government advisers and observers alike suggested an immediate need for stone terraces and windbreaks on the smaller island. By 1966, surface horizons had been removed completely from much of the soil of Nevis.[41] The smaller island was also more susceptible to environmental hazards, mainly drought. In May 1947, drought in Nevis killed several cows and their calves, and in some parts of the island, water for public use was available only one hour per day.[42] In 1955, six months of drought followed hurricane Alice, which had destroyed much of Nevis's cotton crop.

Labor disturbances upset the St. Kitts sugar-cane industry in 1947 and 1948. Ten percent of the 1948 crop was destroyed by cane fires. Union members refused to tend estate animals or to offload incoming ships bringing sugar-industry equipment. It was once again time for an outside inquiry, this time to investigate the state of the St. Kitts sugar industry. The visitors noted workers' poverty and the dependence of the island on imported food, but they were "convinced" that St. Kitts should continue to be a sugar-cane island. The cane fields and the central mill, after all, employed one-half the people of working age, and the "wealth" created by the industry would produce many more jobs.[43] These conclusions were neither imaginative nor surprising. The 1949 report and the several that have followed have all been written from a metropolitan viewpoint and have generally called for a "modernization" and intensification of the sugar-cane industry rather than a growing accommodation to subsistence needs on St. Kitts. Only in the decade of the 1970s have local spokesmen come forth with constructive plans for true agricultural reorientation. [44]

The investigators in 1949 noted with approval the growing mechanization of the sugar-cane industry on St. Kitts. Until the mid-1930s oxen had accomplished most of the hauling and transportation requirements on the estates. By 1949, tractors and trucks had replaced about half of the animals. Mechanization, however, also eliminated jobs, and although the labor union objected, their position was continuously undermined by the emigration of their most able workers. Liberal use of imported fertilizers seasonally revitalized the Kittitian soil that had by now supported sugar-cane crops for three centuries. Imported herbicides kept down weeds, and pesticides eliminated insects in the cane fields. The insects now moved on to the hillside provision grounds, placing further stress on laborers' subsistence production. [45]

Mechanization and large-scale use of chemicals were accompanied by further estate consolidation. The number of estates diminished on St. Kitts from more than 50 at the turn of the century to 47 in 1949 and 38 in 1968. By 1968 the control of sugar-estate land was even more centralized than estate data revealed. Intermarriage and interfamily ownership among planter families had placed the St. Kitts canelands in a relatively few hands. [46] Wade Plantations, Marshall Plantations, Blake Plantations, and Farara Plantations each owned two or more estates, with Wade Plantations owning four and having personal links with a fifth. More significant, by 1968 the Thurston and Horsford retail and wholesale companies in Basseterre managed the majority of the island's canelands. The year before, these two mercantile houses together had had a direct financial interest in 40 percent of the island's 1967 sugar-cane crop. [47] The concentration of land ownership on St. Kitts had followed a trend of monoculture begun in the seventeenth century. By the 1970s, uniformity of cultivation, land ownership, and sugar production had created on St. Kitts a near homogeneous sugar-cane production unit with a black workforce laboring under essentially centralized control and the crop focused toward the single sugar factory.

The homogeneity of the sugar-cane industry on St. Kitts was paralleled by growing agricultural diversity on Nevis. The lack of a central mill and deteriorating soil conditions, made sugar cane less and less viable on the smaller island. Typically, in the 1940s, harvested Nevisian cane was loaded onto donkeys then taken by truck to either the Newcastle or Charlestown pier. Then the cane was lightered across to St. Kitts, offloaded, and trucked to the central factory. Uncertain shipping arrangements, however, often left the cane on piers to become sodden or rat-infested. Even the most robust agriculture on the most fertile soils could hardly absorb such transshipment costs. Nevis's cane acreage steadily dwindled. The last commercial crop was harvested in 1969, when a few tons were shipped across the channel. That year the single cane lighter was inoperable for most of the harvest season. By May, most Nevis cane farmers were using their crops—now seriously desiccated—as animal feed.

Cotton fared little better on the smaller island. Besides contributing to soil erosion, cotton crops were subject to widely fluctuating prices that were depressed for several years after World War II.[48] Since then, cotton cultivation on Nevis as a whole has been measured in minuscule totals such as hundreds of acres and scores of bales, and the demand is always uncertain. The crops themselves have been alternately ravaged by insects, birds, hurricanes, and drought.

Emigration to Great Britain saw some Nevis land sold off to provision farmers, but other land was abandoned. Many of the island's stonewalls that had separated fields for decades had tumbled by mid-century, leaving wide strips of stone through formerly cultivated fields. By the 1960s, acacia weeds colonized abandoned cotton lands.[49] Uncontrolled grazing, for decades an ecological threat on Nevis, became even more prevalent as cultivated lands became weed patches. As in the nineteenth century, investment of remitted money in livestock ensured cash at a later date. Nevis's livestock population had also been indirectly increased by St. Kitts's growing mechanization; Nevis had for years provided oxen as beasts of burden for the sugar-cane plantations on the larger island, but the animals were no longer necessary. In sum, Nevis was becoming overrun with livestock, which in turn compounded soil erosion (Figure 7). Most Nevisian livestock herders, who sold animals for cash on nearby islands, expanded stocks in accord with foreign market demand rather than the local environment's carrying capacity, and commonly, scores of animals died during the recurring droughts.

The first three-quarters of the twentieth century witnessed St. Kitts and Nevis on divergent ecological paths with remarkably similar results. "Modernization" on St. Kitts occurred via mechanization, massive and recurring doses of fertilizers and chemicals, and an almost synthetic de-

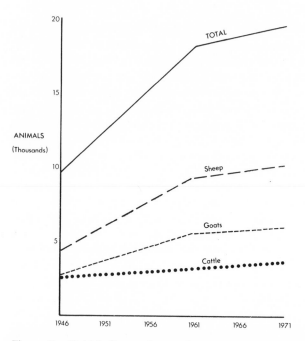

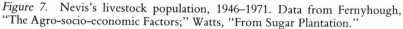

Figure 7. Nevis's livestock population, 1946–1971. Data from Fernyhough, "The Agro-socio-economic Factors;" Watts, "From Sugar Plantation."

pendence on foreign capital for both infrastructural modernization and cash wages. The precarious nature of monoculture was once again exemplified in 1975 when world sugar prices fell sharply after reaching record levels the year before. Nevis, in the meantime, continued to suffer dramatic environmental deterioration. The smaller island's native forests had been cleared long before, but with the disappearance of a sugar-cane cover and the proliferation of thousands of grazing animals, Nevis's vegetation and soil had now been modified and washed away. Foodcrops and livestock on Nevis, always subject to climatic uncertainty, had thus been relegated to a deteriorated ecological base.

From Colony to Associated State

The Caribbean-wide labor disturbances of the 1930s inspired laborers' political movements in every British colony of the region. The St. Kitts Workers' League was organized in 1932 as an advocate of political and social reform in general and to promote the welfare of the working class in particular. An earlier law had prohibited trade unions, but when the law was rescinded in 1940 the St. Kitts–Nevis Trades and Labour Union was established. In April 1940, workers at the Basseterre sugar factory struck for higher wages, and seventy-five were fired after the strike.[50] In the next decade more strikes marked a growing resentment to economic and political domination by white planters, businessmen, and government administrators. The *Union Messenger* assumed an increasingly militant, even strident, tone in its editorials, orchestrating job actions and anti-planter opinion. A three-month strike on St. Kitts in 1948, marked by sporadic cane fires, was ostensibly against the methods of payment for cane cutters. In reality it reflected the impoverishment and frustration of the island's working class.

In 1937, for the first time, popular local candidates had been elected to the St. Kitts–Nevis Legislative Council, although there were still stringent property and income requirements. Most of these requirements were eased for elections in 1946, and several union leaders then became members of the council.[51]

In October 1950, a rally in Basseterre entitled "Operation Blackburne" protested to the British colonial office: Britain had declined to accept the suggestion that local elected leaders be consulted about the appointment of governors and administrators to Caribbean colonies.

The organizer and leader of the demonstration was Robert L. Bradshaw, a Kittitian labor leader who had been elected to the legislative council in 1946. Bradshaw eventually guided the two islands to associated statehood and became the state's first premier. The prototype of a self-educated West Indian labor leader, he was active during the struggles of the 1930s and he eventually led his country partly through the process of political decolonization. Born in 1916 in St. Paul's village, near Sandy Point, Bradshaw was apprenticed to the Basseterre sugar factory's machine shop in 1932. He was active in the Workers' League and was one of those dismissed after the labor action in 1940. Bradshaw was prominent in ensuing strikes, and, as president of the local union, he testified in London in 1948 before the commission investigating the St. Kitts sugar industry.

After general elections in 1956, Bradshaw became the minister of trade and production for St. Kitts–Nevis–Anguilla, which in that year became a separate colony; the former colony of the Leeward Islands in which St. Kitts–Nevis had been a "presidency" had been abolished. Bradshaw, long an interested participant in possible pan-Caribbean federation, resigned his local position to become the minister of finance of the West Indies Federation, of which the three islands were members until the federation's dissolution in 1962. He then became the chief minister of St. Kitts–Nevis–Anguilla after the elections in 1966. When the three islands became an Associated State with Great Britain on February 27, 1967, he was its first premier.

Bradshaw lived to see his own St. Kitts Labour party government take direct control of the island's sugar-cane industry, whose owners he had battled for more than four decades. The government took over the land in 1975 and the next year assumed control of the central sugar factory, which was renamed the St. Kitts Sugar Manufacturing Corporation. The central factory, now sixty-five years old, was a rundown, ramshackle relic of the bright new sugar mill of 1911 that had been the focal point of St. Kitts's land consolidation during the twentieth century. Like the lands on both islands, it had seen its better days, when it had paid years of handsome profits to the few local estate owners and British stockholders.

Unlike some other West Indian political leaders, Robert Bradshaw had never been a labor migrant himself, but he was acutely aware of the importance of migration to the people of both islands, and he relied heavily on the political endorsement throughout St. Kitts of men who had become village leaders by virtue of their successful migrations and returns. Bradshaw once visited former Kittitians in the Dominican Republic who had remained after the depression years, and during his occasional visits to the United Kingdom he met with emigrant Kittitians.[52]

Upon Bradshaw's death, in 1978, his long-time associate, C. Paul Southwell, was appointed premier. Southwell died suddenly in May 1979, almost exactly one year after Bradshaw. Born in Dominica, Southwell had gone to St. Kitts as a youth and early had assumed an active role in the labor movement. Southwell also worked in the St. Kitts central sugar factory, and in 1947 his proposed dismissal became a cause around which grew a dispute over Basseterre dock workers' wages and a threatened general factory strike.[53] Southwell had been at Bradshaw's side throughout strikes and turmoil, and he was chief minister of the three-island colony when Bradshaw occupied a federal ministership.

Although Robert Bradshaw and other St. Kitts Labour party leaders are fondly remembered by Kittitian cane workers, similar affection was never forthcoming from people on Nevis. During the three decades of Labour party rule, Nevisians considered themselves thoroughly abused. Most residents of the smaller island opposed full political independence in partnership with St. Kitts because they feared they would have no recourse to London if Kittitian politicians mistreated them. The extent of Nevisian discontent was exemplified by the results of the 1975 elections. Candidates of the Nevis Reformation party (NRP) ran on one issue—avowed secession from political union with St. Kitts—and carried 80 percent of the vote on Nevis, althought the Labour party won the general election.[54]

St. Kitts–Nevis political rivalries would have aroused little excitement elsewhere had it not been for the earlier Anguilla affair. Within one month after the associated statehood act of 1967 created the three-island state, Anguilla (population 6,000 and three Dutch islands away from St. Kitts) "rebelled" against St. Kitts by sending the Kittitian police force home. Relations between Anguilla and St. Kitts deteriorated, eventually leading to the intervention by British soldiers in 1969.[55] Reports of the incident by metropolitan news correspondents and novelists, intrigued by what they considered a zany political furor, created anger on St. Kitts, embarrassment in Great Britain, and acrimony about "recolonization" throughout the Caribbean.[56] Anguilla received a new constitution from Great Britain in February 1976 and was reinstated as a crown colony in December 1980. Nevisian politicians have since found valuable predecent in the Anguilla case, insisting it would eventually justify their own secession from St. Kitts.

Nevisian secessionist sentiment has been modified by the election results of February 1980. For the first time, the Labour party—now without the planter class as its traditional political target after government takeover of the sugar industry—has fallen from power. A coalition government has taken its place. Dr. Kennedy Simmonds of St. Kitts, leader of the People's Action Movement (PAM)—a party said to derive most of its support from merchants and shopkeepers in Basseterre—is the state's new premier. A lawyer, Simeon Daniel of the NRP, is the minister of finance. The PAM–NRP coalition may soon lead Kittitians and Nevisians together to full political independence.

Still, an ephemeral political coalition has by no means solved cultural and political problems that exist between peoples of the two islands. In the late summer of 1981, Labour party demonstrations in Basseterre protested against the present government, and there have been dark hints of revolution. Cultural differences between the two islands will not be bridged easily. Further compromise will be necessary before St. Kitts and Nevis can achieve peaceful independence as a two–island state.

The usual explanation for traditional rivalries between St. Kitts and

Nevis dwells on their social and economic differences—the rural proletarian image of the Kittitian versus the perception of the sturdy peasant of Nevis, the two having little in common on which a two-island state could be based. The political troubles between the two islands are by no means isolated instances in the Commonwealth Caribbean, where all of the multi-island states in the aftermath of colonialism have shown similar signs of stress, invariably involving secessionist sentiment from the smaller islands. The most dramatic example of interisland rivalries overshadowing potential pan-Caribbean political alignment was the immediate break-up of the West Indies Federation itself.

The failure of multi-island political union is difficult to explain in light of the common struggles of the region's people. Why, for instance, do interisland rivalries exist among the same people who have together resisted colonial domination for centuries? The term *failure,* first of all, is perhaps better suited to the federation plans of outsiders than it is to local people's unwillingness to accept these plans. Tiny insular societies that appear homogeneous to colonial officials and even other West Indians display much more internal differentiation at closer sight. And in some ways the vociferous wranglings of small Caribbean islanders may be an advertisement of this differentiation and the individuality that colonial planters denied them for centuries. Probably more important in explaining insular rivalry is that it manifests jealous protection of island resources. On Nevis only in this century, and on St. Kitts only in the past decade, the lands have come under the control of the people who have worked them for centuries. Land connotes freedom and signifies at least partial protection against world economic oscillations. Despite its deterioration on both islands, the land is a crucial medium for survival. Individual access to the land, whether owned, rented from an estate owner, or allotted by a planter, has been vital to individual survival on St. Kitts and Nevis for decades. Working local land has been half of the usual survival strategy of the people. The other half has been the world outside, which the men and women of St. Kitts and Nevis have tapped for a century and a half. For people who have only recently gained control over part of their livelihood, the idea of possibly giving it up again—even to fellow West Indians—is difficult to accept.

CHAPTER SEVEN

Migration as Livelihood: Response, Continuity, and Survival

I$_N$ THE LATE TWENTIETH CENTURY the people of St. Kitts and Nevis have finally gained control of their own lands after three and one-half centuries of remarkably persistent plantation domination. The achievement is somewhat hollow because Kittitians and Nevisians have inherited physically impoverished environments. The ecological degradation there is the end result of the history of people and land on the two islands, a combination which is itself a distressing interrelationship. The contemporary inhabitants' ancestors, West African slaves, were first introduced to St. Kitts and Nevis for the express purpose of clearing the protective insular forests to make way for fields of cane and cotton. And the subsequent ecological deterioration of the two islands—typical of most of the Commonwealth Caribbean—can be explained not so much by the fact that people and land have been historically combined, but that they have been separated. Plantation owners, not slaves or workers, have until this century made most land-use decisions in West Indian islands. World markets, not local subsistence needs, have dictated crop identity and production modes. The land has been a vehicle for profit, not husbanded for future generations. This outside control of Caribbean environments, whose biotic communities were usually fragile to begin with, has led directly to their physical degradation. This is the ecological dimension of the Caribbean's singular colonial history. Indigenous West Indians were destroyed upon contact or shortly thereafter, calling for the subsequent importation of "native" workforces. The Caribbean thus lacks an indigenous ecological tradition by which its common people might have been able to mediate and buffer the demands of colonialism. The ancestors of contemporary West Indians never had the luxury of slowly coming to grips with encroaching modernization or seeking refuge in their own traditional economic systems. Unique in the annals of colonialism, Caribbean lands and peoples became immediate adjuncts of larger European economies as they were colonized.

The establishment of postslavery "reconstituted peasantries" in the region partly compensated for this. Where uncontested lands lay idle after slavery or indenture, native groups formed village enclaves in partial refuge against outside economic control. This response has been, not surprisingly, most effective in areas where sizable amounts of land have been available, such as in the highlands of Jamaica, the forest fringes and swamps of Trinidad, and abandoned stretches of the reclaimed littoral of Guyana. A village adaptation was also moderately successful in the Windwards, where limited land areas supported reconstituted peasantries. In contrast, on St. Kitts and Nevis, as we have seen, land was unavailable to freedmen at emancipation. Save for village yard animals and tiny subsistence plots legally controlled by planters, freed slaves on the two islands could muster no local line of economic defense against planter domination. At emancipation, Kittitians and Nevisians thus resorted to a largely extralocal means of response, a livelihood strategy they have now pursued for one and one-half centuries. Only recently on either island has land become available in large enough quantities to support a "peasantry." On Nevis, extralocal economic pursuits still compensate for drought, crop failure, overgrazing, and a host of other ecological uncertainties.[1]

This outside means of livelihood has, of course, involved migration and then, often, return. I do not wish to posit a facile small-to-large West Indian island typology that "explains" human migration rates in the region, but it is important to stress that—for the postemancipation peoples of these small Caribbean islands—oscillating migration has always been a basic economic strategy. By traveling away and returning the people have been able to cope more successfully with the vagaries of man and nature than they would have by staying at home. The small islands of the region are the most vulnerable to environmental and economic uncertainty. Time and again in the Lesser Antilles, droughts, hurricanes, and economic depressions have diminished wages, desiccated provision grounds, and destroyed livestock, and there has been no local recourse to disease or starvation. Men and women of the small West Indian islands have thus been obliged to travel away, to face the stresses and challenges experienced by migrants everywhere. And like migrants everywhere, they have usually considered their travels temporary, partly because they have never been greeted cordially in host communities. In migrating away and then coming back in response to local changes and uncertainties, they have—through remarkable tenacity and persistence—supported viable insular societies.

Natural and man-made hazards often vary significantly in their impact according to one's social standing, and the Caribbean region provides vivid examples of class-susceptibility to these superficially impersonal events. In the West Indies, vulnerability and the likelihood of suffering or being destroyed increases as one descends the social hierarchy, and vulnerability also seems to increase as islands become smaller. A member of the black laboring class on one of the smallest islands is likely to be among those affected most adversely by periodic economic depression or physical disaster. These generalizations are rooted in the region's plantation history. During slavery, for instance, periodic drought or disruptions in shipping led to failed crops and diminished revenues for the planters on St. Kitts and Nevis. The same events often meant famine or death for the slaves. Hazards have exerted roughly similar class selection since emancipation. The upper and middle classes have often departed permanently, as they did in the early twentieth century when hundreds of middle-class shopkeepers, artisans, and their families emigrated to the United States. The strategy of migration and return has more often been adopted by the black "lower classes."

The outside world has, moreover, influenced a class selection on the different kinds of human movements from St. Kitts and Nevis. North American immigration rules have favored particular skills for prospective immigrants, skills often associated with job permanency in the Caribbean and thus the middle class. Skilled workers were also the ones most likely to emigrate to the United Kingdom during the 1950s. In contrast, dark-skinned workers from the two islands, as much because of their skin color as of their lack of permanent job skills, were barred from permanent entry into Bermuda and the Dominican Republic early in this century. Therefore, white and middle-class migration from St. Kitts and Nevis has usually been permanent, while temporary back-and-forth movements from the two islands have been undertaken by the black working classes. The latter are the special people who have successfully migrated and returned, demonstrating livelihood responses elicited by both local and external influences.[2]

Although those who now reside elsewhere often help to sustain the two islands' cultures through their periodic visits and occasional remittances, the islands themselves are now dominated by the descendants of the special people. The middle classes have largely been lost through attrition, their ranks continuously thinned by occasional but permanent migrations. All of the journeys away from St. Kitts and Nevis, whether or not they have ended in return, have influenced those remaining. The local migration traditions began with yearnings for freedom during slavery when migration was next to impossible. Then, at emancipation, men and women of the two islands undertook the bold, successful sailing adventures to Trinidad. These voyages were assertions of freedom that left a lasting cultural imprint on the black population of St. Kitts and Nevis.

The viable migration tradition on the two islands persists because it has been a successful livelihood strategy for individuals in every generation. The earliest exodus to Trinidad is not itself remembered and celebrated by Kittitians or Nevisians, nor are there physical monuments dedicated to the event. But each successive generation of migrants—to Trinidad, Bermuda, Santo Domingo, the United States, the Netherlands Antilles, Great Britain, and the Virgin Islands—have traveled out where and when they can, thereby reinforcing "tradition." Family and community ceremony routinely sustain the importance of migration and return. Christmas parties and carnivals are often celebrations to welcome returning kinsmen and friends. Funerals periodically reunite spatially dispersed families. Money received by mail reminds everyone of the importance of migration. Old men who have earned local prestige by migrating and returning exhort younger men to follow in their footsteps. All of these events are meaningful, since Kittitians and Nevisians must continuously respond to opportunities abroad in order to compensate for the precarious livelihood at home. Learned cultural responses thereby maintain a migration ethos on St. Kitts and Nevis that is not only valuable in coping with contemporary problems but also provides continuity with the past.

Most of the young emigrants today fly from their home islands to work destinations. But sea travel is routine for short trips, and it is a constant reminder of the hazards that had to be overcome in the past. Local fishermen daily risk drowning. Even the voyage between the two islands is always potentially dangerous. On Saturday, August 1, 1970, the scheduled passenger boat *Christena,* badly overloaded with holiday passengers from both islands, sank in the straits on its way from Basseterre to Charlestown. Although 92 survived the tragedy, 227 persons drowned, leaving few families on either island that did not suffer the loss of relatives or loved ones.[3] In grim irony, the celebration of Emancipation Day four generations later by the descendants of Kittitian and Nevisian slaves—who had themselves celebrated their own freedom by sailing away—had ended in a sunken ship and mass drowning.

The distinction between permanent emigration on one hand and return migration on the other is also the distinction between "genuine" migration and what is simply "mobility" or "circulation" in the opinion of a probable majority of scholars who deal with problems of human movements. Among the innumerable and rarely agreed upon definitions of human migration, there is a strong tendency to include a degree of permanency in the movement—the mover must change habitat or address—before the motion is "really" migration. Other familiar ingredients of conventional migration definitions—advancement in social standing, gravitation to bright lights, crossing political boundaries, and getting ahead economically—betray the culture-bound background and bias with which many social scientists, who are either Western or Western-trained, view movements of their fellow human beings.

Another view of non-Western migration, a view that might be loosely termed a neo-Marxist stance, sees these movements as part of changes in world economic structures—shifts and dislocations of peoples inevitably controlled by metropolitan economic forces. Individual migration is not "simply a question of individual choice" but "a manifestation of a world-wide shift from a rural agrarian base to an urban-industrial base in the economies of most Third World countries."[4] In West Africa, for instance, modern labor circulation has been interpreted as a direct product of economic exploitation leading to movements of "labour, not of people."[5] This kind of notion seems to fit St. Kitts, Nevis, and the rest of the Caribbean better; Kittitians and Nevisians, after all, owe their West Indian presence to the abduction of their ancestors by early slave traders, and subsequent migration from and return to the two islands since 1838 has served metropolitan-controlled labor needs. Yet neither the conventional view of "migration as getting ahead" nor concepts derived from dependency theory adequately depict the movements of Kittitians and Nevisians. The city lights of London, Port of Spain, and New York have not always attracted Kittitians and Nevisians, some of whom have been repelled by them. Similarly, the portrayal of labor movements from St. Kitts and Nevis as part of a pathetic human drift from one circum-Caribbean wage source to another gives migrants from the two islands much less credit than they deserve. For instance, their postemancipation journeys away from home have usually been in opposition to—rather than a calculation of—the local planter class.

More important than force-fitting the movements of Kittitians, Nevisians, and other Caribbean migrants into pre-existing definitions is to stress that their migrations and returns are fundamental to local livelihood.

Long-distance movements of West Indians from small islands are, from their standpoint, not so much manifestations of world-wide, macroeconomic shifts or disequilibria as they are ongoing livelihood adaptations to ensure survival on small, worn-out, and precarious resource bases. This is, obviously, stressing a micro-scale approach to human migration, an approach that seeks to understand migrants' behavior in their own right. In contrast, many Western observers, from their socially constrained vantage points as members of uniquely bounded, sedentary, affluent nations, often view the movements of Third World peoples as perturbations, departures from the norm, or "problems" seeking solutions. This attitude is often misleading in categorizing many of the human movements in Third World areas and even becomes a source of conflict when applied to "help" such areas. In the western highlands of Papua New Guinea, for example, traditional subsistence cultivators periodically have coped with plant-killing frost by migrating for relatively brief periods into lowland areas. In 1972 the colonial Australian government, whose interests lay in the "development" of the highlands, stopped the movement.[6] Hill tribes of Southeast Asia, whose shifting agricultural techniques have always called for periodic movement, are now branded as "insurgents" by governments whose heretofore ill-defined political boundaries they inadvertently cross.[7]

Western misconceptions of human livelihood mobility are not confined to underdeveloped areas. All developed countries of North America and Western Europe experience ongoing problems of "illegal" immigration and devise elaborate schemes to monitor and deport unwanted immigrants who enter their countries with the presumed intent of remaining. Yet a number of studies of "illegal" migrants suggest that, from the migrants' viewpoints, the movements are temporary—means of bettering life in their home areas to which they plan eventually to return.[8]

In a more enlightened vein, students of the movements of Pacific islanders have found human mobility there so routine that they now employ the term *circulation* rather than *migration*.[9] Indeed, some Pacific and Australasian specialists seriously doubt the utility of analyzing Third World mobility characteristics in terms of models derived from Western observations. Rather than studying the patterns or artifacts of human migration routes, it has been suggested that a more profitable emphasis might be to see "how people use spatial and temporal strategies to meet their life needs."[10] Such an approach will be no less useful in Caribbean migration studies.

One could possibly dismiss the migrations of Kittitians and Nevisians as simply products of history; the broad strokes of Caribbean colonization and global economic trends are doubtless useful and insightful frameworks within which to view their livelihood migration patterns. Yet it is misleading to portray Caribbean colonial history as outlining a rigid template defining the movements of Kittitians and Nevisians in a predetermined way. It is similarly fruitless to employ the sterile "theoretical" analogs of iron filings, protons, and electrons, or pushes and pulls, because these men and women have struggled and succeeded in skillful, stubborn, and ingenious ways in coping with a world they do not control. The world outside, although indifferent, complex, and often hostile, has presented a variety of external resources that they have exploited successfully and creatively. In short, within the broad guidelines laid out by North Atlantic power holders, the common people of St. Kitts and Nevis have written their own histories.

This is not to suggest that migrants from St. Kitts and Nevis have defied the laws of nature by asserting the glory of the human spirit to emerge victorious against all odds. Kittitians and Nevisians are far too practical and have been too preoccupied with survival to rely on such unproductive sentiment.[11] Neither have they spelled out their migration histories in absurd quests that end in failure. Rather, they have tapped external resources by overcoming natural and social constraints through the imaginative use of their skills and their intelligence, by becoming "temporizer(s) in the interests of survival."[12] The early migration route to Trinidad, although not known personally by the first freedmen to make the trip, led to a reliable source of wages. And migrants from the two islands have thereafter sought work destinations closer to home rather than those far away. In 1900 the Bermuda dockyards, for instance, were relatively accessible to Kittitians and Nevisians, so few of them traveled to the Panama Canal like so many other West Indians. Shortly thereafter, cane cutters found Santo Domingo more accessible than Cuba, and banks and post offices in the Dominican Republic were reliable means of sending money home. During World War II, young men and women from the two islands sought work in Antigua and the Virgin Islands before traveling to Trinidad. In some cases external destinations have been unavailable, and potential migrants from the two islands have gone no place. Pointing out the constraints, influences, and restrictions on Kittitian and Nevisian migrants by no means lessens the individual assertion, courage, and skill that the islanders have displayed in their travels. A successful migrant—

one who travels away, earns and saves money in a foreign place, and then returns—has had to be acutely aware of the pitfalls and the promises along the way.

Black Kittitians and Nevisians first learned the art of survival in adversity during slavery. After emancipation they boldly expanded their livelihood space in order to enhance their survival capacity in the face of continuous pressures and demands by the planters on their home islands. In good times at home—when wages were reasonable—the space contracted. In bad times locally or when greater opportunity existed abroad, it enlarged.

As an ethnically distinct group—and as economic competitors—black workers from the two islands have been continuously scorned and abused abroad as "old islanders" in Trinidad, undifferentiated "coloured West Indians" in Bermuda, "cocolos" in the Dominican Republic, "niggers" in Great Britain, "garots" in the Virgin Islands, and "aliens" everywhere. The ill-will and contempt they have received on the personal level have been similarly forthcoming from government spokesmen, who have condemned them as "nuisances" or "criminal-prone" or simply excess labor saturating the local market, although their presence has, not surprisingly, been tolerated and even encouraged when large amounts of semiskilled labor has been necessary. Afterward, in the eyes of colonial or metropolitan immigration officials, they have epitomized the seemingly aberrant migratory "problems," and they have then been barred or sent away. Yet being strangers in other areas has helped as well as hindered Kittitians and Nevisians. In alien countries they have often undertaken work shunned by locals. Migrants from St. Kitts and Nevis, unmindful of or simply not heeding local convention or propriety, have thus been able to view foreign wage possibilities in a possibly more objective light than have local competitors. Single men and women from the two islands working abroad have tolerated, precisely because of their temporary status, living conditions that they would not consider at home. This toleration has meant more money saved for the home area. All-male barracks life, for instance, is a means of saving rent but palatable only so long as it is acknowledged as temporary.

Migrating men and women from St. Kitts, Nevis, and the other small Caribbean islands have, first and foremost, represented themselves and their families in their travels. Earlier in history their movements were often "illegal" or only semilegal. Kittitians and Nevisians have thus often had no means of recourse to harm or mistreatment abroad other than what they themselves could muster. Passports were not required of migrants from the two islands until the second decade of this century. At about that time nominal consular services became available to them in the Dominican Republic, but this gave migrants from the two islands relatively little support or consolation. Since then, travel documents have proliferated both at home and abroad, conferring greater "legality" on outside travel but also reducing the flexibility of earlier days.

Without a free village community tradition and without formal, institutional government support, the peoples of St. Kitts and Nevis have usually had to rely on informal social networks for subsistence and survival.[13] Kinsmen and friends, not banks or government-sponsored financial institutions, have usually financed travels abroad. Interpersonal relationships—not relations with a wider, bureaucratized government—have thus been crucial for individual Kittitians and Nevisians. The establishment and maintenance of a home area or "group" has been important for individual migrants, but the group has been maintained only through perseverance and tenacity. Although individual migrants have had to be aware of opportunities elsewhere, they have also been called upon to sustain the group at home.

Formal, home-based organization on St. Kitts and Nevis to support and facilitate migration has improved somewhat in the twentieth century. Land (on Nevis) and savings institutions have become available as investment possibilities. A reasonably reliable postal system has, since at least the 1890s, allowed migrating workers to remit money from abroad. Church-based friendly societies have pooled small sums of money since emancipation.

But in the traditional absence of strong formal support for Leeward migrants, the exploitation of a wide livelihood space has demanded much energy of the individual migrants themselves. Unlike, for instance, the formal expansion of colonial or business control over a geographical region, whereby a complex organization acts as a retrieval system to bring goods to a central point, livelihood expansion of Kittitians and Nevisians has called for individual dispersion and return. Of course, Kittitians and Nevisians have none of the control that governments or corporate business interests have, and such expansion has been principally horizontal with little in the way of a vertical organizational component. The household or village level organization for economic sojourns abroad has come from the cumulative migration cultures of the peoples themselves, including the potential prestige earned at home by going away.

The ecologist Paul Colinvaux interprets the Neolithic revolution as "niche expansion," whereby humans came to dominate several levels of the food chain, diverting energy in the form of biological production solely for human use. This broader-based subsistence production for humans as a whole was soon supported by organizational complexity and a social hierarchy designed to produce and allocate food and other goods.[14] This hierarchy, in turn, demanded role specialization among individuals. It may not be improper to suggest that a widened livelihood space at emancipation for black Kittitians and Nevisians was also, in very general terms, a case of niche expansion but without accompanying formal organizational complexity.[15]

As one would expect, greater economic generalization for the black freedmen of St. Kitts and Nevis accompanied the postemancipation widening of most individuals' livelihood space; as new destinations became available, new skills were required of each individual migrant, resulting in the "occupational multiplicity" so common throughout the Commonwealth Caribbean. Individual Kittitians and Nevisians thereby became roving jacks-of-all-trades, like the French handyman or *bricoleur,* performing "a large number of diverse tasks" and making do with "whatever is at hand."[16] Complexity resulting from an enlarged livelihood space came to reside in each individual—not the group.

The individuality and mobility of black migrants from St. Kitts and Nevis are also expressed in family life. Households are traditionally dominated by females, since males have been working abroad much of the time. The "evil" habit of mating and living together without the benefit of formal marriage has been observed (and deplored) time and again by colonial administrators ever since emancipation, and "illegitimacy" is still the rule rather than the exception in contemporary St. Kitts and Nevis. This type of family unit, found throughout the Commonwealth Caribbean, is not simply a social extension of the slavery era but a form adapted to the necessities of migration as livelihood.[17] Ever alert to economic opportunities elsewhere and always ready to travel to them, men and women have been less able to invest the time and energy necessary to maintaining family households than have the peoples of the more sedentary societies of Europe and North America.

Heightened occupational mobility and individuality have been mirrored throughout the Caribbean by the region's diffuse political parochialism. A probable factor in the Caribbean islands' inabilities to agree on forms of federation and mutual aid is the difficulty in maintaining any kind

180

of large-scale group organization. To be sure, there are strong feelings of mutual solidarity among the people of the Caribbean against common foes; the planter-worker dichotomy is perhaps the single most important social fact in the region. Yet group action against plantation owners, beginning in slavery, has always been subordinated to individual livelihood and survival.[18] Even in the Santo Domingo days, when men of all the English-speaking islands became aware of their mutual problems and antagonists, potential group activities against planters either there or at home were always defused every six months by the need to travel away to the other destination. The recurring strike actions manifested by overt mass violence aimed at the St. Kitts planter class in 1834, 1896, 1935, and the 1940s seem to have been more ad hoc, formless group expressions of frustration and despair than articulated, organized reactions to events. Most notably, these disturbances have always occurred when migrants have been forced to remain at home because of a lack of outside job opportunities. In other times, when individuals have traveled elsewhere and returned only on occasion, there has been little opportunity for group action. Mobility and individualism have together exerted an apparent depoliticizing effect.

But at the core of group incoherence lies individual strength. A lack of formal indoctrination, only loosely organized tradition, and a notable absence of group pressure toward individual conformity has increased the propensity for individual adaptability to the many hazards and novel circumstances that a Kittitian or Nevisian has had to face. Similar to other Afro-American societies in which resource opportunities are ephemeral, externally controlled, and always subject to change, individuality and flexibility are advantageous characteristics.[19] Individuals among the migrating black populace of St. Kitts and Nevis have rarely been guided to conform to a narrow band of acceptable behavior, thus allowing them the freedom to respond quickly to perturbation, hazard, or potential reward. Thus unencumbered by stifling or immobilizing dogma, a Kittitian or Nevisian possessed of keen wit and intelligence has thus responded remarkably well to the hazards and complexities of inhabiting a tiny, worn-out, and drought-prone island. In short, in a complicated game with few rules, he has emerged as a master of survival. Through individual mobility, underspecialization, and above all, through an ability to respond to the continuous yet changing pressures brought to bear by both man and nature, the people of St. Kitts and Nevis have rarely prospered, but they have survived and endured.

In coping with an unknown future whose outlines are only dim visions, the mobile livelihood characteristics and general adaptability found in each Kittitian and Nevisian are vital assets. Unlike most members of "advanced" societies, who are specialists in narrow economic pursuits and enmeshed in a complex web of technical and social inelasticity for survival, the migrant laborers of the tiny Caribbean islands are flexible, innovative, and responsive to immediate change. These characteristics that have served them well in the past provide insurance against the unknown though certainly precarious events that lie ahead. In the late twentieth century, in the face of growing world material shortages and ongoing international tensions, gloomy world scenarios are common. Prospects have often been gloomy for small islanders of the West Indies, but in the future as well as the past they will probably find a way to persist and survive. Kittitians, Nevisians, and other small Caribbean islanders, peoples who have so often been victimized by the past, may well be peoples of the future.

Next Christmas season, hundreds—possibly thousands—of former island residents now living abroad will return to St. Kitts and Nevis to spend the holiday season with family, friends, and loved ones. In late December the villages and towns of the two islands will come alive. The temporary presence of so many young and middle-aged people will augment the usual preponderance of grandparents and small children who reside there all year round. To the pleasure of old friends and acquaintances, those who have not been home for years will appear. Boisterous parties and celebrations will be marked by renewed friendships, debts paid and incurred, rum consumed, and greetings exchanged. After the dances, fetes, and carnival celebrations have subsided, family members will exchange stories of life and work abroad. Young men will discuss hardships, layoffs, and discrimination on St. Thomas or St. Croix but also their hopefulness of finding a job next month. Young women will explain that London, Toronto, or New York are not so much better in themselves, but they at least provide better economic prospects than those of certain unemployment at home. Old men, inspired by these conversations, will retell anecdotes about good times and bad in the La Romana days in the cane fields of Santo Domingo. Children who have not yet been abroad will listen attentively. All too soon the holidays will be over. As the visitors depart there will be tearful good-bys and promises to come back. St. Kitts and Nevis will once again return to a slow pace after the young people travel away again as they always have before.

182

Notes

Chapter One

1. *Metropolitan* and *metropole* are used in this book to connote the home territory of a sovereign colonial power (e.g., Britain, France) rather than strictly an urban area.

2. Mintz, *Caribbean Transformations,* 146–56.

3. The terms *freedman* and *freedmen* are used here to indicate those nonwhite West Indians who were not slaves before emancipation and also to describe the former slave population after emancipation. See Handler, *The Unappropriated People,* 5–6.

4. Patterson, "Migration in Caribbean Societies."

5. Lowenthal, "Caribbean Views," 4.

6. Augelli, "The Rimland-Mainland Concept."

7. Howard, "The Vegetation of the Antilles."

8. Sauer, *The Early Spanish Main,* 58–59.

9. Rouse and Allaire, "Caribbean," 465.

10. Price, "Caribbean Fishing and Fishermen."

11. Crosby, *The Columbian Exchange.*

12. Wallerstein, *The Modern World System,* 33.

13. Sauer, *The Early Spanish Main,* 206–7.

14. Sheridan, *Sugar and Slavery,* 107.

15. Harris, "Plants, Animals, and Man."

16. Curtin, "Epidemiology and the Slave Trade," 215.

17. Harris, "Plants, Animals, and Man," 193.

18. Deerr, *The History of Sugar,* I, 166.

19. Pulsipher, "The Cultural Landscape of Montserrat," 103–4.

20. Coke, *A History of the West Indies,* 4–5.

21. Watts, "Persistence and Change in the Vegetation," 101.

22. Goveia, *Slave Society,* 329.

23. Higman, *Slave Population and Economy,* 2.

24. Curtin, *The Atlantic Slave Trade,* 87; Inikori, "Measuring the Atlantic Slave Trade"; Drescher, *Econocide,* 205–13.

25. *Richard Schomburgk's Travels,* 61–62; Handler and Lange, *Plantation Slavery in Barbados,* 95–97.

26. Dirks, "Resource Fluctuations," 134–35.

27. Handler and Lange, *Plantation Slavery in Barbados,* 86–91.

28. Patterson, *The Sociology of Slavery,* 159–64.

29. Higman, *Slave Population and Economy,* 168.

30. Price, ed., *Maroon Societies.*

31. Although many planters opposed it, black military regiments were formed in the British Caribbean before emancipation. See Buckley, *Slaves in Red Coats.*

32. Color and class remain extremely intricate and varied in the Commonwealth Caribbean. In this book, I use the term *black* to indicate persons of solely or predominantly Negroid ancestry and *colored* for persons of mixed ancestry. Lowenthal, *West Indian Societies,* 76–143.

33. Price, "Caribbean Fishing and Fishermen."

34. Hill, *The Impact of Migration,* 206.

35. Eltis, "The Traffic in Slaves."

36. Shyllon, *Black Slaves in Britain.*

37. Burn, *Emancipation and Apprenticeship,* 179.

38. Mintz, *Caribbean Transformations,* 234–36.

39. Farley, "The Rise of Peasantry."

40. Richardson, "Livelihood in Rural Trinidad," 246–47.

41. Thome and Kimbell, *Emancipation in the West Indies,* 46.

42. Light to Colebrooke, St. Christopher Council Minutes, March 1838 to January 1843, entry for June 13, 1840.

43. Richardson, "Freedom and Migration."

44. Roberts, "Emigration from the Island of Barbados," 261.

45. Proudfoot, *Population Movements in the Caribbean,* 14–15.

46. Stephens, "Cotton Growing."

47. Proudfoot, *Population Movements in the Caribbean,* 14.

48. *St. Kitts Daily Express* Jan. 9, 1909.

49. Peach, *West Indian Migration,* 19, 112.

50. Midgett, "West Indian Ethnicity"; Philpott, *West Indian Migration,* 17.

51. Davison, *Black British,* vii.

52. Segal, ed., *Population Policies in the Caribbean,* 219; Chaney and Sutton, eds., *International Migration Review.*

53. Segal, ed., *Population Policies in the Caribbean,* 219.

54. Frucht, "Community and Context"; Hill, *The Impact of Migration;* Carnegie, "Strategic Flexibility"; Midgett, "West Indian Migration and Adaptation"; Myers, "I Love My Home Bad"; Philpott, *West Indian Migration;* Rubenstein, "Black Adaptive Strategies"; Tobias "How You Gonna Keep."

55. Lowenthal, "The Range and Variation."

56. Philpott, "Remittance Obligations," 467.

57. Lowenthal, *West Indian Societies,* 222.

58. Frucht, "Emigration, Remittances, and Social Change."

59. Wilson, *Crab Antics,* 155.

60. Comitas, "Occupational Multiplicity."

61. Philpott, *West Indian Migration,* 101.

62. Lowenthal, *West Indian Societies,* 221.

63. Richardson, "The Overdevelopment of Carriacou," 396.

64. González, "Family Organization" and *Black Carib Household Structure.*

65. Philpott, "The Implications of Migration," 15.

66. Lowenthal and Comitas, "Emigration and Depopulation," 210.

67. Singham, *The Hero and the Crowd,* 153.

68. Proudfoot, *Population Movements in the Caribbean*, 23.
69. Segal, ed., *Population Policies in the Caribbean*, 10–11.
70. Marchione, "Food and Nutrition Policy," 4.
71. Ibid., 6–10.
72. Blaut, et al., "A Study of Cultural Determinants," 405.
73. Philpott, *West Indian Migration*, 80.
74. Berleant-Schiller, "The Social and Economic Role of Cattle," 300.
75. Nietschmann, "Ecological Change, Inflation, and Migration."

Chapter Two

1. Frucht, "Community and Context," 179.
2. "Digest of Statistics no. 9," table 5; Gussler, "Nutritional Implications."
3. "Digest of Statistics no. 9," table 2. E.C. (Eastern Caribbean) $2.70 equals U.S. $1, as of July 1976.
4. Ibid., table 10.
5. "Annual Report of the Chief Medical Officer," 16, 41.
6. Lang and Carroll, *Soil and Land-Use.*
7. Aronoff, "The Cane Cutters."
8. *A Technical Survey of the Sugar Estates of St. Kitts*, I, 13.
9. Data courtesy of William F. Dore.
10. Edwards, "The Agricultural Census 1975," 14.
11. Gussler, "Nutritional Implications," 107.
12. Fernyhough, "The Agro-socio-economic Factors," 13.
13. Figures courtesy of Johnny Clarke, Superintendent of Agriculture, Nevis.
14. "Vendors of Cotton 1975/76."
15. Frucht, "Community and Context," 114.
16. Fernyhough, "The Agro-socio-economic Factors," 35.
17. Figures courtesy of Tom Molyneaux, Central Housing Authority, Basseterre.
18. Edwards, "The Agricultural Census 1975," 14–15, 43–44.
19. Frucht, "Emigration, Remittances, and Social Change," 200.
20. Aronoff, *Psychological Needs*, 31.
21. Data from the Immigration Department, Basseterre police station.
22. *St. Kitts/Nevis Territorial Plan T1*, 20–21.
23. "The Invisibles," *Labour Spokesman*, May 17, 1960.
24. Data from postal remittance records, Basseterre post office. During 1975 the E.C. dollar was worth U.S. $0.47.
25. Data from the Statistical Unit, Government Health Department, Basseterre, St. Kitts.
26. Gussler, "Nutritional Implications," 98.
27. González, "Family Organization," 1273.
28. Aronoff, "The Cane Cutters," 55.
29. Richardson, "Migration and Death Ceremonies."
30. Personal interview by the author, April 12, 1976.

Chapter Three

1. Sheridan, "Africa and the Caribbean," 21.
2. C.O. 152/20, "State of the Leeward Islands," vol. 46, p. 159.
3. Pares, *A West-India Fortune,* 106.
4. Dunn, *Sugar and Slaves,* 320.
5. Pitman, "Slavery on the British West India Plantations," 639.
6. Dirks, "Resource Fluctuations;" Higman, *Slave Population and Economy;* Craton, *Searching for the Invisible Man,* 97–99.
7. Ibid., 166–67.
8. Eltis, "The Traffic in Slaves," 61.
9. Bridenbaugh, *No Peace,* 42–43.
10. Merrill, *The Historical Geography,* 32–35.
11. Branch, "Aboriginal Antiquities in Saint Kitts and Nevis."
12. Goodwin, "The Lesser Antillean Archaic."
13. Jeaffreson, ed., *A Young Squire of the Seventeenth Century,* 322–23.
14. Rochefort, *Histoire naturelle et morale,* 30–40.
15. Dunn, *Sugar and Slaves,* 33.
16. Bridenbaugh, *No Peace,* 249–56.
17. Deerr, *History of Sugar,* II, 279.
18. Bridenbaugh, *No Peace,* 354–55; Dunn, *Sugar and Slaves,* 317.
19. Sheridan, *Sugar and Slavery,* 158.
20. Riddell, *Voyages to the Madeira and Leeward Caribbean,* 22–23.
21. Dunn, *Sugar and Slaves,* 139.
22. Coke, *A History of the West Indies,* 4–5.
23. Pares, *A West-India Fortune,* 78–79, 103, 353.
24. Thomas Woodcock, "Estimate of an Estate," 383.
25. Pares, *A West-India Fortune,* 129.
26. Pitman, "Slavery on the British West India Plantations," 632–33.
27. Goveia, *Slave Society,* 139.
28. Dirks, "Resource Fluctuations," 148–49.
29. Goveia, *Slave Society,* 196, 235–36.
30. Patterson, "Migration in Caribbean Societies," 134.
31. Cox, "The Shadow of Freedom," 166.
32. Abrahams, "Christmas Mummings on Nevis," 120.
33. Goveia, *Slave Society,* 134–35.
34. Cox, "The Shadow of Freedom," 94–95.
35. Dirks, "Resource Fluctuations," 155.
36. Goveia, *Slave Society,* 129.
37. Ibid., 95.
38. Pares, *A West-India Fortune,* 92.
39. Pitman, "Slavery on the British West India Plantations," 626.
40. Furley, "Moravian Missionaries and Slaves," 12.
41. Goveia, *Slave Society,* 167.
42. Wilson, *Crab Antics,* 192.
43. Cox, "The Shadow of Freedom," 112–13.

44. Pitman, "Slavery on the British West India Plantations," 598.
45. Pares, *A West-India Fortune,* 118.
46. Schaw, *Journal of a Lady of Quality,* 129.
47. Price, "Caribbean Fishing," 1378.
48. Coke, *A History of the West Indies,* 47–48.
49. Goveia, *Slave Society,* 228.
50. Cox, "The Shadow of Freedom," 59, 69; Hall, *Five of the Leewards,* 8.
51. Handler, *The Unappropriated People,* 40; Goveia, *Slave Society,* 172–73; Pares, *A West-India Fortune,* 132.
52. Cox, "The Shadow of Freedom," 149, 152.
53. Ibid., 69; Pares, *A West-India Fortune,* 350.
54. Patterson, *The Sociology of Slavery,* 163.
55. Pares, *A West-India Fortune,* 154.
56. Phillips, "A Jamaica Slave Plantation," 238.
57. Goveia, *Slave Society,* 172, 221.
58. Ibid., 147.
59. Eltis, "The Traffic in Slaves," 55.
60. In 1800 the St. Kitts Council was distraught over the many slaves escaping on foreign vessels. Goveia, *Slave Society,* 257.
61. Nevis Assembly Minutes, September 24, 1823–April 24, 1827, entries for October 14, 1824, and March 2, 1826.
62. Handler, *The Unappropriated People,* 39.
63. Hall, *Five of the Leewards,* 25.
64. Frucht, "Emancipation and Revolt."
65. Leeward Islands Duplicate Despatches (St. Kitts Government Archives) 1834/1842, pp. 412, 449–50.
66. Ibid., 401, 403, 407, 409–10, 412.
67. Hall, *Five of the Leewards,* 28.

Chapter Four

1. Leeward Islands Duplicate Despatches 1834/1842, pp. 651–55, 680–81.
2. Beck, "The Bubble Trade".
3. Lowe, *The Codrington Correspondence,* 79.
4. Sturge and Harvey, *The West Indies in 1837,* 9, 15–16.
5. P.P. 1839/XXXVII, "Papers Relative to the West Indies," 161.
6. C.O. 323/53, "Law Officer's Reports," 52.
7. C.O. 884/1/iv/ app. 3, "Opinions of the Law Officers," 8.
8. P.P. 1842/XIII, "Report from the Select Committee on West India Colonies," testimony of George Estridge, 232.
9. C.O. 323/54, "Law Officer's Reports," 587.
10. Nevis, *Blue Book,* 1842, pp. 52–53.
11. P.P. 1839/XXVI, "Papers Relative to the West Indies," 227.
12. Ibid., 197, 203.
13. St. Christopher Assembly Minutes, Jan. 1836 to June 1840, pp. 737–38.
14. P.P. 1839/XXXVII, "Papers Relative to the West Indies," 224.

15. Ibid., 205–6.

16. Ibid., 250.

17. Hall, *Five of the Leewards,* 55.

18. P.P. 1842/XIII, testimony of George Estridge, 229, 231.

19. Wood, *Trinidad in Transition,* 53.

20. Cunningham to Legislative Council St. Kitts, St. Christopher Assembly Minutes, July 1840 to Sept. 1842, pp. 72–73.

21. P.P. 1840/XXIV, "Copy of a Circular Despatch . . . Relative to Immigration into Trinidad," 363.

22. Adamson, *Sugar Without Slaves,* 43.

23. Speech of Lt. Gov. C.J. Cunningham, Dec. 22, 1840 in St. Christopher Council Minutes, Mar. 1838 to Jan. 1843, p. 316.

24. P.P. 1839/XXXVII, "Papers Relative to the West Indies," 289, 302.

25. P.P. 1842/XIII, testimony of George Estridge, 232.

26. P.P. 1842/XXIX, "Papers Relative to Trinidad," 454.

27. Nevis Council Minutes, 1840 to 1844, entry for Sept. 29, 1842.

28. P.P. 1842/XXIX, testimony of Thomas F. Johnston, 453–54.

29. St. Christopher Assembly Minutes, July 1840 to Sept. 1842, pp. 110–14.

30. Adamson, *Sugar Without Slaves,* 44.

31. P.P. 1842/XIII, testimony of Henry Barkly, 204.

32. P.P. 1844/XLVI, "Tables of the Revenue, Population, Commerce, etc. . . . ," 317.

33. P.P. 1839/XXXVII, "Papers Relative to the West Indies," 190.

34. P.P. 1846/XXVIII, "State of the Labouring Population," 295.

35. *The Reports . . . of Her Majesty's Colonial Possessions. Transmitted with the Blue Books for the Year* [hereafter cited as *The Reports] 1854* (London: HMSO 1855), excerpt from "The Report of the Commissioners for Taking the Census . . . ," 154.

36. Martin, *Statistics of the Colonies,* 88, 95.

37. St. Christopher, *Blue Book,* 1843, p. 134; Nevis, *Blue Book,* 1842, p. 130; P.P. 1845/XXXI, "Colonial Population Censuses," 331.

38. P.P. 1842/XIII, testimony of George Estridge, 232.

39. Nevis Council Minutes, 1840 to 1844, entry for Dec. 23, 1843.

40. P.P. 1845/XXXI, "Correspondence Relative to the Labouring Population of the West Indies," 575.

41. P.P. 1842/XXIX, testimony of Dr. Meikleham, 421; Lionel Lee, 450; and Thomas F. Johnston, 454.

42. P.P. 1845/XXXI "Correspondence Relative to the Labouring Population of the West Indies," 480.

43. Wood, *Trinidad in Transition,* 122–25.

44. *The Reports, 1847,* Harris to Grey, 175.

45. P.P. 1846/XXVIII, "State of the Labouring Population," 283.

46. *The Reports, 1854,* "Report of the Commissioners for Taking the Census," 154.

47. P.P. 1862/XXXVI, report from Lt. Gov. Benjamin Pine of St. Kitts, 84.

48. *The Reports, 1853,* reports from President Charles Kenney of Nevis, 149.

49. *The Reports, 1854,* Dr. Thomas H. Cooper's report on cholera in St. Kitts, 139–51.

50. P.P. 1874/XLIV, report by President James S. Berridge of St. Kitts, 128.

51. P.P. 1867/XLVIII, Pine to Carnarvon, 84.

52. P.P. 1877/LIX, report by Alex M. Moir, 101.

53. Nevis Council Minutes, 1840 to 1844, entry for Feb. 18, 1841.

54. Asiegbu, *Slavery and the Politics of Liberation,* 129–30.

55. P.P. 1867/XLVIII, Pine to Carnarvon, 85.

56. *The Reports, 1849,* report by R.J. Mackintosh from St. Kitts, 47.

57. P.P. 1846/XXVIII, report of J.T. Pedder, stipendiary magistrate of St. Kitts, 282; ibid., "Immigration of Labourers into the West Indian Colonies and the Mauritius," 481.

58. *The Reports, 1854,* p. 158.

59. P.P. 1867/XLVIII, Pine to Carnarvon, 85; P.P. 1872/XLII, report by C.M. Eldridge, 143.

60. P.P. 1859, Sess. 2/XXI, "Accounts and Papers Relating to West Indies and Mauritius (Immigration), 31 May–13 Aug. 1859," pp. 151, 155.

61. *The Reports, 1847,* report of Willoughby Shortland in Nevis, 139–40.

62. *The Reports, 1849,* report of R.J. Mackintosh in St. Kitts, 47.

63. P.P. 1870/XLIX, report by Gov. H.W. Cairns of St. Kitts, 88.

64. *The Reports, 1860,* report by Lt. Gov. Benjamin Pine of St. Kitts, 83.

65. P.P. 1867/XLVIII, Pine to Carnarvon, 85.

66. Nevis, *Blue Book,* 1874, no p. number; P.P. 1880/XLVIII, report from Nevis, 199; P.P. 1884–85/LII, report by Acting President C.M. Eldridge of Nevis, 175.

67. P.P. 1843/XXXIII, "Further Papers Relative to the Earthquake in the West Indies," 236.

68. Nevis, *Blue Book,* 1863, p. 60.

69. P.P. 1868–69/XLIII, Mackenzie to Hill, 89.

70. P.P. 1874/XLIV, report by President James S. Berridge of St. Kitts, 127–28.

71. P.P. 1883/XLV, report by Acting President C.M. Eldridge of St. Kitts, 105–6.

72. P.P. 1846/XXVIII, "State of the Labouring Population of the West Indies," 297.

73. *The Reports, 1854,* "Report of Census," 154.

74. P.P. 1857–58/XL, report by Isidore P.L. Dyett, visiting magistrate on Nevis, 123.

75. Beachey, *The British West Indies Sugar Industry,* 104.

76. St. Kitts and Nevis, *Blue Book,* 1871–80.

77. Nevis, *Blue Books,* 1876, p. 127; 1877, p. 156; 1878, no p. number.

78. Nevis, *Blue Book,* 1879, p. 69; St. Kitts, *Blue Book,* 1879, p. 53.

79. *The Reports, 1852,* p. 151.

80. Ramesar, "Patterns of Regional Settlement."

81. *The Reports, 1850,* report by Willoughby Shortland in Nevis, 119.

82. Myers, "I Love My Home Bad," 81.

83. P.P. 1865/XXXVII, Pine to Hill, 90.

84. Hoetink, "The Dominican Republic in the Nineteenth Century," 108.
85. Hall, *Five of the Leewards,* 113–14; Green, *British Slave Emancipation,* 254–55.
86. P.P. 1864/XL, Hill to Rumbold, 92.
87. Nevis, *Blue Book,* 1864, p. 292.
88. P.P. 1857–58/XL, despatch from President Arthur Rumbold of Nevis, 122.
89. P.P. 1862/XXXVI, report of Lt. Gov. Benjamin Pine of St. Kitts, 88.
90. P.P. 1845/XXXI, report of Stipendiary Magistrate Osborn on St. Kitts, 557.
91. P.P. 1857/X, Robinson to Hamilton, 198.
92. P.P. 1862/XXXVI, report of Lt. Gov. Benjamin Pine of St. Kitts, 87.
93. St. Kitts, *Blue Book,* 1881, p. 228.
94. Nevis, *Blue Book,* 1866, p. 279.
95. P.P. 1862/XXXVI, report of Lt. Gov. Benjamin Pine of St. Kitts, 87.
96. Nevis, *Blue Book,* 1862, p. 273.
97. Paton, *Down the Islands,* 50.
98. Leeward Islands, *Blue Book,* 1895, p. Q3.
99. Beachey, *The British West Indies Sugar Industry,* 68, 77.
100. P.P. 1857/X, despatch from President Frederick Seymour on Nevis, 202.
101. Frucht, "Community and Context," 71–72.
102. P.P. 1862/XXXVI, report of Lt. Gov. Benjamin Pine of St. Kitts, 85.
103. P.P. 1857/X, Robinson to Hamilton, 195.
104. P.P. 1862/XXXVI, report of Lt. Gov. Benjamin Pine of St. Kitts, 85.
105. P.P. 1864/XL, Hill to Rumbold, 92.
106. Nevis, *Blue Book,* 1863, p. 278; St. Kitts, *Blue Book,* 1867, p. 233.
107. P.P. 1857/X, despatch by President Frederick Seymour of Nevis, 206.
108. P.P. 1867/XLVIII, Pine to Carnarvon, 85.
109. *The Reports, 1854,* report by President Frederick Seymour of Nevis, 170.
110. P.P. 1857/X, despatch by President Frederick Seymour of Nevis, 206–7.
111. P.P. 1862/XXXVI, report by Lt. Gov. Benjamin Pine of St. Kitts, 88.
112. *The Reports, 1860,* report by Lt. Gov. Benjamin Pine of St. Kitts, 85.
113. Beachey, *The British West Indies Sugar Industry,* ch. 2.
114. P.P. 1892/LV, Smith to Knutsford, 479.
115. Saul, "The British West Indies in Depression," 14–15.
116. Cox to Todd, Mar. 19, 1900, St. Kitts archives.
117. Frucht, "Emigration, Remittances, and Social Change," 196.
118. *Chief of the Bureau of Statistics,* report ending Mar. 31, 1882, pp. 378, 380; report ending June 30, 1887, p. 890.
119. *Saint Christopher Advertiser and Weekly Intelligencer,* Aug. 28, 1894.
120. Letter from W.L.R. Lewis, *St. Kitts Daily Express,* Sept. 30, 1898.
121. C.O. 884/1/iv/ app. 3, pp. 6–7; *St. Christopher Advertiser and Weekly Intelligencer,* Mar. 2, 1896.
122. C.O. 884/1/iv/ app. 3.
123. P.P. 1899/LXI, "Correspondence Relating to the Hurricane on 10th–12th September, 1898," p. 180.
124. P.P. 1901/XLV, "Report on the Blue Book," 45–46.

Chapter Five

1. Saul, "The British West Indies in Depression," 24.
2. Myers, "I Love My Home Bad," 86, quoting Robert Kuczynski, *Demographic Survey of the British Colonial Empire,* III (New York: Oxford University Press, 1953), 6.
3. *St. Kitts Daily Express,* Oct. 20 and 21, 1910.
4. C.O. 884/6/100, "Agreement with Messrs. Pickford and Black to Establish a Steamship Service between Canada and the West Indies," 3–7.
5. "Destitute West Indians in Bermuda," *Saint Christopher Advertiser and Weekly Intelligencer,* June 26, 1894.
6. *Saint Christopher Gazette and Charibbean Courier,* Nov. 23, 1903.
7. P.P. 1901/XLV, annual report for Bermuda for 1900, p. 139.
8. P.P. 1902/LXIV/147; P.P. 1903/XLIII/61; P.P. 1904/LVI/87; P.P. 1905/LI/151, annual reports for Bermuda, 1901–4.
9. Letter from "Several Labourers," *St. Kitts Daily Express,* Oct. 31, 1901.
10. Annual reports for Bermuda, 1901–4.
11. "Several Labourers," *St. Kitts Daily Express,* Oct. 31, 1901.
12. "Bermuda Money," *Saint Christopher Gazette and Charibbean Courier,* Dec. 4, 1903.
13. P.P. 1901/XLV, annual report for Bermuda for 1900, p. 139.
14. Letter from "One Going by Next Canadian Steamer," *St. Kitts Daily Express,* Nov. 7, 1901.
15. P.P. 1904/LVI, annual report for Bermuda for 1903, p. 87.
16. *Saint Christopher Gazette and Charibbean Courier,* Nov. 23, 1903.
17. Letter from "An Artisan," *St. Kitts Daily Express,* Nov. 21, 1901.
18. "The Biter Bitten," *St. Kitts Daily Express,* Nov. 19, 1901.
19. *St. Kitts Daily Express,* Nov. 12, 1901.
20. P.P. 1906/LXXIII/483; P.P. 1907/LIII/197; P.P. 1908/LXVIII/301, annual reports for Bermuda, 1905–7.
21. *St. Kitts Daily Express,* Oct. 29, 1901.
22. Munro, *Intervention and Dollar Diplomacy,* 17.
23. Knight, *The Americans in Santo Domingo,* 139.
24. Much of the information in the next several paragraphs comes from letters from "Un Ingles" to the Bassterre *Union Messenger,* June 15, 1927, and Aug. 24, 1927, and from interviews with older men of the two islands. I am particularly indebted to Edgar S. Bridgewater for an interview in Basseterre, Feb. 12, 1976.
25. *St. Kitts Daily Express,* Nov. 18, 1912.
26. Knight, *The Americans in Santo Domingo,* 137.
27. Ibid., 157, 188.
28. "Notice. Santo Domingo Labourers," *St. Kitts Daily Express,* Jan. 13, 1913.
29. Letter from "Un Ingles," *Union Messenger,* June 15, 1927.
30. Knight, *The Americans in Santo Domingo,* 144.
31. "On the Crest of a Crime Wave," *Union Messenger,* Sept. 26, 1923.

32. "The Emigrant Labourer's Protection Act, 1924," *Union Messenger*, Apr. 2, 1924.

33. "Editorial" on the Emigrants Protection Act, no. 10 of 1929, *Union Messenger*, Jan. 7, 1931.

34. "Destitute West Indians," *Union Messenger*, May 15, 1935.

35. *St. Christopher Advertiser and Weekly Intelligencer*, July 17, 1900.

36. Philpott, *West Indian Migration*, 81.

37. Reid, *The Negro Immigrant*, 239–40.

38. Interview, May 23, 1976.

39. *St. Kitts Daily Express*, June 25, 1909.

40. Reid, *The Negro Immigrant*, 12.

41. "A Reminder," *Union Messenger*, Apr. 22, 1925.

42. Reid, *The Negro Immigrant*, 42.

43. "Hard Times," *Saint Christopher Gazette and Charibbean Courier*, Sept. 14, 1903.

44. Frucht, "Emigration, Remittances, and Social Change," 198.

45. *St. Kitts Daily Express*, June 21, 1909.

46. DuBois, "Inter-racial Implications," 92; Weatherly, "The West Indies as a Sociological Laboratory," 299.

47. "America, the Land of Opportunities," *Union Messenger*, Jan. 2, 1924.

48. Reid, *The Negro Immigrant*, 58–59.

49. "St. Kitts C.C. Champions of 1924 in New York County Cricket League," *Union Messenger*, Feb. 11, 1925.

50. "Great Throng at Casino Protests B.W.I. Peonage," *Union Messenger*, June 25, 1924.

51. Reid, *The Negro Immigrant*, 32–33, 289.

52. *Union Messenger*, Dec. 6, 1937.

53. Reid, *The Negro Immigrant*, 66.

54. St.-Johnston, *From a Colonial Governor's Note-Book*, 121–22.

55. Leeward Islands, *Blue Book*, 1901–2, p. X2.

56. *A Technical Survey of the Sugar Estates of St. Kitts*, I, 6.

57. "Estates and Labour," *Union Messenger*, June 27, 1923.

58. Leeward Islands, *Blue Book*, 1901–2, p. X2.

59. *Union Messenger*, Sept. 3, 1924; Leeward Islands, *Blue Book*, 1924, sect. 22, p. 11.

60. "Sea Island Cotton Crisis," *Union Messenger*, Sept. 7, 1927.

61. "Nevis as We See It," *Union Messenger*, Jan. 14, 1925.

62. Frucht, "Community and Context," 77.

63. Ibid., 79–80; Leeward Islands, *Blue Book*, 1934, sect. 22, p. 2.

64. G.H. King, "Nevis and Her Possibilities," *Saint Christopher Gazette and Charibbean Courier*, Feb. 3, 1908.

65. *Saint Christopher Gazette and Charibbean Courier*, Aug. 22, 1904.

66. Leeward Islands, *Blue Book*, 1930, sect. 22, p. 11.

67. "Land Settlement in St. Kitts," *Union Messenger*, Dec. 10, 1938.

68. "Our Returned Labourers," *Union Messenger*, Aug. 3, 1932.

69. *Report of the Commission Appointed to Enquire into The Organisation of the Sugar Industry of St. Christopher,* 2, 6–10, 64–5.

70. R.E. Kelsick, "Soil Erosion," *Union Messenger,* May 14, 1938.

71. *Report of the Commission . . . Sugar Industry of St. Christopher,* 8.

72. "Labourers on Strike," *Saint Christopher Gazette and Charibbean Courier,* Jan. 23, 1905, and Feb. 1, 1905.

73. Auty, "Scale Economies and Plant Vintage," 156–57.

74. *Union Messenger,* Feb. 9, 1935.

75. "Letter of Appreciation," *Union Messenger,* Feb. 28, 1935.

76. "Despatch from the Governor of the Leeward Islands to the Secretary of State for the Colonies," *Union Messenger,* Aug. 17, 1935.

77. "Immigrants Deported from the Dominican Republic," *Union Messenger,* Apr. 8, 1935.

Chapter Six

1. P.P. 1938–39/XV "Labour Conditions in the West Indies," 826–30, 860–61.

2. P.P. 1951–52/XXIV "British Dependencies in the Caribbean and North Atlantic 1939–1952," p. 167.

3. "Industrial Relations Report (As of December 31, 1948)," Lago Oil and Transport Company of Aruba.

4. "Emigration to Netherlands Island, Aruba," *Union Messenger,* Apr. 8, 1938; "Emigration to Curaçao," *Union Messenger,* May 9, 1938.

5. Singham, *The Hero and the Crowd,* 153.

6. *Union Messenger,* Dec. 1, 1944.

7. Leeward Islands, *Blue Book,* 1945, sect. 15, p. 4, and sect. 33, p. 5.

8. *Union Messenger,* Sept. 14, 1938.

9. Prest, *War Economics,* 263.

10. Proudfoot, *Population Movements in the Caribbean,* 23.

11. P.P. 1944–45/VI, West India Royal Commission Report, 413–14.

12. "Government Planning Reign of Tyranny against Labour," *Union Messenger,* Oct. 8, 1949.

13. Banton, "Recent Migration."

14. Data from local travel agents in Basseterre showed the following numbers emigrating to Great Britain from St. Kitts, Nevis, and Anguilla combined. 1955: 891; 1956: 717; 1957: 1,095; 1958: 1,231; 1959: 1,410; 1960:2,472; 1961: 3,533; 1962: 2,800; 1963: 312; 1964: 251.

15. "74 Leave for U.K.," *Democrat,* Apr. 23, 1960.

16. Lowenthal, *West Indian Societies,* 224–25.

17. "Acute Unemployment Problem in U.K.," *Labour Spokesman,* Mar. 10, 1960.

18. Patterson, *Immigration and Race Relations in Britain,* ch. 2.

19. Mills, "The Development of Alternative Farming Systems," 64.

20. "U.K. or U.S.A.?" *Democrat,* Apr. 22, 1961.

21. "The Invisibles," *Labour Spokesman,* May 17, 1960.
22. Foner, *Jamaica Farewell,* 76–77, 225.
23. Dominguez, *From Neighbor to Stranger,* 71.
24. Foner, "West Indians in New York City and London," 293.
25. Figures from the Immigration Department, Basseterre Police Department.
26. Henry, "The West Indian Domestic Scheme in Canada."
27. "Agents Have Hard Times Checking Alien Influx in U.S. Virgin Islands," *Union Messenger,* Oct. 21 and Nov. 11–12 and 15, 1949.
28. "Alien Workers in the Island of St. Thomas United States' Virgin Islands," *Labour Spokesman,* July 17, 1960.
29. Lewis, *The Virgin Islands,* 220; Green, "Social Networks in St. Croix," 83.
30. "Annual Statistical Report," St. Thomas, Virgin Islands, 2.
31. Figures from Immigration Department, Basseterre Police Department.
32. Dirks, "Ethnicity and Ethnic Group Relations."
33. Lewis, *The Virgin Islands,* 218.
34. De Albuquerque and McElroy, "West Indian Migration," 36.
35. Crist, "Static and Emerging Cultural Landscapes."
36. "Land Settlement in St. Kitts," *Union Messenger,* Dec. 10, 1938.
37. *Report of the Commission . . . Sugar Industry of St. Christopher,* 10.
38. P.P. 1944–45/VI, West India Royal Commission Report, 106.
39. *Report of the Agricultural Department, St. Kitts, Nevis and Anguilla. . .* 1950, p. 16.
40. "Heavy Rain in St. Kitts," *Union Messenger,* Sept. 6, 1949.
41. Lang and Carroll, *Soil and Land Use Surveys,* 15.
42. "Effect of Drought," *Union Messenger,* May 14, 1947.
43. *Report of the Commission . . . Sugar Industry of St. Christopher,* 3.
44. Mills, "The Development of Alternative Farming Systems."
45. Ibid., 102.
46. Bai, "The Dialectics of Change," ch. 5.
47. *A Technical Survey of the Sugar Estates of St. Kitts,* 11.
48. Frucht, "Community and Context," 179.
49. Watts, "From Sugar Plantation to Open-Range Grazing."
50. Joseph N. France, "From Apprentice to Premier," *Labour Spokesman,* May 27, 1978.
51. Universal suffrage came to St. Kitts and Nevis in 1952, although ultimate political authority still rested with the appointed British governor.
52. "Mr. Robert Bradshaw, Premier of St. Kitts-Nevis-Anguilla," *The Times* (London), May 25, 1978.
53. *Union Messenger,* Basseterre, Mar. 19, 1947.
54. Richardson, "St. Kitts-Nevis."
55. Clarke, "Political Fragmentation."
56. "Britain's Bay of Piglets," *Time,* Mar. 28, 1969; Westlake, *Under an English Heaven.*

Chapter Seven

1. Frucht, "Caribbean Social Type."
2. Frucht, "Emigration, Remittances, and Social Change."
3. *Report on the Circumstances Surrounding the Sinking of the M.V. "Christena."*
4. Safa, "Introduction," 1.
5. Amin, "Introduction," 66.
6. Waddell, "How the Enga Cope with Frost."
7. Geddes, *Migrants of the Mountains.*
8. Piore, *Birds of Passage,* 50–51.
9. Bedford, *New Hebridean Mobility.*
10. Ward, "Migration, Myth, and Magic," 120.
11. Meeker, "Picaresque Science and Human Ecology."
12. Abu-Lughod, "Comments," 205.
13. Graves and Graves, "Adaptive Strategies in Urban Migration," 132–35.
14. Colinvaux, *Why Big Fierce Animals Are Rare,* ch. 18.
15. Dirks, "Resource Fluctuations."
16. Lévi-Strauss, *The Savage Mind,* 17.
17. González, *Black Carib Household Structure.*
18. Perhaps this is why biographical studies of individuals have portrayed Caribbean cultures so vividly: Beck, *To Windward of the Land;* Levine, *Benjy Lopez;* Mintz, *Worker in the Cane;* Wilson, *Oscar.*
19. Dirks, "Networks, Groups, and Adaptation," 568; Whitten and Szwed, "Introduction," 44–45.

Bibliography

Newspaper sources are cited in the notes. Local newspapers from St. Kitts and Nevis are in the archives at the government headquarters in Basseterre, St. Kitts: *The Democrat, The Labour Spokesman, The Saint Christopher Advertiser and Weekly Intelligencer, The Saint Christopher Gazette and Charibbean Courier, The St. Kitts Daily Express,* and *The Union Messenger.* Early council and assembly minutes from both islands are also in the St. Kitts archives. The British Colonial Office and the British Sessional Papers or Parliamentary Papers are abbreviated in the notes as C.O. and P.P., respectively.

Abrahams, Roger D. "Christmas Mummings on Nevis," *North Carolina Folklore Journal* 21 (1973):120–31.

Abu-Lughod, Janet. "Comments: The End of the Age of Innocence in Migration Theory." In Brian M. DuToit and Helen I. Safa, eds., *Migration and Urbanization,* 201–6. The Hague: Mouton, 1975.

Adamson, Alan H. *Sugar Without Slaves: The Political Economy of British Guiana, 1838–1904.* New Haven: Yale Univ. Press, 1972.

Amin, Samir. "Introduction," in Amin. ed., *Modern Migrations in Western Africa,* London: Oxford Univ. Press, 1974.

"Annual Report of the Chief Medical Officer and Registrar General for the Year Ending 31st December 1972," St. Kitts-Nevis-Anguilla. Mimeographed.

"Annual Statistical Report," Alien Certification Office, St. Thomas, U.S.V.I., 1976. Mimeographed.

Aronoff, Joel. "The Cane Cutters of St. Kitts," *Psychology Today* 4 (1971):53–55.

———. *Psychological Needs and Cultural Systems: A Case Study.* Princeton, N.J.: Van Nostrand, 1967.

Asiegbu, Johnson U.J. *Slavery and the Politics of Liberation, 1787–1861: A Study of Liberated African Emigration and British Anti-Slavery Policy.* New York: Africana Publishing Corp., 1969.

Augelli, John P. "The Rimland-Mainland Concept of Culture Areas in Middle America." *Annals of the Association of American Geographers* 52 (1962):119–29.

Auty, R.M. "Scale Economies and Plant Vintage: Toward a Factory Classification." *Economic Geography* 51 (1975):150–62.

Bai, David H. "The Dialectics of Change in Plantation Society: Production Organization and Politics in St. Kitts, West Indies." Ph.D. diss., Univ. of Alberta, 1972.

Banton, Michael. "Recent Migration from West Africa and the West Indies to the United Kingdom." *Population Studies* 7 (1953): 2–13.

Beachey, R.W. *The British West Indies Sugar Industry in the Late 19th Century.* 2d ed. Westport, Conn.: Greenwood Press, 1978. (Original edition 1957.)

Beck, Horace. "The Bubble Trade." *Natural History* 85 (Nov. 1976): 38–47.

Beck, Jane C. *To Windward of the Land: The Occult World of Alexander Charles.* Bloomington: Indiana Univ. Press, 1979.

Bedford, R.D. *New Hebridean Mobility: A Study of Circular Migration.* Canberra, Australia: Research School of Pacific Studies, 1973.

Berleant-Schiller, Riva. "The Social and Economic Role of Cattle in Barbuda." *Geographical Review* 67 (1977): 299–309.

Blaut, James M., et al. "A Study of Cultural Determinants of Soil Erosion and Conservation in the Blue Mountains of Jamaica: Progress Report." *Social and Economic Studies* 8 (1959): 403–20.

Branch, C.W. "Aboriginal Antiquities in Saint Kitts and Nevis." *American Anthropologist* 9 (1907): 315–33.

Bridenbaugh, Carl, and Roberta Bridenbaugh. *No Peace Beyond the Line: The English in the Caribbean, 1624–1690.* New York: Oxford Univ. Press, 1972.

Buckley, Roger Norman. *Slaves in Red Coats: The British West India Regiments,* New Haven: Yale Univ. Press, 1979.

Burn, W.L. *Emancipation and Apprenticeship in the British West Indies.* London: Jonathan Cape, 1937.

Carnegie, Charles. "Strategic Flexibility and the Study of Caribbean Migration." Paper presented at meetings of the Caribbean Studies Association, Curaçao, Netherlands Antilles, May 1980.

Chaney, Elsa M., and Constance L. Sutton, eds. *International Migration Review* 13 (Summer 1979). Special edition on Caribbean migration to New York.

Chief of the Bureau of Statistics. Quarterly reports ending March 31, 1882, and June 30, 1887, Washington, D.C.: Government Printing Office.

Clarke, Colin G. "Political Fragmentation in the Caribbean: The Case of Anguilla." *Canadian Geographer* 15 (1971): 13–29.

Coke, Thomas. *A History of the West Indies.* London: Thomas Coke, 1811.

Colinvaux, Paul. *Why Big Fierce Animals Are Rare: An Ecologist's Perspective,* Princeton, N.J.: Princeton Univ. Press, 1978.

Comitas, Lambros. "Occupational Multiplicity in Rural Jamaica." In Comitas and David Lowenthal, eds. *Work and Family Life: West Indian Perspectives,* 157–73. New York: Doubleday, 1973.

Cox, Edward L. "The Shadow of Freedom: Freedmen in the Slave Societies of Grenada and St. Kitts, 1763–1833." Ph.D. diss., Johns Hopkins Univ., 1977.

Craton, Michael. *Searching for the Invisible Man: Slaves and Plantation Life in Jamaica.* Cambridge, Mass.: Harvard Univ. Press, 1978.

Crist, Raymond E. "Static and Emerging Cultural Landscapes on the Islands of St. Kitts and Nevis, B.W.I." *Economic Geography* 25 (1949): 134–45.

Crosby, Alfred W. *The Columbian Exchange: Biological and Cultural Conse-*

quences of 1492. Westport, Conn.: Greenwood Press, 1972.

Curtin, Philip D. *The Atlantic Slave Trade: A Census.* Madison: Univ. of Wisconsin Press, 1969.

————. "Epidemiology and the Slave Trade." *Political Science Quarterly* 83 (1968): 190–216.

Davison, R.B. *Black British: Immigrants to England.* London: Oxford Univ. Press, 1966.

De Albuquerque, Klaus, and Jerome L. McElroy. "West Indian Migration to the United States Virgin Islands: Demographic Impacts and Socio-Economic Consequences." Paper presented at meetings of the Caribbean Studies Association, St. Thomas, U.S.V.I., May 1981.

Deerr, Noel. *The History of Sugar.* London: Chapman and Hall Ltd., 1949.

"Digest of Statistics no. 9, January–December, 1973." St. Kitts: Statistical Dept. Mimeographed.

Dirks, Robert. "Ethnicity and Ethnic Group Relations in the British Virgin Islands." *The New Ethnicity: Perspectives from Ethnology,* 95–109. Proceedings of the American Ethnological Society, 1973. St. Paul, Minn.: West Publishing, 1975.

————. "Networks, Groups, and Adaptation in an Afro-Caribbean Community." *Man* 7 (1972): 565–85.

————. "Resource Fluctuations and Competitive Transformations in West Indian Slave Societies." In Charles D. Laughlin and Ivan A. Brady, eds., *Extinction and Survival in Human Populations,* 122–80. New York: Columbia Univ. Press, 1978.

Dominguez, Virginia R. *From Neighbor to Stranger: The Dilemma of Caribbean Peoples in the United States.* Antilles Research Program, Yale Univ., Occasional Papers no. 5, 1975.

Drescher, Seymour. *Econocide: British Slavery in the Era of Abolition.* Pittsburgh: Univ. of Pittsburgh Press, 1977.

DuBois, W.E.B. "Inter-racial Implications of the Ethiopian Crisis." *Foreign Affairs* 14 (October 1935): 82–92.

Dunn, Richard S. *Sugar and Slaves: The Rise of the Planter Class in the English West Indies, 1624–1713.* Chapel Hill: Univ. of North Carolina Press, 1972.

Edwards, Cecil H.R. "The Agricultural Census, 1975, St. Kitts-Nevis-Anguilla." Basseterre: Dept. Agriculture, 1976. Mimeographed.

Eltis, David. "The Traffic in Slaves between the British West Indian Colonies, 1807–1833." *Economic History Review* 25, 2d series (1972): 55–64.

Farley, Rawle. "The Rise of Peasantry in British Guiana." *Social and Economic Studies* 2 (1954): 87–103.

Fernyhough, D. "The Agro-socio-economic Factors Influencing the Planning of Change in Agriculture in St. Kitts–Nevis: The Effects of History and Prospects for the Future." M.S. thesis, Univ. of Reading, England, 1974.

Foner, Nancy. *Jamaica Farewell: Jamaican Migrants in London.* Berkeley: Univ. of California Press, 1978.

————. "West Indians in New York City and London: A Comparative Analysis." *International Migration Review* 13 (1979): 284–97.

Frucht, Richard. "Caribbean Social Type: Neither 'Peasant' nor 'Proletarian.' " *Social and Economic Studies* 16 (1967): 295–300.

———. "Community and Context in a Colonial Society: Social and Economic Change in Nevis, West Indies." Ph.D. diss., Brandeis Univ., 1966.

———. "Emancipation and Revolt in the West Indies: St. Kitts, 1834." *Science and Society* 34 (1975): 199–214.

———. "Emigration, Remittances, and Social Change: Aspects of the Social Field of Nevis, West Indies." *Anthropologica* 10 (1968): 193–208.

Furley, Oliver W. "Moravian Missionaries and Slaves in the West Indies." *Caribbean Studies* 5 (July 1965): 3–16.

Geddes, W.R. *Migrants of the Mountains: The Cultural Ecology of the Blue Miao (Hmong Njua) of Thailand.* Oxford: Clarendon Press, 1976.

González, Nancie L. Solien. *Black Carib Household Structure: A Study of Migration and Modernization.* Seattle: Univ. of Washington Press, 1969.

———. "Family Organization in Five Types of Migratory Wage Labor." *American Anthropologist* 63 (1961): 1264–80.

Goodwin, R. Christopher. "The Lesser Antillean Archaic: New Data from St. Kitts." *Journal of the Virgin Island Archaeological Society* 5 (1978): 6–16.

Goveia, Elsa V. *Slave Society in the British Leeward Islands at the End of the Eighteenth Century.* New Haven: Yale Univ. Press, 1965.

Graves, Nancy B., and Theodore D. Graves. "Adaptive Strategies in Urban Migration." *Annual Review of Anthropology* 3 (1974): 117–51.

Green, James W. "Social Networks in St. Croix, United States' Virgin Islands." Ph.D. diss., Univ. of Washington at Seattle, 1972.

Green, William A. *British Slave Emancipation: The Sugar Colonies and the Great Experiment, 1830–1865.* Oxford: Clarendon Press, 1976.

Gussler, Judith D. "Nutritional Implications of Food Distribution Networks in St. Kitts." Ph.D. diss., Ohio State Univ., 1975.

Hall, Douglas. *Five of the Leewards, 1834–1870: The Major Problems of the Post-Emancipation Period in Antigua, Barbuda, Montserrat, Nevis and St. Kitts.* Barbados: Caribbean Universities Press, 1971.

Handler, Jerome S. *The Unappropriated People: Freedmen in the Slave Society of Barbados.* Baltimore: Johns Hopkins Univ. Press, 1974.

Handler, Jerome S., and Frederick W. Lange. *Plantation Slavery in Barbados: An Archaeological and Historical Investigation.* Cambridge, Mass.: Harvard Univ. Press, 1978.

Harris, David R. "Plants, Animals, and Man in the Outer Leeward Islands, West Indies: An Ecological Study of Antigua, Barbuda, and Anguilla." Ph.D. diss., Univ. of California, Berkeley, 1963.

Henry, Frances. "The West Indian Domestic Scheme in Canada." *Social and Economic Studies* 17 (1968): 83–91.

Higman, B.W. *Slave Population and Economy in Jamaica, 1807–1834.* Cambridge: Cambridge Univ. Press, 1976.

Hill, Donald R. *The Impact of Migration on the Metropolitan and Folk Society of Carriacou, Grenada.* New York: Anthropological Papers of the American Museum of Natural History 54, no. 2 (1977): 191–391.

Hoetink, Harmannus. "The Dominican Republic in the Nineteenth Century: Some Notes on Stratification, Immigration, and Race." In Magnus Mörner, ed., *Race and Class in Latin America*. New York: Columbia Univ. Press, 1970.

Howard, Richard A. "The Vegetation of the Antilles." In Alan Graham, ed., *Vegetation and Vegetational History of Northern Latin America*, 1–38. Amsterdam: Elsevier, 1973.

"Industrial Relations Report (As of December 31, 1948)." Lago Oil and Transport Company of Aruba. Mimeographed.

Inikori, J.E. "Measuring the Atlantic Slave Trade: An Assessment of Curtin and Anstey." *Journal of African History* 17 (1976): 197–223.

Jeaffreson, John Cordy, ed. *A Young Squire of the Seventeenth Century: From the Papers of Christopher Jeaffreson*. London: Blackett, 1808.

Knight, Melvin M. *The Americans in Santo Domingo*. New York: Vanguard Press, 1928.

Lang, D.M., and D.M. Carroll. *Soil and Land-Use Surveys no. 16, St. Kitts and Nevis*. Trinidad: University of the West Indies, Imperial College of Tropical Agriculture, 1966.

Levine, Barry B. *Benjy Lopez: A Picaresque Tale of Emigration and Return*. New York: Basic Books, 1980.

Lévi-Strauss, Claude. *The Savage Mind*. Chicago: Univ. of Chicago Press, 1962.

Lewis, Gordon K. *The Virgin Islands: A Caribbean Lilliput*. Evanston, Ill.: Northwestern Univ. Press, 1972.

Lowe, Robson. *The Codrington Correspondence, 1743–1851*. London: Robson Lowe, 1951.

Lowenthal, David. "Caribbean Views of Caribbean Land." *Canadian Geographer* 5 (1961): 1–9.

———. "The Range and Variation of Caribbean Societies." *Annals of the New York Academy of Sciences* 83 (1960): 786–95.

———. *West Indian Societies*. New York: Oxford Univ. Press, 1972.

Lowenthal, David, and Lambros Comitas. "Emigration and Depopulation: Some Neglected Aspects of Population Geography." *Geographical Review* 52 (1962): 195–210.

Marchione, Thomas J. "Food and Nutrition Policy in Self-Reliant National Development." Paper presented at the American Anthropological Meeting, Washington, D.C., 1976.

Martin, Robert Montgomery. *Statistics of the Colonies of the British Empire*. London: Allen, 1839.

Meeker, Joseph W. "Picaresque Science and Human Ecology." *Human Ecology* 5 (1977): 155–59.

Merrill, Gordon C. *The Historical Geography of St. Kitts and Nevis, West Indies*. Mexico City: Instituto Panamericano de Geografia e Historia, 1958.

Midgett, Douglas K. "West Indian Ethnicity in Great Britain." In Helen I. Safa and Brian M. Du Toit, eds., *Migration and Development*, 57–81. The Hague: Mouton, 1975.

———. "West Indian Migration and Adaptation in St. Lucia and London." Ph.D. diss., Univ. of Illinois, 1977.

Mills, Frank L. "The Development of Alternative Farming Systems and Prospects for Change in the Structure of Agriculture in St. Kitts, West Indies." Ph.D. diss., Clark Univ., 1974.

Mintz, Sidney W. *Caribbean Transformations.* Chicago: Aldine, 1974.

———. *Worker in the Cane: A Puerto Rican Life History.* New Haven: Yale Univ. Press, 1960.

Munro, Dana G. *Intervention and Dollar Diplomacy in the Caribbean, 1901–1921.* Princeton, N.J.: Princeton Univ. Press, 1964.

Myers, Robert Amory. "I Love My Home Bad, But . . . : The Historical and Contemporary Context of Migration on Dominica, West Indies." Ph.D. diss., Univ. of North Carolina, 1976.

Naipaul, V.S. *The Middle Passage.* London: Andre Deutsch, 1962.

Nietschmann, Bernard. "Ecological Change, Inflation, and Migration in the Far West Caribbean." *Geographical* Review 69 (1979): 1–24.

1970 Population Census of the Commonwealth Caribbean, Jamaica: University of the West Indies, 1973.

Oliver, Vere Langford. *Caribbeana.* London: Mitchell, Hughes, and Clark, 1912.

Pares, Richard. *A West-India Fortune.* 2d ed. Hamden, Conn.: Archon Books, 1968. (Original edition 1950.)

Paton, William A. *Down the Islands: A Voyage to the Caribees.* London: Kegan Paul, Trench & Co., 1888.

Patterson, Orlando. "Migration in Caribbean Societies: Socioeconomic and Symbolic Resource." In William H. McNeill and Ruth S. Adams, eds., *Human Migration: Patterns and Policies,* 106–45. Bloomington: Indiana Univ. Press, 1978.

———. *The Sociology of Slavery: An Analysis of the Origins, Development, and Structure of Negro Slave Society in Jamaica.* London: MacGibbon & Kee, 1967.

Patterson, Sheila. *Immigration and Race Relations in Britain, 1960–1967.* London: Oxford Univ. Press, 1969.

Peach, Ceri. *West Indian Migration to Britain: A Social Geography.* London: Oxford Univ. Press, 1968.

Phillips, Ulrich Bonnell. *The Slave Economy of the Old South.* Baton Rouge: Louisiana State Univ. Press, 1968.

Philpott, Stuart B. "The Implications of Migration for Sending Societies: Some Theoretical Considerations." *Migration and Anthropology,* 9–20. Proceedings of the 1970 Annual Spring Meeting of the American Ethnological Society.

———. "Remittance Obligations: Social Networks and Choice among Montserratian Migrants in Britain." *Man* 3 (1968): 465–76.

———. *West Indian Migration: The Montserrat Case.* London: Athlone Press, 1973.

Piore, Michael J. *Birds of Passage: Migrant Labor and Industrial Societies.* New York: Cambridge Univ. Press, 1979.

Pitman, Frank Wesley. "Slavery on the British West India Plantations in the

Eighteenth Century." *Journal of Negro History* 11 (1926): 584–668.

Prest, A.R. *War Economics of Primary Producing Countries,* Cambridge: Cambridge Univ. Press, 1948.

Price, Richard. "Caribbean Fishing and Fisherman: A Historical Sketch." *American Anthropologist* 68 (1966): 1363–83.

Price, Richard, ed. *Maroon Societies: Rebel Slave Communities in the Americas.* Garden City, N.Y.: Doubleday, 1973.

Proudfoot, Malcolm J. *Population Movements in the Caribbean.* Port of Spain, Trinidad: Kent House, 1950.

Pulsipher, Lydia M. "The Cultural Landscape of Montserrat, West Indies, in the Seventeenth Century: Early Environmental Consequences of British Colonial Development." Ph.D. diss., Southern Illinois Univ., 1977.

Ramesar, Marianne D. "Patterns of Regional Settlement and Economic Activity by Immigrant Groups in Trinidad: 1851–1900." *Social and Economic Studies* 25 (1976): 187–215.

Reid, Ira De A. *The Negro Immigrant: His Background, Characteristics, and Social Adjustment, 1899–1937.* New York: Columbia Univ. Press, 1939.

Report of the Agricultural Department, St. Kitts, Nevis and Anguilla for the Year Ended 31st December 1950. Antigua: Government Printing Office, 1952.

Report of the Commission Appointed to Enquire into the Organisation of the Sugar Industry of St. Christopher. London: Crown Agents for the Colonies, 1949.

Report on the Circumstances Surrounding the Sinking of the M.V. "Christena". St. Kitts: Government Printery, 1970.

Richard Schomburgk's Travels in British Guiana, 1840–1844. Trans. Walter E. Roth. Georgetown, British Guiana: "Daily Chronicle" Office, 1922.

Richardson, Bonham C. "Freedom and Migration in the Leeward Caribbean, 1838–48." *Journal of Historical Geography* 6 (1980): 391–408.

———. "Livelihood in Rural Trinidad in 1900." *Annals of the Association of American Geographers* 65 (1975): 240–51.

———. "Migration and Death Ceremonies on St. Kitts and Nevis." *Journal of Cultural Geography* 1 (Spring/Summer 1981): 1–11.

———. "The Overdevelopment of Carriacou." *Geographical Review* 65 (1975): 390–99.

———. "St. Kitts-Nevis." In Robert J. Alexander, *Political Parties of the Americas.* Westport, Conn.: Greenwood Press. Forthcoming.

Riddell, Maria. *Voyages to the Madeira and Leeward Caribbean Isles with Sketches of the Natural History of These Islands.* 1802. Reprint. New Haven: Research Publications, 1975.

Roberts, G.W. "Emigration from the Island of Barbados." *Social and Economic Studies* 4 (1955): 245–88.

Rochefort, Charles E. *Histoire naturelle et morale des Iles Antilles de l'Amérique.* Rotterdam, 1653.

Rouse, Irving, and Louis Allaire. "Caribbean." In R.E. Taylor and Clement W. Meighan, *Chronologies in New World Archaeology,* 431–81. New York: Academic Press, 1978.

Rubenstein, Hymie. "Black Adaptive Strategies: Coping with Poverty in an Eastern Caribbean Village." Ph.D. diss., Univ. of Toronto, 1976.

Safa, Helen I. "Introduction." In Safa and Brian M. DuToit, eds., *Migration and Development,* 1–14. The Hague: Mouton, 1975.

St.-Johnston, Sir Reginald. *From a Colonial Governor's Note-Book.* London: Hutchinson, 1936.

St. Kitts/Nevis Territorial Plan T1. Antigua: United Nations Development Program, Physical Planning Project, 1975.

Sauer, Carl O. *The Early Spanish Main.* Berkeley: Univ. of California Press, 1966.

Saul, S.B. "The British West Indies in Depression, 1880–1914." *Inter-American Economic Affairs* 12 (Winter, 1958): 3–25.

Schaw, Janet. *Journal of a Lady of Quality, Being the Narrative of a Journal from Scotland to the West Indies, North Carolina, and Portugal, in the Years 1774 to 1776,* ed. Evangeline Walter Andrews and Charles McLean Andrews. New Haven: Yale Univ. Press, 1923.

Segal, Aaron L., ed. *Population Policies in the Caribbean.* Lexington, Mass.: Lexington Books, 1975.

Sheridan, Richard B. "Africa and the Caribbean in the Atlantic Slave Trade." *American Historical Review* 77 (1972): 15–35.

———. *Sugar and Slavery: An Economic History of the British West Indies, 1623–1775.* Baltimore: Johns Hopkins Univ. Press, 1973.

Shyllon, F.O. *Black Slaves in Britain.* London: Oxford Univ. Press, 1974.

Singham, A.W. *The Hero and the Crowd in a Colonial Polity.* New Haven: Yale Univ. Press, 1968.

Stephens, S.G. "Cotton Growing in the West Indies during the 18th and 19th Centuries." *Tropical Agriculture* 21 (Feb. 1944): 23–29.

Sturge, Joseph, and Thomas Harvey. *The West Indies in 1837.* London, 1838.

A Technical Survey of the Sugar Estates of St. Kitts. London: Bookers Agricultural and Technical Services, Ltd., 1968.

Thome, Jas. A., and J. Horace Kimbell. *Emancipation in the West Indies. A Six Months' Tour in Antigua, Barbadoes, and Jamaica in the Year 1837.* New York: American Anti-Slavery Society, 1838.

Tobias, Peter M. "How You Gonna Keep Em Down in the Tropics Once They've Dreamed New York? Some Aspects of Grenadian Migration." Ph.D. diss., Rice University, 1975.

"Vendors of Cotton 1975/76 as at May 19, 1976," Nevis: Dept. Agriculture. Mimeographed.

Waddell, Eric. "How the Enga Cope with Frost: Responses to Climatic Perturbations in the Central Highlands of New Guinea." *Human Ecology* 3 (1975): 249–73.

Wallerstein, Immanuel. *The Modern World System: Capitalist Agriculture and the Origins of the European World-Economy in the Sixteenth Century.* New York: Academic Press, 1976.

Ward, R. Gerard. "Migration, Myth and Magic in Papua New Guinea." *Australian Geographical Studies* 18 (1980): 119–34.

Watkins, Henry. *Handbook of the Leeward Islands.* London: West India Committee, 1924.

Watts, David. "From Sugar Plantation to Open-Range Grazing: Changes in the Land Use of Nevis, West Indies." *Geography* 58 (1973): 65–68.

———. "Persistence and Change in the Vegetation of Oceanic Islands." *Canadian Geographer* 14 (1970): 91–109.

Weatherly, U.G. "The West Indies as a Sociological Laboratory." *American Journal of Sociology* 49 (1923): 290–304.

Westlake, Donald E. *Under an English Heaven.* New York: Simon and Schuster, 1972.

Whitten, Norman E., Jr., and John F. Szwed, "Introduction," In Whitten and Szwed, eds., *Afro-American Anthropology: Contemporary Perspectives,* 23–60. New York: Free Press, 1970.

Wilson, Peter J. *Crab Antics: The Social Anthropology of English-Speaking Negro Societies of the Caribbean.* New Haven: Yale Univ. Press, 1973.

———. *Oscar: An Inquiry into the Nature of Sanity.* New York: Random House, 1974.

Wood, Donald. *Trinidad in Transition: The Years After Slavery.* London: Oxford Univ. Press, 1968.

Woodcock, Thomas. "Estimate of an Estate . . . ," *Annals of Agriculture* 31 (1798): 381–84.

Index

Caribbean Migrants was composed into type on the Mergenthaler Linotron 202N phototypesetter in ten point Bembo with two points of spacing between the lines. The book was designed by Larry Hirst, composed by Williams of Chattanooga, printed offset by Thomson-Shore, Inc., and bound by John H. Dekker & Sons. The paper on which the book is printed bears the watermark of S.D. Warren and is designed for an effective life of at least three hundred years.

The University of Tennessee Press : Knoxville